P9-CMO-250

The Minister as Crisis Counselor

Revised and Enlarged

DAVID K. SWITZER

Abingdon Press
Nashville

THE MINISTER AS CRISIS COUNSELOR
REVISED AND ENLARGED

Copyright © 1974 by Abingdon Press
Revised edition copyright © 1986 by Abingdon Press

All rights reserved.
No part of this work may be reproduced or transmitted in any form or by any means, electronic or mechanical, including photocopying and recording, or by any information storage or retrieval system, except as may be expressly permitted by the 1976 Copyright Act or in writing from the publisher. Reequests for permission should be addressed in writing to Abingdon Press, 201 8th Avenue South, Nashville, TN 37203.

This book is printed on recycled acid-free paper.

Library of Congress Cataloging-in-Publication Data

SWITZER, DAVID K., 1925–
    The minister as crisis counselor.
    Bibliography: p. Includes indexes.
    I. Pastoral counseling. 2. Crisis intervention
(Psychiatry) I. Title.
BV4012.2.S9   1986   253.5   85-15827

ISBN 0-687-26954-7 (pbk.: alk. paper)

Scripture quotations are from the Revised Standard Version of the Bible, copyrighted 1946, 1952, © 1971, 1973 by the Division of Christian Education of the National Council of the Churches of Christ in the U.S.A. and are used by permission.

00 01 02 03 04 05 06 07—20 19 18 17 16 15 14 13

MANUFACTURED IN THE UNITED STATES OF AMERICA

To
my children,
Rebecca and Eric

CONTENTS

I t has been a source of considerable gratification to me that *The Minister as Crisis Counselor* has continued to be used by ministers and seminary students as well as a few others. Of course, numerous students have had no great choice in the matter, but periodically I have heard from some of them, representing several different seminaries, that the book has been useful. That was, and is, the point. We ministers work with people in crisis much of the time, and we fail our calling if we do not do all within our power to be as effective as possible in our pastoral ministry.

In the ten years since the book was first published, a number of things have happened, many of them to me. First, as I have referred back to this book time and again in teaching and have read and heard students discussing it, I have been increasingly offended by the exclusively masculine language. In the mid-seventies, women students at Perkins School of Theology began to make a sensitizing impact on me in regard to certain women's issues that I had not really been aware of before. Language was one of these. By about 1975 I was beginning to try always to use gender-inclusive language, and this revision (as well as my books published in 1979 and 1980) reflects my present convictions about this matter.

I have also learned more about crisis counseling from a number of sources. Persons in crisis who have allowed me to be their pastor and counselor have contributed much. In addition, I have been enlightened by a large number of ministers who have attended some twenty-five or more workshops I have led in different parts of the country and who have shared their experiences with me. Some of these insights have been worked into the present text.

In the Preface to the first edition, I stated, "Other books are bound to follow, and I welcome them." They did, and I have. Some of them have made significant contributions to my thinking and are referred to in this revision. However, it is surprising to me that only two of the books, as far as I am aware, have been written by active ministers for the practicing minister.[1] At least two other authors have a ministerial background, but their books are not directed specifically toward the clergy, although one has an excellent chapter, "Crisis Intervention by Clergy."[2] Since there is still no glut on the crisis-book-for-ministers market, and since there are enough differences between Stone's book and mine (although I understand our theory and practice to be very close if not identical), I believe an updating of *The Minister as Crisis Counselor* is warranted. Gerkin's book, while relevant to the practice of crisis counseling, makes its unique contribution in the nature and quality of its theological emphasis.

My total thank-you list is too long to be published. I shall try, though, to point out major areas of indebtedness. My own specific introduction to crisis theory and intervention came in a course offered to the clergy by the Los Angeles County Department of Mental Health and the Mental Health and Clergy Committee of Los Angeles. Many of the course leaders' names are found in the footnotes. My fear is that some of their material, which got into my head from their lectures and our discussions, might have found its way into the text of two of my chapters without appropriate reference, as I assimilated in my own practice and thinking what they were teaching me. Let this then be the reference as well as my expression of appreciation.

Some of this book already has a public history. Parts of chapters 2 and 3 were first a very brief article in the *Christian Advocate* and later a longer article in *Pastoral Psychology*. Chapter 7 was published with only slight variations in *Omega: An International Journal for the Psychological Study of Dying, Death, Bereavement, Suicide, and Other Lethal Behaviors*. The editors of these journals have given permission for the publication of the articles in revised form here.

Several years spent training lay people for telephone crisis intervention at Contact and at Suicide Prevention Center, both twenty-four-hour telephone counseling services in Dallas, gave feedback on the practical usefulness of the approach utilized here; and an invitation to give two presentations on crisis theory and therapy as a part of the Timberlawn Psychiatric Residency Program Guest Lecture Series provided the opportunity to test the ideas and organization of chapters 2 and 3 with a sophisticated audience and contributed to their final shape. Chapter 6 was developed originally as a lecture to the Southwest Regional Interseminary Movement Conference in 1972, with additional research adding to its form in this book.

I am appreciative of the continued opportunities afforded me by various members of the medical staff at Timberlawn Psychiatric Hospital to work with patients. In the focused therapy on grief and in other occasional crises, and in the related conversations with those psychiatrists and other professionals, I have learned much.

Several persons have contributed directly to the content and form of certain portions of this book. I take this opportunity to express gratitude to Dr. Edwin Shneidman and Dr. Karl Slaikeu for their time in reading sections which refer to their work, for their suggestions, and for their helpful responses; also to Dr. Emma Justes and the Reverend Abigail Carlisle for allowing me to read what at the time was unpublished material, and for the opportunity to discuss some of those issues with them.

I am especially indebted to my spouse, Dr. Theresa McConnell, also an ordained United Methodist minister and pastoral counselor, not only for her insights as we have discussed pastoral ministry, but for the quality of her love and caring, which nourish and energize me.

Finally, I am grateful to those persons who have allowed me to participate with them in their struggles in times of stress, anxiety, and pain, those who have either sought me out or responded to my initiative with openness, sharing intimate details of their own feelings of distress and trouble in such a way that their crises have been resolved and have, at the same time, contributed to my own growth as a human being and a professional. These relationships have developed into continuing friendships of great meaning.

David K. Switzer

CHAPTER 1

THE MINISTER
AS CRISIS COUNSELOR

In one way or another, the Christian pastor throughout the centuries has been involved with persons in time of crisis and distress. The clergy have always in this sense been counselors. This is hardly news to anyone who might be reading this book. Nor is there, in these days, a setting in which ordained ministers work where they are not called upon, at least occasionally, to engage themselves with someone who is hurting in some way. Certainly in the local pastorate and in many specialized ministries, the demand is constant. They may seek this form of pastoral work or attempt to avoid it; they may be well or poorly trained for it; they may do it effectively or rather badly. But there is no escape from the counseling responsibility, short of escape from the ministry itself. Actually, most ministers place a high value on the importance of their role as pastors and the helping relationship with persons; they feel this to be one of the most satisfying activities in which they participate.[1]

What Is Pastoral Counseling?

If we take the professional psychotherapist as a model for comparison, the minister is a strange kind of counselor indeed, and he or she comes to this function by a professionally circuitous route. In order to get to the point of understanding the minister as crisis counselor, it may be enlightening to look first at the unique meaning of the term *pastoral counselor*. Perhaps a diagram will be helpful.

Paul Tillich has properly pointed out the nature of caring as a general and universal human characteristic. As he puts it, caring "is going on always in every moment of human existence."[2] Caring is transformed into pastoral care by reference both to motivation and context. It is the conscious acting out toward one another of the love

11

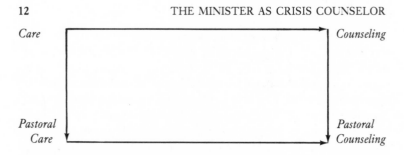

Care   *Counseling*

Pastoral   *Pastoral*
Care   *Counseling*

that God has shown to us in Jesus Christ, and it is done within and also as a representative of the community of faith. This moves us in one direction beyond the general human characteristic of care, as another dimension is added to it.

But there are certain types of situations of human distress for which the general human quality of caring, or even pastoral caring, is not sufficient to produce healing. Therefore specialized techniques of caring have been developed which have the potential to produce change in human life even when there are deep and persistent problems. This kind of caring is called counseling or psychotherapy. Thus another dimension is added, in another direction, to the everyday mutual caring of persons for one another.

Now, moving from the position of counseling in the direction of the pastoral motivation and context, and from the position of pastoral care in the direction of the specialized function of counseling, we find that the intersection of the lines indicates what ministers are doing when they engage in pastoral counseling.

Counseling "in General"

Even though in many ways the pastoral counselor may be distinguished from the situation and functioning of the professional psychotherapist, there are certain aspects of the counseling process and relationship that are identical, no matter who the counselor might be, if effective counseling is taking place. At the risk of being too elementary, perhaps the word *counseling* itself should be further clarified. Let it be understood from the very beginning that no one particular methodology is intended. Although there are methods and techniques, there is no single way to counsel. Counseling is a relational process. It is being a person to and for another person. It is providing a model of personhood in contrast to an emphasis on techniques. Even Karl Menninger, as a psychoanalyst, writes, "In my opinion the most important thing in the acquisition of psychoanalytic technique is the development of a certain attitude or frame of mind."[3] And Theodore Reik, another psychoanalyst, emphasizes the point, in what really must be something of an overstatement, that there are no techniques, only persons. I say overstatement because, certainly within the ministry, which may occasionally be inclined toward the error of overemphasizing this particular aspect of truth to the exclusion of the counterbalances necessary for it to *be* the truth, it is important to avoid the overly simplistic, erroneous, and potentially harmful conclusion that "because I'm such a great person whom everyone automatically loves, I am a highly competent counselor." This is, of course, not necessarily so. Still, with this corrective statement, the *human* element is at the center of the counseling process.

Robert Carkhuff, building upon the work of Carl Rogers and carrying it further, states—as a result of extensive research with clients—that there are several essential ingredients of effective psychotherapy. One of these is genuineness.[4] He is referring to the counselor's own genuineness as a person, the capacity to be in touch with oneself, aware of what is going on in oneself at any given moment, and the ability to communicate oneself, not merely one's ideas, clearly and appropriately to others. Jourard is traveling the same route when he speaks of "real-self interpersonal behavior" and *"being* in the presence of another."[5] This implies patterns of behavior with others in which one person relates without anxiety or defensiveness, so that the anxiety of the other is reduced, barriers to self-disclosure are removed, and self-disclosure itself is facilitated. Such a form of relating provides the atmosphere for change, because the process of self-exploring and self-revealing is that which is inherently healing in the person. Jourard's point is that a person is healthy to the degree that she or he is open, can be transparent to others. The masked, self-enclosed counselor (or, for that matter, preacher) has a built-in barrier to the process in which he or she claims to be engaged.

Counseling is acceptance of and love for another. It is the facilitation of communication—not just the use of words, even intellectually precise ones—but the art of understanding and being understood. This includes emotional meanings as well as intellectual ones. It is quite clear from this that the counselor is not merely a detached observer of a process but rather a related participant, albeit more objective than the other person, though not totally objective, since there is no such thing. Sullivan uses the term "participant observer" to describe the therapist's role.[6] Counseling is entering into a dynamic process. It is giving one's time, therefore sharing a part of one's life with another, reliving part of another person's life along with him or her, entering into new life with the other. A counselor, in order to be helpful, needs to avoid becoming snared in the same emotional trap in which the counselee is caught, but does enter into that person's emotional world. The counselor is a mirror for the other. But she or he is more than that. The counselor not only reflects feelings, but feels, not only reflects meaning, but participates in the creation of meaning. The counselor is not the aggressive molder of another individual into a preconceived pattern, but is not neutral about the outcome of the process, either. The counselor is committed to the person with whom he or she is involved. Yet the counselor's own selfhood must never be threatened by the failure of the other person to respond as the counselor thinks that person should.

All this is to say that counseling is a dynamic personal relationship in which both persons participate and both persons change. Even in what we might judge failure, the counselee is not unaffected, nor is the counselor ever left unchanged. The counselor gains insights, recognizes his or her own responses, learns from the other, and is confronted by the other.

The Uniqueness of the Minister as Counselor

When we consider counseling in these terms, however, there is nothing at all unique about ministers. Nevertheless, there are a number of ways in which clergy are quite distinct from other counselors. Actually, it is not at all clear that the professional psychotherapist should be our primary model, any more than the premodern minister should be. In fact, there are already in process of development new models that are something of a fusion of the two, and one of these is precisely what this whole book seeks to elaborate. This new model is one that is in keeping with the pastor's traditional role throughout the centuries and is very much related to the rather extensive involvement with persons granted to pastors in their role as ministers of local congregations. At the same time, it also includes a technical knowledge of personality dynamics, psychopathology, and contemporary counseling approaches.

Because of their role, ministers come much closer to total involvement therapeutically with larger numbers of persons with a greater variety of problems than any psychologist or psychiatrist or other psychotherapist. Contrasted with these professionals, ministers either know to some degree a relatively high percentage of people with whom they engage in counseling, or will have some form of continuing extraoffice relationship with them, a point that will be referred to later. Most psychotherapists are infrequently directly involved in a helping way with grief situations triggered by death, premarital counseling, supportive counseling of the physically ill and the dying, the most frequent problems of aging, or even with suicide and alcoholism in ways of functioning that are open to the clergy. Yet ministers are, or should be, almost always significantly related to persons in these situations. In addition, there are other ways in which clergy are quite distinct from other psychotherapists, and these particularly contribute to their potential effectiveness in situations of crisis: symbol power; pastoral initiative; prior personal relationship with many of the persons into whose lives they now enter in this unique relationship; the availability and value of the community of faith; and a theological perspective. There are also aids such as the growing practice and acceptance of the role of the laity in pastoral care, with ministers as teacher-supervisors, and the increase in telephone counseling, which are peculiarly available to the clergy. These will be discussed in later chapters.

The Symbol Power of the Minister. The first and, in my thinking, primary uniqueness of the minister, and one that is a source of peculiar strength in pastoral relationships, apart from the power of personal presence, is her or his power as a symbol.[7] The fact that the counselor is an *ordained minister* is a datum that usually has some impact upon a person. All professionals with clients (or in this instance, parishioners) are not only who they are, but who other persons feel them to be—not only at a level of conscious awareness but also of unconscious process. The pastor is not only a person but a symbol.

Tillich lists a number of characteristics of symbols in the context of his declaration that "ultimate concern must be expressed symbolically, because symbol alone is able to express the ultimate." The first characteristic is the most obvious one, that a symbol points beyond itself to something else. Second, however, unlike a simple sign, a symbol participates in that to which it points. There is somehow a direct, inseparable relationship between the two. The third characteristic of symbol is that it opens up levels of reality that otherwise are closed for us. And fourth, it also unlocks dimensions and elements of our inner being that correspond to the dimensions and elements of reality. What Tillich seems to be expressing here, without using this sort of language, is that, as a result of the symbol's participation in the reality to which it points, it also has the power to communicate something of that reality to the person for whom the symbol is meaningful.[8]

It is important that ordained clergy be aware that they are symbols of the reality that underlies the meaningfulness of Christian faith. In other words, quite apart from their own being as persons, clergy are perceived by others as being the physical representation to the community of faith and, at least to some extent, to the larger community of the reality of God. Their very physical presence has the power to stimulate those internal images which, through early learning in a highly emotionally charged relationship of dependence, have become a part of an individual's intrapersonal dynamics. These primitive images are a part of that individual's internal resources and are strong unconscious forces, affecting every aspect of his or her life.[9] Now to be sure, it must be recognized that in the development of quite a number of people, these images have negative forces attached to them, but even in many of these people, as well as in a large number of others who have been related to a religious community, they are positive. Ordained ministers are physical representations of the whole community of faith, of the tradition, of a way of viewing the meaning of life, of the dynamic power of faith, and even of God. This is a significant factor not to be overlooked when the minister engages in counseling or intervenes in crises. Because of this symbol power, there may be unconscious negative forces to be dealt with, worked through, and overcome, as well as unconscious positive forces that actually become available to many persons in strengthening and healing ways during their times of distress. While other mental health professionals are also symbols, because of the long-term history of religious communities, the relationship between religion and culture, and the total exposure of many persons when they are children to the religious community, its collection of symbols, its ritual, and its ministry, and the way in which all this exposure is integrally tied into the nuclear family itself, the symbol of the pastor seems to be of a different order in terms of its strength.

Pastoral Initiative. Another aspect of the uniqueness of the minister as a counselor may be termed *pastoral initiative*, both as it relates to the establishment of precounseling relationships and to active crisis intervention. This is an aspect of the minister's functioning that too many all too often take for granted, although all clergy utilize it more or less consciously in a variety of ways. A minister is rare among professionals, in that he or she is expected to go where people are, and at least usually will have some entrée. Our social forms have provided this type of expectation, and it is a significant one when utilized sensitively and responsibly in the establishment of precounseling relationships, in active intervention in crisis, and in the follow-up which plays such an important role in crisis counseling. It also allows the freedom to schedule more or less formal counseling appointments in the homes of the persons involved, rather than in the office, something a few marriage and family therapists are beginning to do with considerable success and satisfaction. Home, hospital, and job visitation can give a minister a breadth and depth of relationships, an opportunity to know people and be known by them, that no psychiatrist or psychologist can match. These visits in themselves occasionally turn rather quickly into brief or even longer counseling sessions. Certainly they provide an excellent basis for persons to call on the ministers later for help, or for the ministers to return later on their own initiative, if they believe their presence can be helpful. With their entrée to homes, pastors, through sensitive questioning and responsive listening, are able to discover a number of problems in their early stages. In this way they may be useful in preventing the development of more serious problems. It is interesting that after so many centuries of this tradition in the ministry, there are now a few places where psychiatric emergency teams are beginning to call in people's homes and are being sent to families of persons who have committed or attempted suicide.

It is also interesting to note the way ministers are expected to intervene in certain crisis situations on their own initiative and without specific invitation. They certainly are expected to do so at times of physical illness and in grief situations. People may tend to be somewhat more surprised if they also turn up when someone is intoxicated or there is a family fight going on. There is an obvious danger in using initiative in these unexpected ways. Pastors may on some occasions be resented and resisted and even rejected. They may in fact fail, and no one likes to fail. But there are also tremendous possibilities for service. Many times in the midst of great stress there is a sense of relief upon the appearance of the minister. Perhaps an individual or family had not even thought of calling the pastor, but his or her presence is genuinely welcomed. On other occasions, even when there is initial resistance to intrusion, barriers can sometimes be broken down and a relationship established or reestablished, permitting constructive interaction to take place. Certainly at times like these the depth and quality of a prior relationship are of major significance. The degree of trust, confidence, sincerity, genuine helpfulness, real friendship make it possible for intervention into the crisis by a pastor's own initiative to be of a constructive nature. Even where there may be resistance and rejection, it should not be assumed that the intervention is without its unseen positive effects.

Relationships with Persons. There is a third way ministers are different from professional psychotherapists. In many of the settings in which clergy function, they frequently have a prior relationship with a person, an ongoing, out-of-therapy relationship during the span of the counseling, as well as a continuing relationship when the counseling itself is concluded. There are, of course, some exceptions, but it is often the case that the person or persons in need of help are parishioners, fellow workers, friends, neighbors. Some of the implications of this have already been referred to in terms of the possibilities for preventing the growth of more serious problems and the quality of uninvited intervention. In addition, the prior and continuing relationship has implications both for the development of transference and for the usual ways of working through separation at the conclusion of counseling.

Transference, in its simplest terms, refers to the situation in which a person in therapy, without being aware of it, "transfers" onto the therapist feelings originally directed toward the parents and now repressed. These may be hostility, love (including sexual feelings), and dependence, often with the expectation of magical omnipotence. In traditional psychoanalysis, where the analyst is theoretically a neutral figure—not known as a person before, during, or after the therapy—such transference of repressed feeling is invited. Where there has been a prior relationship, as in the case of parishioner and minister, although there may already be some elements of transference growing out of the minister's position and the way the parishioner unconsciously views this, the minister also is known as a person, and he or she continues to be known as a person in contacts outside the counseling sessions. Under these circumstanes, the depth and strength of transference may be reduced. Some psychotherapists understand such a reduction in transference as being a potential aid in the establishment of a less distorted helping relationship, one in which there may possibly be less magical expectation and less resistance to the process.[10] This positive potential may, of course, be more fully realized when the minister is willing to be known as the human being she or he truly is.

In addition, the fact that there will be a continuing relationship after the counseling is completed means that termination of counseling does not produce the sharp and absolute loss of relationship, but rather a transformation from one form to another. Recognizing that a parishioner in such an intimate relationship may in fact view it as a loss, still when this perception and the feelings attached to it are verbalized, there are important and potentially quite positive and meaningful carry-over values into the relationship that continues to exist.

The Community of Faith. An obviously unique resource which the minister has as crisis counselor is the availability and value of the community of faith. In the first place, there are the precounseling advantages. In the education program, in preaching, and in the quality and forms of relating to persons in business meetings and the variety of other small groups, the minister has the opportunity to invite people in indirect ways to come for counseling. There is also the opportunity to train people in the art of the anticipation and identification of problems in their early stages and ways to deal with them when they arise. No other professional person regularly has this sort of platform or organizational context in which to do sound education for mental health and problem solving, or to open doors for people to talk openly about these issues. Beyond this, there is the supportive community, which forms a strengthening context for many people who are in individual or marriage or family counseling with the minister as they continue to participate in the life of the community of which they are already a part. When crises arise, they are already actually in the midst of many of the resources they will need. For those who come to the minister from outside the church, there is the community into which at least some of them may be effectively integrated as an additional resource for strength. The small group structures are especially helpful at this point, and the value of those that include sound education and fellowship and a focus on spiritual life ought not to be overlooked. There is also the possibility of developing, as many churches have already done, the unstructured small groups of a semitherapeutic or therapeutic nature, which form the social context for a person's testing of insights and new forms of relating as they arise during individual counseling.[11]

Clearly, none of these other factors which lend uniqueness to the pastor's role would be fully meaningful or helpfully effective were it not for the theological perspective out of which the pastor views human life and destiny. In addition, it would be rare for a psychotherapist who is a person of faith and a member of the church to have the sophistication that is properly expected of the well-trained minister in the areas of biblical interpretation, Christian ethics, and the theologizing process, and the ways these may be usefully discussed with persons, families, and groups grappling with the meaning of their lives and their relationships. Paul Pruyser, a clinical psychologist, emphasizes this unique contribution of the minister:

> By virtue of [many persons'] choice of first seeking pastoral help, are they not asking for their problems to be placed in a pastoral perspective?

> In seeking a pastoral answer, even if recognizing that [it] may be only a first or tentative answer, are they not placing themselves voluntarily into a value system, and into an ambiance of special tradition and communion which they consider relevant?[12]

Pruyser's point is that the theological perspective out of which to view persons, their situations, and their behavior is a legitimate and, for many people, an important one. Evaluations of specific persons and specific situations made from a theological point of view and often phrased in the language of faith may be enlightening in terms of the person's increased self-understanding, decision making, and behavior. This does not mean that psychological insights are cast aside; rather, the theological and psychological may be laid alongside each other and interact, with the theological dimension being a significant addition to the evaluation and helping process. Pruyser states that

> pastors, like all other professional workers, possess a body of theoretical and practical knowledge that is uniquely their own, evolved over years of practice by themselves and their forebears. Adding different bits of knowledge and techniques by borrowing from other disciplines, such as psychiatry and psychology, does not undo

the integrity and usefulness of their own basic and applied sciences. Adding clinical insights and skills to their pastoral work does not—should not—shake the authenticity of their pastoral outlook and performance.[13]

Other writers have been calling our attention to the contributions of the Bible to our understanding of the human situation. Oglesby selects a few major themes of Scripture in order to shed light on critical human experiences: initiative and freedom, fear and faith, conformity and rebellion, death and rebirth, risk and redemption. And Capps notes how the pastoral care process itself may be shaped and made more effective by a study of the literary forms in which biblical material is presented.[14]

The well-educated minister is unique among helping professionals, not merely by viewing life through the eyes of faith (numerous ones in other professions have such a perspective), but by being specifically trained to assist others to see themselves in their particular situations from a theological perspective, and by the fact that some large numbers of people expect ministers to help them in this particular way.

Pastoral Counseling and Secular Psychotherapy

Some of the first generation leaders of the modern pastoral care movement, those who sought to bring to the unique role of the minister the insights and methodology of certain forms of contemporary psychotherapy, are still with us. It was only shortly before and during World War II that the work of a few persons in this new field began to be represented in the curriculum of several theological seminaries, and only after the war did the demand for and the availability of competent teachers begin to come together in such a way that pastoral counseling began to move in the direction of becoming the expected and accepted part of seminary education that it is today.

The undergirding theoretical-practical approach, already in the process of being developed by Dicks, Cabot, Hiltner, and others, was supported and stimulated by secular counseling in the work of Carl Rogers.[15] While modern methods of pastoral counseling were not directly derived from Rogers initially, they were given impetus by his work, as could be seen in the important books of the well-known pioneers which followed.[16] The change in designation of Rogers' contribution from nondirective to client-centered counseling indicated a transition from an emphasis on technique to the centrality of a particular quality of relationship, an observation that had already been made in the pastoral care and counseling field, but which was increasingly substantiated by Rogers' research data.[17] The training of young ministers in the seminaries in this field was permeated by the client-centered understanding of the counseling relationship and process.

At times there intruded into this seminary scene some of the complex concepts of Freud, frequently more for the purpose of adding "depth" to the theoretical foundation of personality dynamics than in suggesting that the parish minister adapt psychoanalytic therapy to pastoral counseling practice. Both Rogerian and Freudian therapy, however, seemed to assume that the therapeutically oriented minister, when confronted by a "serious" problem, would need to arrange for a series of many weekly sessions before significant positive change could come about, or refer the person to another therapist who would follow that procedure.

Short-term Therapy

In recent years strong challenges have arisen both to client-centered (as formerly understood) and psychoanalytic therapy, on theoretical and on practical levels, from sources that are really quite diverse. Even within psychoanalysis itself, practitioners have developed new techniques of short-term therapy.[18] On the whole, the trend has been toward greater personal involvement by the therapist, with fewer sessions.

This is good news for pastors, for on the one hand, their essential role calls for a more active involvement with persons, and on the other hand, these overly busy practitioners of the multiple functions that are demanded by the local church very rarely do any of the long-term therapy they might have learned about in seminary. Even if they were quite well trained and emotionally prepared for a depth-counseling relationship of some length, they simply do not often have the time for its regular demands. Personal experience and discussion of counseling practices with many other ministers has led me to conclude that the typical minister sees very few persons for more than six consecutive weekly sessions of one hour. In a period of 15 months as a pastoral counseling specialist on a church staff, only

15 out of 154 different individuals, couples, or families who came to me were seen for more than six sessions.

In addition, in eight years as the designated counselor to students and their families at Perkins School of Theology, a very specialized counseling ministry, only 14 percent of the over 800 different persons I saw came for more than six consecutive sessions. In most of the workshops I have conducted for ministers throughout the country, informal polls showed that most parish pastors do not see even one person during a year for six or more consecutive weekly counseling sessions. A more systematic study surveyed 105 Protestant ministers in one southern and one nothern city (including inner city, suburbs, and nearby small communities). Results indicated that these ministers saw people in counseling for an average of only 3.5 times per problem per person, with the most common frequency of scheduling being two, three, and four times per month, in that order.[19] The upshot of these data is that most parish ministers see people in counseling for very few consecutive sessions. Longer-term counseling is very seldom done in the parish, or even in most other pastoral settings.

Our need as ministers is to become skilled in assisting people to work through a number of painful, frustrating, anxiety-producing, problematic situations by means of a variety of approaches that will take only a few sessions.

Happily, in recent years, new approaches to the resolution of many personal problems have been offered by professionals in the fields of pastoral counseling, psychology, and community and emergency psychiatry. More and more, the inadequacy of traditional methods of long-term individual psychotherapy to deal with the constantly increasing mental-health needs of the nation has become apparent. In proportion to the total population and to the total number of persons in need, there is a decreasing percentage of psychiatrists, clinical psychologists, and psychiatric social workers and nurses. There are at least two directions to go in search of an answer: new methods and new co-laborers.

One large group of co-laborers which this book (and a number of other books also, by the way) proposes as at least a partial answer to the increasing mental-health needs, is the clergy. They are already on the firing line. They live and work in all areas of the cities, small towns, and rural countryside. Many people already know them personally. Their presence is visible through the obvious existence of church buildings, through church services, and through their many community activities. A reasonably large number of people have some image of the minister as a person to turn to for help. Many ministers see themselves in the role of helper to all persons, regardless of their relationship to the church, their education, race, or social or economic standing. They are usually available twenty-four hours a day, and usually without cost to the person seeking help. A rather large number of them have at least a modest amount of training in various forms of helping, and that number is rapidly increasing.

There are also new perspectives and new methods for dealing effectively with people's pressing needs in a short period of time. Irving Janis details the theory, research, and procedures for helping people arrive at decisions concerning various aspects of their health, career, marriage, and other problematic areas of their lives, and assisting them in carrying out difficult decisions already decided upon.[20] These two aspects of decision making and action are already components of much long-term psychotherapy. However, focusing on only the decision-making process and the carrying out of the decisions at the time the needs arise makes an immediate contribution to the reduction of confusion, stress, and anxiety, and opens up new vistas in people's lives. This results in increasing their quality of life and reducing the probability of more complex problems later.

Ministers will certainly not be surprised to discover that Janis includes them in his list of different professionals regularly involved in this kind of counseling. Ministers deal very frequently with people who bring to them the very sorts of issues Janis discusses—people whom they see only a few times, often only once or twice. Janis, however, now provides the insights and procedures pastors need in order to have a higher probability of helping more people in a shorter period of time.

Clinebell has recently published a revision of his classic book, *Basic Types of Pastoral Counseling.*[21] One could in fact say that in many ways, it is a new book. It is a gold mine of perspectives on pastoral ministry, with an emphasis on pastoral counseling, broadly conceived, with details on the procedures appropriate to the needs of particular persons in their own particular relationships and situations. With few exceptions the helping processes Clinebell describes are those that are consistent with the pastor's traditional role and require at most only a few formal counseling sessions. Often enough, some of the same needs are effectively responded to during informal contacts or regular pastoral visitation as well. He gives attention to the facilitation of spiritual wholeness, supportive care, the exploration of ethical, value, and meaning issues, bereavement, marriage and family relationships, and others.

There is yet another area of human need and a specific method of helping that has proved to be quite effective for those ministers who have become acquainted with it. This is crisis intervention, also discussed by Clinebell.[22] For pastors, this approach, along with those Janis and Clinebell have described, presents a modality that ministers and other mental health professionals have found extremely helpful.

The term *crisis intervention*, although it may carry a novel ring, when pondered for a moment, is not at all a surprising one to apply to the work of ministers, who are continually intervening in some crisis, and who do so both by invitation and by their own initiative. It is no more than stepping into a disturbed situation or the life of a disturbed person, a family, or other group at an opportune time, in such a way as to stop the downward spiral of a deteriorating situation or condition, bringing love, support, assurance, and insight, in an effort to lead to decisions that can redirect life. Ministers have already been doing this in critical illness, serious accident, a major move or vocational change, family disruption, death and dying, suicide, grief, intense emotional distress and its accompanying behavioral changes.

Now, however, as a result of the systematic work of several groups of mental health practitioners, a clear model of operating procedure is being offered to ministers for testing, adaptation, use, and perhaps modification. It is the theory and methodology of crisis intervention, particularly as it relates to the work of the clergy, especially the parish minister, that this book will seek to examine and elaborate. First, crisis theory as such will be discussed, for the theory is directly tied to practice. Next, the details of crisis intervention will be presented in the context of important understandings of the necessary ingredients for all effective counseling. The major portion of the rest of the book will look at specific situations of crisis and how the minister may appropriately and helpfully function in these situations.

Finally, the important issue of ministers and their relationship to those community agencies and resources appropriate to their work in the various crisis areas will be discussed, along with the significance of their own constant context, the community of faith. It is hoped that this book will enable ministers to function with increased competence with persons in distress, not as "baptized" traditional psychotherapists, but in ways consistent with their vocational identity as ministers, perhaps utilizing some new concepts and methodologies and certainly learning from new research, but combining these with their uniqueness as *pastoral* counselors in potently healing ways.

To state the purpose of the book in these terms is neither to overlook nor to depreciate the highly significant point made by Jernigan that "pastoral care, as the total ministry of the religious community to individuals and families in crisis, should include both ministries of healing and comfort and ministries of preparation." He goes on to indicate that pastoral care oriented exclusively or primarily toward pathology or evident situational trouble spots is a quite inadequate response to the larger and long-range goals of the church in relation to the total needs of individuals, families, the congregation, and the larger community.[23] There is no question in my mind that he has thrown out a challenge for the development of a comprehensive church program and quality of congregational life and activity that has implications reaching farther than the major emphasis of this particular book. However, day by day ministers and members of congregations continue to be confronted by the hurt, distress, panic, and sense of hopelessness that persons and families experience when a crisis is actually upon them. There is the continual need to understand and work effectively with these persons. To increase such understanding and to facilitate such work is the limited but still important intent of these pages.

CHAPTER 2

CRISIS THEORY:

DEFINITION, DESCRIPTION,

DYNAMICS

Case #1

Ms. A, a doctoral student in clinical psychology, came to see her pastor about three weeks after the fall semester began. She described to him her pervasive feeling of sadness, crying spells at different times of the day, inability to concentrate on her work, and her loss of interest in what she was doing. She even wondered if she were fit to be a psychologist. She had no idea why she was feeling this way. An exploration of her situation over the last few weeks led to the discovery that she had been feeling this way only since school had begun and that the group of students, both men and women, of which she was a part, and who were very close friends, had broken up. One had recently been married and four had left to do their nine-month clinical placement in other locations; one of these was planning a wedding in the near future. She also spoke of her longing for a love relationship with a man and was even thinking of quitting school.

Case #2

Mr. B, a young businessman, had gradually begun to behave somewhat erratically at his office. He had been a reliable and competent worker. Now he was occasionally late, work was left unfinished, and now and then he would say something his co-workers thought was somewhat out of place, not connected to anything else. Nothing was too much out of line, but after a few weeks his superior told him she had noticed all this and wondered if something were wrong. He assured her that he was perfectly all right, that he had just gotten a bit lax, that he would pay more attention in the future. For another few weeks all went well. Then he missed a day of work without calling in, and when he did not appear the second day, his supervisor called his home. After the phone rang a number of times, it sounded as though someone had picked it up, but there was no verbal answer. She called back several times during the morning, but the line was busy. She asked one of the man's friends to go over to Mr. B's residence during lunch. The friend rang the bell. There was no response. He looked through the window and saw Mr. B. sitting in a chair, staring straight ahead. The friend rapped on the window, but again there was no response. He reported this to the supervisor, who called the company doctor. The doctor and Mr. B's friend met an ambulance and a police car at Mr. B's house. When they got no response after ringing the bell and knocking, the police officer broke in. Mr. B was still sitting there. The police officer stepped out of the house, and the doctor and friend tried to talk Mr. B into coming with them. He then became violent and had to be restrained in order to be taken to the hospital. A search of his recent history turned up no event that could be identified as traumatic or threatening.

Does either of the above stories portray a person in crisis? If so, which one? Or do both? How does one make such a determination? Does it matter?

The clear preference for many people in most situations is definitely not to get bogged down in the detail of theoretical considerations. The practical matters are what count. However, it is of some real importance to get the meaning of crisis clearly in mind, primarily because, as self-evident as it may sound, the methodology of crisis intervention does not work very well unless the person needing help is actually in a crisis. The how-to is tightly tied to the theory. Therefore the minister must be able to identify the characteristics of crisis and understand what the person is experiencing, in order, first, to make the decision to utilize the methodology, and second, to function effectively.

The Development of Crisis Theory

It is ironic that the major impetus to the development of contemporary crisis theory and modes of intervention being proposed to ministers as a means of upgrading the quality of their counseling practice actually grew out of a psychiatrist's involvement in an area of human distress that is usually the domain of ministers—namely, grief. Numerous writers have recounted the events first reported by Dr. Erich Lindemann in an article in 1944.[1]

Very briefly, survivors of the disastrous Cocoanut Grove nightclub fire of 1942, in which more than 490 persons finally died, were taken to Massachusetts General Hospital, where Dr. Lindemann began to notice certain characteristic responses on the part of those who had lost close relatives. These were the familiar symptoms of grief, which show the behavior of personality decompensation in response to the loss of an emotionally significant person. Both realistic and unrealistic methods of coping with this loss were called up, and where realistic methods were ineffective, unrealistic defenses and methods of escape and denial took over. When these unrealistic mechanisms were dealt with by the psychiatrist's facilitating the person's grief work—that is, in relationship with the grief sufferers, helping them test reality with its pain and find new patterns of rewarding interaction—the persons once again established themselves and reentered life with new resources for dealing with crisis. Again, in all this there is nothing particularly new for the sensitive and faithful minister, but it was systematized so that further psychiatric investigation of crisis could be made.

Religious Origins

It is also ironic that the concept of crisis was not more familiar to ministers, as well as to psychiatrists, prior to that time, since material was already available in the work of Anton Boisen. As early as 1923 he published his evolving ideas based on his own experience and observations, which were presented in their more developed form later. Essentially, he recognized the increasing tension of inner conflicts, which were neither good nor bad in and of themselves, but which comprised an intermediate stage a person must pass through in order to reach a higher level of development. The higher level meant a reintegration of the individual's personality, bringing greater insight, new perspectives, and additional strength. However, there were dangers, and if the reintegration did not take place, the result was decompensation, the moods and behavior of mental illness.[2] Still without using the word *crisis*, in 1936 Boisen developed these ideas in detail in his classic and provocative *The Exploration of the Inner World.* Here, in the context of the examination of the relationship between religious experience and psychosis, he reiterated the make-or-break nature of a high level of anxiety, to the point of panic. There were always possibilities in the conflict, because old and inadequate methods of coping were challenged and barriers to growth were removed. Even when there was breakdown to the point of psychosis, it could be viewed as a problem-solving possibility, as a person sought "to assimilate hitherto unassimilated masses of life experience." The outcome, Boisen believed, was dependent "upon the presence or absence of an acceptable nucleus of purpose around which the new self can be formed."[3]

The most complete presentation of his theory of crisis came in 1945 with the publication of *Religion in Crisis and Custom*, partially based on papers published during the late 1930s. Here he outlines three categories: normal developmental crises, situational frustration, and intrapsychic conflict.

The developmental crises are those we would expect: adolescence, marriage, birth of children, aging, bereavement, death. There are the heightened emotions of any crisis period, the need for readjustment, the attempt to find meaning, the potential for positive and negative outcome.[4]

Situational crises are reactions to the serious frustrations produced by specific external events, such as marriage disruption, business or job failure. Frustration is a condition of growth, and the way people handle and assimilate these reactions is determinative of their direction in life.[5]

Finally, Boisen takes into consideration the personality aspects of individuals that form barriers to effective dealing with stressful events.[6] This is not precisely what his outline would have led us to believe, in that the crisis is not caused by "intrapsychic conflict," but Boisen is correct in introducing those factors that make persons particularly vulnerable to stress and limit their appropriate and constructive responses.

Crisis is characterized by anxiety, self-blame, and frequently a sense of personal failure and guilt, which lead to a constricted perspective on accumulating problems. There is the combination of tremendous emotional impact, along with a diminishing ability to see the problems clearly and deal with them. There is, of course, danger to the person, and it may be a shattering experience. However, because there is also a speeding up of the emotional and intellectual processes, there is the potential for new insights, and therefore not only a solution of the problems but also a reorganization of personality around a new center and on a higher level. At this point, Boisen appropriately introduces religious experience as one form the crisis and its resolution may take.[7]

It is clear that while Boisen has made a unique contribution, there are elements of his theory of crisis and their relationship both to personality decompensation and to religious experience that have their roots in the studies of James, Starbuck, and others, around the turn of the century.[8]

Psychiatric Origins

The major figure in the systematic development of crisis theory within psychiatry was Gerald Caplan, who, with Lindemann, established a community mental health program in the Cambridge, Massachusetts, area in 1946. Much of what has been done in this field during the last decade has been an elaboration of, or at least somehow in response to, Caplan's work.[9] A crisis, according to Caplan, arises out of some change in a person's life space that produces a modification of one's relationship with others and/or one's perceptions of oneself. Such a change may come about relatively slowly, as a result of rather normal and inevitable experiences of growing and developing physically and socially, or quite rapidly, as a result of some unforeseen and traumatic event. These two concepts have been differentiated by referring to them as *developmental* and *accidental* crises.

Erikson has elaborated the former in detail. He proposes that life is to be thought of as a series of eight stages, each of which has significance in and of itself; but each also contributes to or detracts from the achievement of the goal of "integrity," as he has designated the positive goal of the final stage. Each of these stages has its task and outcome characterized by contrasting terms—one emphasizing the positive need and the positive outcome if the need is successfully met, and the other, a possible negative result. For example, the series of stages of childhood are basic trust versus mistrust, autonomy versus shame and doubt, initiative versus guilt, and industry versus inferiority. The needs and conflicts of adolescence are penetratingly and helpfully elaborated in the discussion of identity versus self-diffusion. Adulthood consists progressively of intimacy versus self-absorption, generativity versus stagnation, and finally, integrity versus despair. It is made clear that if a person is to accomplish the tasks and have the needs of one of these stages adequately met, it is important that basic trust has been established in the very first stage, and that the outcome of each successive stage be more on the positive side than on the negative. Each of these stages is a developmental crisis because each is both the opportunity for significant growth and an occasion for the dangers of the failure to grow. Each has its own particular emotional stress. As long as a person is alive, there is no possibility of avoiding having to deal with the external and internal situations presented by each stage.[10] While the developmental crises are significant periods in a person's life, and each has implications for the total ministry of the church (sacrament and ritual; fellowship, growth, and study groups; personal and group counseling), it is not the purpose of this book to discuss them in further detail.

Categories of Crisis

Since specific procedures of helping are directly related to the particular dynamics and behavior of a given situation, it is essential that there be a precise definition of *crisis*. Some of the difficulty is that there are numerous definitions. The word has been in use for a long time, and in our everyday language we have a tendency to apply it to almost any situation or condition of stress or anxiety or confusion, or a serious problem of any kind. Even in psychiatric literature it has been used in several different ways. Clearly it is not the purpose of this book to describe how ministers may function effectively in all of these. However, because ministers do in fact deal with a broad spectrum of human conditions, it would be useful to point to some of the most usual situations to which the word *crisis* is applied. How ministers then attempt to be helpful will differ according to the particular category of crisis, and the one with which this book will deal exclusively can be clearly distinguished from the others.

Such a systematic classification has been developed by Baldwin.[11] He lists six categories of crisis.

Dispositional. The person feels distressed (anxiety, anger, hopelessness, etc.) as a result of a particular external problematic situation, in which the distress can be immediately removed by direct means: referral to a physician to receive medical treatment or to an agency to receive food or be assisted to find housing, by the giving of information, by medical or psychological education, or by administrative action, such as the restoring of a job.

Anticipated Life Transitions. These are usually normal situations a person knows are going to happen and over which the person may or may not have control: a housing move, a job change, becoming a parent.

Sudden Traumatic Stress. Here a specific external event triggers a very rapid reaction of distress, usually involving extreme anxiety or some amount of depression, or both, and some breakdown in functioning. There may have been the loss of a job; the loss of a person by death, separation, or divorce; or some other event perceived as threatening.

Maturational/Developmental. Because life goes on, a person is required to attempt to make adjustments, with successful moves being in the direction of greater maturity. If there are developmental issues not dealt with adequately in the past, there is greater difficulty in making the new adjustments. Significant issues which keep arising are those that have to do with dependency, values, emotional and sexual intimacy, self-discipline, the sense and exercise of power.

Psychopathological. These crises result primarily from the reactivation of unresolved earlier severe failures in maturation or critical losses and usually result in behaviors to which the term psychotic would be properly applied.

Psychiatric Emergencies. This category refers to the first helping contacts of persons who are becoming psychotic or who are suicidal or homicidal or are behaving in other extreme ways.

It is obvious that there is some overlapping between some of the above categories, but it is both conceptually and functionally useful to classify them in some such way as this. This book is going to deal exclusively with those crises referred to in the third category—Sudden Traumatic Stress—which will be referred to throughout this book as Situational Crisis.

Applying Baldwin's terms and descriptions to the two brief cases which opened this chapter, we can see that #1 involves Sudden Traumatic Stress, or in our terms, a situational crisis. The break-up of Ms. A's support group has led her to feel abandoned and alone; those feelings and the accompanying thoughts and behavior began recently and quite quickly.

In contrast, no such precipitating event was discovered in Mr. B's recent history; though the changes in his behavior are fairly recent, they developed more slowly. It is very likely that his condition would be located under Baldwin's categories "Psychopathological" and "Psychiatric Emergencies."

The Situational Crisis: Description and Dynamics

A situational crisis differs from a developmental crisis primarily in the source of stress and the element of time. There is a more rapid modification of perception of one's self and one's world, frequently including relationships with other persons, and usually initiated by some type of personal loss perceived as a threat to the self. Along with this form of external event, or in place of it, there may be some other sudden change in a situation that challenges one's self-concept or sense of identity. In either case, there is the self-perception of being threatened, with movement in the direction of feeling unable to cope with the situation with the usual repertoire of behavioral responses at one's disposal.

Thus, according to Rapoport, "There are three sets of interrelated factors that can produce a state of crisis: (1) a hazardous event which poses some threat; (2) a threat to instinctual need which is symbolically linked to earlier threats that resulted in vulnerability or conflict; (3) an inability to respond with adequate coping mechanisms."[12]

The threat-producing event, in other words, has the power, because of its similarity to prior events in our lives, to arouse earlier feelings of anxiety that have been repressed or covered over in some way. Therefore, in the present we have the sense of a double fear with sufficient cumulative power to make us feel highly vulnerable. An inevitable part of this experience of increasing vulnerability is one's perception of oneself as being less and less capable of coping with this event and the feelings that have been aroused. The crisis, then, is not necessarily inherent in the external situation itself. To be sure, there are certain events involving serious personal loss which usually trigger the response of crisis in most people. However, it should be made clear that the crisis itself is the *internal reaction* to the external event, and events that may be very threatening for some may not be for others.

In crisis theory there is the assumption that there are a number of physical, psychosocial, and sociocultural needs that contribute to the fundamental ego integrity of a person. The physical needs are rather obvious. Among the most important psychosocial needs are those that cluster around a person's relationship with others in the family and outside the family, so that cognitive and emotional development are stimulated, need for love and affection is met, behavioral guidelines are given, personal support is supplied, reality-testing takes place, and opportunities are provided to work with others on tasks seen to be significant. The sociocultural supplies include the influence of the customs and values of society on personal development and behavior. These help to locate one's position in the social order and afford an external structure and an inner security as the context for living out one's life. The sudden shutting off of one or more of these supplies cues a perception of threat to one's basic integrity as a person. This condition produces a series of adaptational struggles in order to preserve one's identity.[13]

For example, physical illness often produces crisis. Two factors seem to be involved. One is the relationship between the concept of body image and the whole self. The first major step in the development of the self is the infant's finally coming to the place where he or she can distinguish between what is outside the skin and what is inside, the delineation of the infant's own body, the setting it off from the rest of the world. The full psychosocial self of the adult is preceded in time by the recognition of the physical self, and therefore the body image forms the foundation of and is incorporated into what later comes to be the total self. Thus, any change in or attack upon the body is perceived to be an attack upon one's whole being. The observable physical changes of early adolescence are first experienced as a changing of the self, and these call for readjustment. The same is true of other stages of the aging process, of illness, surgery, or accident. The perception of this threat is experienced as anxiety, and in the case of the medical patient, it is not always proportionate to the medically diagnosed seriousness of the disorder.

A second factor involved is that in the face of this anxiety there is often the beginning of a breakdown of one's personal world. This means the breakdown of that pattern of meaningful relationships in which we exist and by which we live. The patient who is already experiencing a threat to the self as anxiety, if hospitalized, is now taken out of the familiar and somewhat secure context of living and thrust into a new and strange situation, and is relatively isolated. Opportunities for reality testing are minimized, and so a sense of peril and ideas of self-reference have more fertile soil in which to grow. There may be the beginning of the loss of identity, and personal identity is always based upon and in relation to community. This was true developmentally and continues to be true in terms of the relationship of internal dynamics and external social situations throughout life. We come to know who we are because of the communities in which we were born and raised, and frequently during illness, we feel separated from those communities that sustain us as persons.

So the physical illness or other attack upon the body in and of itself is perceived as a threat to the self; but further, there is the loss, to some degree, of previously meaningful extensions of one's self, those objects and persons in the external world with which we have identified—that is, taken into ourselves as a part of our personal identity. In this situation there are heightened demands upon the individual, without an increase of psychosocial supplies. On the contrary, there may be the withdrawal of these supplies. So, in addition to the double sense of threat in the situation, there is the appraisal of one's self as having reduced resources with which to cope with one's feelings. Understanding this, the minister can see, with perhaps greater clarity than before, the overarching importance of visiting the sick, particularly those who are in the hospital as the result of illness or surgery or accident. The pastor not only provides the opportunity for these persons to express their feelings, reduce the pressure of them, and objectify them, but also gives an increased sense of personal support and the support of the community of faith, and of faith itself.

Other situations frequently productive of crisis in somewhat similar terms are the death of an emotionally significant person, change in or loss of job, disruption of a family, and change of role due to developmental or cultural transitions. One study of 108 patients who came into a mental health clinic during a period of a year and a half shows the following most frequent "hazardous situations": loss of a family member, the disturbed behavior of a family member, a new family member, a move, a change of role within or outside marriage, and the isolation of a family from the community. Often there was an additional force which led the person to seek help after beginning to be aware of rising anxiety, such as a talk with a friend, a minister, or a doctor. The anxiety felt was the main motivating force; the desire for relief the primary goal.[14] These observations are quite close to the experiences of most ministers.

Another study made an intensive examination of the precipitating stress that led forty persons to seek treatment in a psychiatric clinic. The purpose was to organize the variety of stresses into descriptive categories.[15] All but one of these are relevant to the onset of crisis. The following are the important broad categories to keep in mind.

The first, already clearly referred to, is object loss or threat of loss.

The second is frustration with a previous source of help. One would presume here that there had not been a crisis, but a need of some kind for which assistance was sought from some person or agency, but for some reason help in the expected form was not forthcoming. At least in some instances, this disappointing result would arouse emotions that could not be expressed appropriately and effectively and that the people now felt incapable of handling. Or there may have been a sense of hopelessness and helplessness produced that had not been experienced before.

The third form of precipitating stress is a product of a person's identification with someone else. When the other person becomes involved in a situation similar to one in the first person's own past, then the original conflict and painful emotions are aroused to an intense degree. There is not always an awareness of what is taking place, or why, and a cry for help is forthcoming. For example, a middle-aged woman may at one time in her life have experienced a very painful divorce, with anger, bitterness, guilt, yet a sense of loss. With remarriage and the passing of the years, those feelings have become deeply submerged and are never consciously felt and seldom thought of. Now, however, the woman's daughter is going through a divorce, and the woman herself is having a severe emotional reaction, with feelings of depression, anger at her daughter, feelings of guilt toward her present husband; and she is quite surprised at her inability to handle her feelings.

A fourth category of precipitating stress is any event that produces a threat to one's present level of adjustment. A person is confronted with a decision, perhaps one which on the surface would seem to hold positive promise, but would still disturb one's present psychological equilibrium. There may be attraction and threat at the same time. One may not only be threatened in this way by the loss of a job or a demotion, but may also be thrown into a state of anxiety and immobility by the offer of a promotion.

Life is to be viewed as a continual series of new experiences, and therefore of demands upon the organism to cope with the internal pressure brought about by our own maturational processes or by the external stimuli of a continually changing environment. Most of these do not place excessive demands upon us, because our past learning includes a repertoire of adaptive responses that have been interpersonally and intrapsychically effective in maintaining a relatively homeostatic condition. (*Homeostasis* refers simply to a relative balance of internal forces with one another, and can be extended even to mean a relative balance between internal and external demands.) The similarity of the external occasion for the present anxiety to earlier occasions, and the knowledge of our own problem-solving resources, lead to an evaluation which includes the expectation of a successful resolution. However, when the novelty of the situation is such, or the personal loss is perceived as being so great that these usual methods of coping do not seem to be appropriate or strong enough, there is a severe disruption of the usual emotional life, which may be compared to the disruption caused by a normal maturational transition. Every developmental state or major life decision, as we have seen, has its stresses: the anxiety of giving up old patterns of responding, the threat of new responsibilities and situations calling for new forms of coping, new relationships with persons, and new relationships between meanings, as well as the creating of new meanings.

An accidental crisis results from a situation that places these same demands upon an individual, but is compressed into a brief period of time. Major alterations in pattern may occur rather rapidly, yet may subsequently persist as new aspects of personality.[16] It is important to note that the determining factor is not merely the difficulty of the situation as such, but its importance to the person, the degree of ego involvement, the amount of threat felt, and the way the person perceives the resources available to remove the threat in the learned, expected period of time. This brief transitional period has the power, due to its emotional intensity, to produce significant personality change. Clinical evidence points to the first six weeks as being vital in giving the direction.[17] This personality change can be positive or negative, adding strength or taking it away from one's ego, depending upon whether new and effective means of coping have been developed or whether there has been an increase in disturbing feelings and a breakdown of one's usual level of functioning.

Caplan has outlined four phases of the crisis situation which give a picture of the process taking place:

1. There is the original rise in tension from the problem stimulus, the experience of anxiety, perceived threat to the self. This calls forth the habitual problem-solving responses which have been learned previously and which might be generalized to this particular problem stimulus.
2. Because of the novelty of the situation and the continuing intensity of the stimulus, there is a lack of success in reducing the anxiety with the usual coping mechanisms in the period of time expected. A feeling of helplessness and ineffectualness results.
3. This is the "hitching up the belt" stage. The person dips deep into a reserve of strength and extends the range of behavior in attempting to maintain ego integrity. A redefinition of the problem may bring it into the range of prior experience. Trial and error behavior, both in

thinking and in overt act, seeks to change or remove the problem stimulus. There may be a redefinition of the person's role, thus a modification of identity. Active resignation may be integrated into the self-image. The problem may be solved in this phase. If it is, the person usually becomes stronger and moves further along the continuum toward mental health, in that methods of dealing effectively with a new and threatening situation have been learned and have been brought into the repertoire of responses.

4. However, if the problem continues with no need satisfaction, the tension produced by the anxiety may take the person beyond the threshold of rational responding, described by the term personality decompensation, where there are exaggerated distortions of one's identity or of the situation, rigid and compulsive and ineffective behavior, socially unacceptable behavior, extreme withdrawal, *et cetera*.[18]

It can be observed that one of the characteristics of crisis, as well as a factor that has the effect of intensifying it, is the narrowing of the usual range of attention, with more and more focus being on the anguish of the condition, emphasizing only a few of the features of the total situation to the exclusion of others, thus causing a greater sense of inadequacy and the hopelessness of it all.

An elaboration of this process is made by Perlman, who has referred to three levels of coping: the unconscious (ego defense mechanisms), the preconscious (those almost automatic responses to stress which can be brought quickly into consciousness and reflected upon), and the conscious (behaviors of which we are quite aware and can use selectively).[19] When we are confronted with a radically new event, or one that triggers earlier unresolved conflicts or anxieties, often the conscious and preconscious behaviors are not effective in changing the situation or reducing anxiety in the expected period of time. The unconscious mechanisms are then activated and begin to function in a rigid, compulsive manner. What has happened is that the conscious and preconscious responses, which are a part of what Perlman refers to as *mastery* of oneself and one's social environment, give way to the responses of *self-protection*, which, in their inflexible extreme, themselves become disruptive of a person's life. What Perlman has described is the deterioration of the usual level of adjustment, with the intensity of the anxiety interfering with the usual patterns of clear thinking and problem solving. A person is no longer in conscious touch with her or his strengths. If the trial-and-error behavior is not effective in reducing anxiety, then that feeling continues to escalate into panic and increasing helplessness and a person may give up, feel hopeless. Hooker has applied theories of learned helplessness in psychiatric depression to the very rapidly stimulated feelings of helplessness in situations of crisis, and gives us an understanding of how the anxiety turns into the depression which is so often seen.[20]

While it is important to be able to note the similarities between human beings, it is essential in looking at a situational crisis to note the uniqueness of this particular person in this particular situation. Karl Slaikeu stresses the necessity of looking not only at the precipitating event and at the person as an individual, but of taking into account the fact that each individual is a system with a number of subsystems, that this individual is a part of several social systems at any one time, and that all these systems interact with one another.[21] Slaikeu proposes a schema useful in evaluating a person in crisis. It is BASIC: the five modalities of *B*ehavioral, *A*ffective, *S*omatic, *I*nterpersonal, *C*ognitive. Within crisis, one or more of the aspects of any one of these modalities may begin to break down or not function well. On the other hand, with anyone in crisis, there are aspects of one or more of these modalities which continue to function well and can be sources of strength. An adequate evaluation of the crisis can take place only as we look at the various aspects of each modality and identify both weaknesses and strengths.

It needs to be stated very clearly that anyone may have a crisis, and in fact, all persons do. No one is so unmovably stable that she or he is not faced with events in life that are radically disruptive. It can also be helpful to realize that people who are already undergoing even severe emotional disorder may, in addition, experience a situational crisis. Obviously, some people may be vulnerable to fewer types of events than others and may respond more constructively and more quickly, have more resources in their personal environment, and move through their crises more quickly than others, but no person is immune.

Behavioral crisis may look like one or a combination of the behaviors of any form of disturbance, ranging from mild to extreme: confusion, lack of attention, the inability to do one's work effectively, irritability, the breakdown of personal relationships, mild to extreme depression, a persistent anxiety or occasional anxiety attacks, withdrawal, loss of interest in sex or eating, sleep disturbances, or even the very extreme behaviors we would ordinarily attribute to psychosis. However, the behavior of crisis is not most accurately conceived of as psychopathology as such, although careful attention needs to be given to suicidal and homicidal impulses. It is more properly to be thought of as the behavior of the transient state of situational crisis.

During the last decade of increased interest in the development of an understanding of crisis and the attempt to develop effective forms of intervention, numerous therapists and other investigators have sought to define and describe it. Some of the results have been somewhat less than useful in clarifying the matter, primarily as a result of some differences in concept and practical evaluation on the part of therapists themselves. It would seem, from the point of view of the minister's own practice, that the need to determine whether or not the reaction of a specific person is a crisis, with obvious implications for the counseling method used with this person, can be met by answering three questions: (1) Has there been a recent (within a few weeks) onset of the troublesome feelings and/or behavior? (2) Have they tended to grow progressively worse? (3) Can the time of onset be linked with some external event, some change in the person's life situation?

Taplin has made an important contribution by viewing the concept of crisis in terms of a perceptual and cognitive disorder. He points out that observations of persons in crisis indicate that a breakdown of thinking begins to take place under a physical or psychological overload, where there is an input of information that is significantly incompatible with one's present pattern of thinking about oneself, one's world, and one's relationships. This inevitably means that the dissonant information interferes with one's usual forms of planning and carrying out effective behavior. Crisis, then, is defined in terms of a cognitive perspective that can include all the presently observed behavior involved in the condition (an identifiable, disorienting perception; a sudden decrease in memory recall and in planning ability; an increase in aimless behavior, emotionality, suggestibility). This conceptuality also provides an accounting for therapeutic procedures which themselves are primarily cognitive in nature: direct teaching of information-processing techniques; the giving of information itself, leading to a more realistic appraisal of one's self and one's world; and the making of appropriate decisions which result in constructive behavior.[22]

After this is said, however, the issue of greatest importance to ministers and to lay workers in helping situations is not the specific technical theory of personality to which they adhere, but whether they are able to identify a crisis, distinguish it from disorders related to longer-standing pathology, understand the dynamics of personality in particular situations, and function effectively in reducing the intensity of emotion and helping those persons to new perspectives on themselves and their situations, and to effective decision making.

The implication throughout this discussion of the nature of crisis is that the power of the intense emotion, and the condition where earlier patterns of structured behavior have broken down, combine to produce a situation in which a person may either go under or experience rapid new growth. One writer has expressed another aspect of the total human picture by saying that "continual gratification of stability does not seem conducive to rapid change or growth."[23] The very nature of crisis is that it forces change and readjustment. A person must learn new methods of coping that become part of increased adaptability, resiliency, and strength.

> At crisis a painfully unstable state of psychological affairs exists and some kind of equilibrium must be established for a person to become oriented effectively to the future. . . . [Therefore it] represents both a need and an opportunity for significant growth and creativity and lowers resistance to utilizing interpersonal experience and other kinds of information in new ways, to seeking newly conceived experiences or accepting formerly rejected ones.[24]

An extremely important factor to keep in mind is that people usually do not face a crisis alone, and therefore they are either helped or hindered in their task of maintaining themselves as persons by the other significant persons about them: family, friends, co-workers, members of the groups to which they belong, and professional workers of various kinds, one of which is the minister, an important figure for many people. Are these persons involved in the sufferer's life in such a way as to give psychosocial need satisfactions that will compensate for the need frustration in other areas? Does the minister, for example, visit in the hospital? Does he or she come by and continue to see people in grief ? Does the pastor work with the family of a person who has been hospitalized with an emotional disorder? Do the minister and other significant persons offer the opportunity for new decisions, new behavioral forms, new roles that are ego-strengthening?

During a crisis, persons are more open to influence by others than at any other time. Their emotional equilibrium is upset, their thinking is unclear, and even a relatively minor force can tip them to the side of resolution of the problem and additional strength, or toward failure and increased vulnerability and potential decompensation of behavior. The presence of significant other persons may have a major effect in determining the choice of coping mechanisms, which in turn influence the outcome of the crisis.[25]

Crisis in Theological Perspective

It is possible to define crisis from points of view and with language that is not exclusively psychological. If ordained clergy do not view human crisis from a theological perspective as well as understanding it in the terms used in this chapter up to this point, they are being untrue to themselves as persons and professionals and are limiting their uniquely pastoral opportunities with persons to whom they minister.

An especially provocative theological approach has been elaborated by Charles Gerkin, who sets the stage for his discussion with the following:

> A crisis situation is, for modern persons, an extreme or boundary situation in which the fundamental contradiction between human aspiration and finite possibilities becomes visible in such a way as to demand attention. In the situational crisis we are confronted with our human vulnerability, our finitude, the utter impossibility of our deepest hopes and wishes. In that situation, a most elemental choice is forced upon persons that is at its core a religious or "faith" choice. Either persons must defend themselves against the contradiction with whatever human defense is possible, be that denial or heroic courage, or they must open themselves to the vulnerability of the unknown future, trusting in the power and care of God coming out of the change and contingency of the unknown.[26]

At the same time that persons find themselves caught between their infinite aspirations and their obvious boundaries of finitude, they often discover they have lost "the power of the image of God's providence" as the "transcendent one who sets and maintains the natural order of things with its boundaries between finite and infinite and . . . who is with us in our contingent life, shielding us from its vulnerability." Gerkin finds in the work of Jürgen Moltmann and Wolfhart Pannenberg a theology that presents the God appropriate and adequate to the human condition as revealed in these situations of crisis. "The image is of future emergence of God's power. . . . To be free is to be open to God's power coming toward us out of the unknown future of his kingdom. It is in the power to transform the present made possible by the coming of the kingdom of God that persons are to find their security in God's purpose.[27]

There are a number of sets of terms by which we may conceive pastoral care theologically. Gerkin's journey through human crises, enabled by a "theology of hope" and our openness to our own new future, which is also God's future, leads him to think of pastoral care as "incarnational acts." From this perspective, pastoral care is understood as that form of helping relationship in which the minister as a human being enters into the human experience of another, while at the same time representing the God who comes into our present out of the future. Crisis ministry is seen by Gerkin as "directed toward opening up avenues of . . . trust in the ultimate outcome of things that can only be secured in the mystery of God's purpose for creation yet to be fulfilled.[28]

Gerkin's exact formulation of crisis as an issue of faith, and the particular statement of the theology that is meaningful to him, are not the only ways of theologically conceiving of and talking about human crisis. However, his approach is both meaningful in itself and stimulating to the minister's own unending path of attempting to see human life realistically in the light of the reality of God, and to the additional task of assisting others in grappling meaningfully with these critical issues for themselves. It is to this helping task that we now turn.

CHAPTER 3

METHODS OF CRISIS
COUNSELING

In a comprehensive overview of the methods of crisis counseling, it is necessary to talk about much more than methods as such and in the narrow sense of the word. Purpose, persons, and process are tied inseparably together. These, along with their corollaries, can be discussed independently of one another, although never without obvious overlap. This is the way it must be, in terms of the practicalities of presentation. Nevertheless, it should be understood at every point that these elements are a part of the unified whole of what crisis counseling is all about. This chapter, then, is to be an examination of the five elements which comprise this whole:

The *goal* of crisis counseling
The *role of words* in the interaction
The *personhood of the minister*
The *facilitative conditions* of the helping relationship
The *process and methods* of crisis counseling

The Goal

The primary goal of *crisis* counseling can be stated very simply and needs only a little elaboration. Very concisely, it is the quickest possible relief of the internal and external symptoms of the crisis and a return to that particular person's usual level of functioning. In actual practice it is recognized that many crises will leave their residue of hurt and therefore residual feelings and occasional behavioral responses to these. In this sense, it is unrealistic to expect a person to be precisely the same as before. Also, in many instances of the successful resolution of crisis, new learning will have taken place; new methods of coping as a by-product of the resolution process will be added to the person's repertoire of behavior designed to deal with stress and loss. So in an additional sense, the person is not the same, and in reality is functioning at an improved level. Therefore it is appropriate to consider some real growth as a reasonable expectation of working directly toward crisis resolution.

The tricky part of defining this goal of symptom relief for any given person is that the feelings and behavior of crisis must be distinguished from the feelings and behavior of the person's precrisis condition. Not only are the methods of crisis intervention inappropriate if there is a chronic pathological condition without crisis, but it must also be understood that a person with a chronic disturbance may also suffer a crisis. In that person, a differentiation between the symptoms must be made, and the crisis counseling directed only at the behavior of the crisis. There must be no attempt to deal with the prior condition at the same time and with the same methods. A specific case to be presented later will seek to illustrate this point as well as demonstrate the basic methods of crisis intervention.

However, in such instances, it is possible that the effectiveness of the minister in working with a person in crisis may in itself provide the stimulus to motivate the person to seek additional help with other problems.

In summary, the goal of crisis counseling contains inherently within it a series of expectations:

1. Symptom relief—the alleviation of immediate distress, the cessation of the maladaptive behavior of the crisis
2. Actual growth through the learning of new coping methods
3. The continuance in counseling with the same or another counselor when there are other problems yet to be resolved.

The Role of Words

It is somewhat amazing to many people, at first brief consideration, to realize that a relationship and a process as potent as that of counseling or psychotherapy takes place chiefly through an exchange of words. Of course, as far as the minister is concerned, something of the same thing could be said for preaching. Interestingly, although pastoral counseling and preaching are clearly distinguishable functions of ministry, there are some amazing similarities: Both are interpersonal processes, personal relationships with similar interpersonal dynamics and procedural steps. From the perspective of faith, God is present and active in both processes, and in both the gospel is expressed. Finally, the use of words is essential in both, and the interpersonal conditions communicated by those words is critical.[1] Therefore it is imperative that we look more deeply at the meaning of the spoken word. When we do so, we discover that a word is never *merely* a word. It is an *act* of the whole person, like any other act. It becomes then a form of delivering ourselves to another person. It is a reflection of who we are, an acting out of our being in relation to another being.

In order to grasp fully this level of meaning, an elaboration of the development of personality and the role of the learning and use of language in the early development of the child would be necessary. Such a detailed elaboration is beyond the scope of this book, and, in fact, is to be found in an earlier work.[2] Only the very briefest summary will be presented here.

Talking is originally learned by every child in the context of the emotionally charged relationship of absolute dependence upon parents. The original meaning of talking then gains its full force from this relationship. It is learned in a very complex process, combining the beginning natural expression of sounds on the part of the child, the imitation of that which the parents are seeking to teach by rewarding certain sounds over certain other sounds, and by the actual identification with the behavior of the parent. This last factor means that the language of the parent and the attitudes the parent has toward the child are incorporated as a part of the child's own self. Language then is literally an integral part of one's self. Talking is practiced by the child first as a necessary means of communicating basic survival and comfort needs; second, as a means of winning and maintaining parental approval; and third, as a means of holding the parents emotionally near even when the child is alone. In all three of these ways, talking is a means of anxiety reduction, a learned method of overcoming separation. Language continues to have something of this affective and relational meaning throughout a person's life. It is important to keep this in mind as the relationship and process of crisis counseling are discussed.

In this context it is easy to see that there is a unity of language and personality. Talking is one of the most important ways we have of establishing meaningful relationships, reducing anxiety, and communicating meaning—emotional as well as intellectual. In human life one act may substitute for another. This is not to say that they are

identical in meaning, potency, and effect, but depending upon the
quality of the act, its context, and a number of other factors, it moves
more or less in the direction of being the same. Talking is an act that
is frequently a substitute for other acts. For example, we speak
angrily or sarcastically or in a demeaning manner, rather than hitting
another person. This, then, is the power of the spoken word in
counseling. It is emotional-relational in its very nature, and it
encompasses all the time dimensions.

Something of the meaning of talking in counseling, as it relates to
the time dimensions, may be shown in the following diagram:

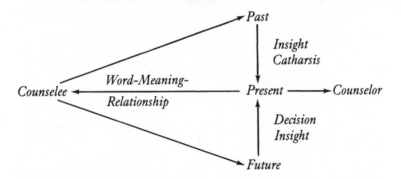

The word is *in* the present; in fact, in the moment of counseling, it
is the present. It is in the context of a personal, affective relationship,
and it is the means of developing and maintaining that relationship, a
security measure, and an ego-fulfilling act.

But the present word frequently refers to the past, either near or
distant. Persons in counseling reach back into their past, have an
image of what took place, speak the present word describing the past,
and therefore in effect, by telling their story, present a contemporary
reenactment of the past: its relationships, acts, feelings. Their words
are present acts substituting for past acts, and within the reenactment
they have the potential for clarifying the past, bringing insight into
the present, and producing catharsis, the pressure-relieving
expression of emotion.

By the same token, the present word may move, indeed *must* move,
into the future in order to bring it into the present for testing. Again,
we have a present act, substituting this time for a future one, testing
future action in the present to try to determine what it *will* be like, but
without all the consequences. Therefore it too has the power to bring
insight into the present and leads to decision making on the basis of

the present testing of the future. Counseling is this kind of present, past-present, and future-present relationship, established and expedited by the use of spoken words.

The Personhood of the Minister

Carkhuff points out that there are four factors which interact to affect the outcome of any counseling: the person needing help; the counselor; the setting of the counseling relationship and process, and the total context that develops out of that relationship and process; and the daily environment of the person in distress (home and family, work, friends, group membership).[3]

In regard to the person needing help, the identifiable common characteristics of crisis have already been discussed, as has the fact that the precrisis condition will differ from person to person. The influence of the total physical environment, the quality of behavior of family, friends, and co-workers in relation to the person in crisis, and the number and degree of meaningfulness of the person's activities, including work, would seem to be rather obvious. Not the least of these factors in potency is the helper. The relationship between the counselor and the person needing help, and what that produces, will be discussed later.

It was stated in Chapter 2 that in the midst of the transition, the unsettled thoughts and the disturbed emotions of a person in crisis, intervention by another person has a potential for tremendous influence. One would naturally expect that those with the most influence would be those who are already linked to the person in crisis by bonds of love and who play a role in his or her particular pattern of needs. Caplan confirms this judgment.[4] The closer one is to the needs of the sufferer, the closer one is to the crisis in terms of time and place, the more likely one is to be called on and the easier it usually is for that one to take the initiative to intervene.

Few are in a more strategic position for intervention in crisis, in terms of visibility, availability, and previously established relationships, than the alert and sensitive minister. Caplan notes this and makes a point of particular value to us in the ministry, who sometimes feel a bit unsure of ourselves as we move into the role of psychotherapists. Caplan believes the forms of crisis intervention should be consistent with the already-defined functions of one's chosen profession. He does not recommend a direct transfer of the methods of perception, assessment, and psychotherapy from the psychiatrist or psychologist to the minister. The basic professional role of the clergy should always be maintained in order to be of greatest value to the persons who understand themselves as talking with a minister. A direct transfer of techniques might entail the modification of perspective integral to the role and functioning of ministers to such a degree that they are robbed of their own unique and helpful perceptions and approaches.[5] This does not mean, of course, that we have nothing to learn from the psychiatric professional. But we must work out, with some clarity, what we may adopt with value for our understanding and technique without damage to our fundamental role. Certainly, too, there should be, beneath every professional role, a genuinely human basis for the sensitive perception of the situation and for methods of dealing with the persons and their problems.

On the other side of the coin, it should be appropriately noted that the way ministers have traditionally functioned and related to persons in need could be studied by other mental health professionals to their advantage. An interesting article by Thomas McGee has outlined four considerations that he feels are an absolute necessity for mental health workers in order to utilize certain techniques of crisis intervention in the most effective way. Although he himself makes no reference to it at all, he makes a superb case for the minister as the present number-one crisis counseling professional; he uses the model of ministers' typical functioning to make his point in regard to the transformation of the operation of at least much of the present community mental health program.

The first consideration he mentions is *location*. The mental health worker "must be located in and involved with a specific community or communities."[6] A person in crisis is much more likely to seek help and to do so more rapidly when this is the case. In any community, few facilities are more universally present or more easily recognized than the church building, and few professionals more visible than the clergy, who have a double tie—with the community of faith itself through persons' voluntary association with the church, and with the larger community through the minister's active participation in it. Every minister has had the experience of people coming for help simply because they live down the block from the church, or were just driving by and saw it, or had seen or heard or met the pastor at some community gathering.

The second consideration is *availability*. A person in distress "must be guaranteed an effective contact . . . rapidly and *during the period of crisis*, not two or three weeks hence."[7] McGee turns thumbs down on the Monday-through-Friday nine-to-five operation as an appropriate schedule for meeting crises. People simply do not pay attention to typical clinic hours as a format for the production of their own crises. Ministers, as we all know, have never been accused, certainly not by their own families, of keeping such hours rigidly. Ministers are available. The importance of immediate access to a helping person at the time of crisis is emphasized by several professionals in the field, pointing to the value of the rapid reduction of some of the dangers of crisis and the rapid establishment of a firm therapeutic working relationship.[8]

The third necessary factor for the fuller meeting of people's crisis needs is *mobility*. "The mental health professional who merely waits in a mental health facility for an individual in crisis to appear is not prepared to engage in comprehensive crisis intervention."[9] Again, the conscientious and dedicated minister is a model: visiting in homes, getting to know persons, opening doors for counseling, sensing needs at an early stage, visiting in the hospital where most persons are experiencing mild to severe crisis, being on call to go to an unbelievable variety of places when asked, and taking the initiative by going to persons wherever they are and whenever there is reason to believe there is need.[10]

The fourth consideration is *flexibility* of procedure. By this McGee is referring specifically to the effective use of the telephone and also to the ready acceptance of walk-ins. Interestingly, he feels it necessary to point out that these and other procedures are not demeaning or beneath one's professional status.[11] This thought probably had never occurred to most ministers, whose usual training and inclination have combined to lead them to do whatever they can whenever they can, if it seems to be the best thing to do for the person in need. Certainly counseling and follow-up on the telephone and accepting people for immediate counseling when they walk into the church is standard operating procedure.

Most ministers not only will accept McGee's points, they will recognize their own methods of operating, which could very well have served as the source for his suggestions. Most ministers function in these ways because they genuinely desire to help others. They have received, out of their own tradition, forms of serving that have proved useful, and they keep an openness to new forms and a readiness to experiment with them and adopt them when they prove useful. Of course, what has been discussed here has related primarily to the minister's role and context and, to some extent, motivation. Still crucial are those elements of pastoral functioning that grow out of the underlying human factors of the minister as helper, each minister's own level of adjustment and manner of relating to other persons: warmth, genuineness, courage, openness. The whole issue of the helper as a human being and how he or she contributes to or takes away from the growth of the person seeking help must be examined honestly.

Many ministers who graduated from seminary some years ago can remember their first courses in pastoral care and counseling. Among the first things we learned was that pastoral counseling was not (1) immediately and automatically applying the forms, symbols, rites, and sacraments of the church as the answer to all problems, nor was it (2) immediate advice as to the course of action a person should take. Once beyond that, a major impression was that if we applied the methodology of nondirective counseling, a number of people would be helped significantly, the great majority would be helped some, and no one would be injured. With qualifications, that may have been very close to the truth. But when we were let loose on real people with real problems, most of us had no supervision, no guidelines to determine whether we were applying that methodology consistently, no data relating the methodology to the *person* who was using it. As a result we fell into many errors, yet we continued to believe that at the very worst, there would be a few people we would not be able to help.

Further research over the years has shown us how wrong we were—that as a matter of fact, counseling is like marriage, it is for better or for worse. In fact, it is like any relationship. It never stays the same; it is always in process. Persons in distress likewise do not remain precisely where they are. They get better or they get worse, and the helping persons have much to do with the direction they go. Research evidence smashes the idea that just any sort of person may learn certain ideas and techniques and thereby become an effective counselor of others. The hypothesis that has been tested, and so far upheld, is that "all effective interpersonal processes share a common core of conditions conducive to facilitative human experiences." These conditions are not just something we do, but are reflections of who we are. It is a rather obvious fact that the counselor is a key ingredient in the process, in that she or he offers a model of a person who is living effectively. There are crucial elements of a relationship necessary for the growth of persons in distress that counselors cannot simply produce by something they *do,* unless somehow that is what they *are,* unless their behavior in the relationship is an authentic expression of their own being.[12]

Carkhuff refers to the three Rs of helping which are appropriate to discuss in the context of the minister's intervention in crisis:

1. The *right* of the helper to intervene in the life of another
2. The *responsibility* of the helper once he or she has intervened
3. The *role* the helper must assume in helping another individual, and at the same time, the various role conflicts encounted in attempting to implement the responsibilities implied by intervention.[13]

We ministers have not too often questioned our *right* to enter into the lives of other persons in a variety of ways, both by invitation and at our own initiative. Somehow we have assumed this right as a proper and inherent given in our being ministers. Carkhuff, however, basing his conclusions on a growing body of research data, states that this right must be based on our ability to help, not just our traditional role. This means that we must be functioning at higher levels of effectiveness ourselves in the relevant areas of concern. "Only the person who is alive and growing can enable the struggling person to choose life at the life and death crisis points."[14] Pastors should not be in the ministry primarily to fulfill, in rather temporary pastoral care and counseling relationships, those needs of their own that are unfulfilled in their personal lives or to find intimacy they cannot find elsewhere. Otherwise, they may end up helping neither themselves nor others.

The matter of responsibility follows hard on the heels of this statement. Persons who intervene primarily out of their own lack of fulfillment act in distorted ways that are reflections of their own incompleteness, and thus their methods of relating to others will be designed more to serve themselves than to serve others. They will subtract from and otherwise distort the meaning of the responses of the person in need, thereby *increasing* the other person's distortions rather than reducing them. This speaks of responsibility, initially to ourselves in regard to our own growth, health, and meaningful relationships, in order that we may have something, mainly ourselves, to offer to the other.

The matter of role is a particularly important issue for ministers, for we have a long history, a tradition, which tells us and the larger society something about who the clergy are. Without going into detail here, we need to clarify the difference between certain of our functions as ordained clergy, and ourselves as individual human beings. We need to be able to utilize the symbolic power of our role and the authority it carries, but without hiding behind it or exploiting people with it. Our role responsibility as pastoral counselors is a commitment to do all we can that will translate into benefits for the person who needs help. Our movement in the process is always from the role first, to the person later, a personal relationship "in which neither person allows himself or the other to be less than he can be."[15]

All this leads to an obvious conclusion. Ministers cannot be effectual crisis counselors merely by learning theory and techniques from a book. They must grow as persons. One of the central functions of the minister at all times, and most certainly in counseling, is to provide for others a model of one who has a purpose in life, who has satisfying relationships, who is able to utilize insights in appropriate action. Most of us as ministers have very little choice as to whether we will or will not be involved with persons in crisis. The only choice is how well we will function for the other's benefit. The obligation is laid upon us to grow in the direction of being the kind of persons who contribute more to the helping process than we take away from it, by taking advantage of whatever opportunities are available to us: clinical training, supervision of our counseling by another professional, growth groups, individual or group therapy. Carkhuff summarizes it succinctly:

> Perhaps the point on which to conclude a consideration of the counselor's contribution to helping processes is the point at which all effective helping begins, that is, with an integrated and growing person, one who is personally productive and creative, one whose life is dominated by personal meaning and fulfillment. Without such persons in the helping role there is no hope in the world or for the world.[16]

It will be seen in the discussion and case study later in this chapter that both the limitation of time and the procedures themselves demand a more active participation on the part of the counselor than do the older traditional approaches in which most ministers have been schooled. An active role in questioning, searching, focusing, keeping the person on the present situation, interpreting, giving information, suggesting, mobilizing resources, and in calling for decision making develops naturally in the process. This is not as easy for many ministers as it may seem merely from reading about the crisis counseling process itself, since many of us tend to be rather passive in many situations and relationships, although not necessarily in all. Kardiner, however, speaks very strongly about the negative, obstructive impact of passivity on the part of the crisis counselor. Rusk and Gerner emphasize the same point, adding that the model of the counselor as a "blank screen" is entirely inappropriate. Wolberg discusses the counselor's need for flexibility in both personality and approach, for spontaneity and creativity, for the ability to move in quickly in relationships and to take the initiative in mobilizing help.[17]

The danger in emphasizing this type of activity and directness and initiative-taking is that it is possible for them to be expressed in ways that communicate paternalism or authoritarianism, which are not merely direct, but rather directive, in the sense of suggesting that the counselor will do for the person what that person must take the responsibility to do for herself or himself. This delicate balance of being direct without being directive, of being active without being authoritarian, of being one upon whom the other can be temporarily dependent while still seeking to nourish an egalitarian relationship, requires attention on the part of the pastor to his or her own personality as well as to particular skills of intervention.

A last absolutely crucial factor needs to be mentioned in this discussion of the personality of the minister who is engaged in crisis counseling, or any other pastoral care, for that matter. It is what might be referred to by the "shorthand" expression, *sex role expectation*. Most certainly such images and expectations of ourselves as male or female, and of others as male or female, are an inevitable and integral part of who we are. In order for ministers to be most effective in any helping process, we need to be aware of the influence on our pastoral relationships of our own learning concerning what it means to be male and female in our society. Our actual relationships with our own parents and our memories of those, both accurate and distorted, affect the way we relate to men and women and the way we expect them to relate to us. In addition, what we learn of gender roles from many sources has the potential for influencing our pastoral care in a negative manner.

Although much of what we read and hear has to do with male counselors and female clients or male pastors and female parishioners (with the exception of only a few psychiatric, psychological, and pastoral counseling writings [18]), with the rapidly increasing number of women clergy, it is important to explore women's learning of male and female roles with regard to pastoral relationships. However, since the large majority of clergy have, to this time, been men, and the majority of persons who seek pastoral counseling have been women, most of the discussion has been focused on those situations.

In her research, Emma Justes interviewed male pastors and role-played with them typical situations in which they might be called upon to help female parishioners. She discovered both conscious and unconscious biases concerning male/female roles, which affect negatively the therapeutic relationship and significantly limit those pastors' ability to assist women in exploring the possible alternatives for themselves in the problem-solving phase of the helping process. For example, she reports an incident involving an attractive woman who reported to her (male) pastor that her husband had beaten her. The minister concluded that the husband would naturally be jealous of a wife so attractive, and the direction taken in his series of responses led very clearly to the conclusion that if *she* would only work harder in the marriage, giving the husband no provocation, then *he* will not beat her. She must try not to *create* jealousy in him (even though her behavior had, in fact, been entirely innocent).[19] One can only imagine the sense of frustration, anger, and perhaps guilt this woman experienced in response to this unbelievable lack of understanding of what she was attempting to communicate about herself and her relationship.

Insensitive and unreflective male pastors may often unthinkingly place more responsibility on the woman than on the man in a marriage or in other male/female relationships. If the *woman* will make the necessary changes, *he*, and, by presumption, the *relationship* will be all right. It all depends on *her*.

Another common way in which both male and female learning roles may have an impact upon pastoral care in general by male ministers with women parishioners is the assumption that men are supposed to take care of women in certain particular ways. It would not be surprising that the two people involved would collude unconsciously in encouraging the woman's dependence upon the minister. This would be particularly critical in crisis counseling, since a feeling of helplessness and the dependence which follows are both common and natural. If the *cultivation* of dependence were to take place, the male minister would fail to empower women in crisis by not assisting them to do as much for themselves as they possibly can. The whole relationship and its outcome would be different if the person in crisis were a man.

Justes makes clear that good skills alone are not sufficient for effective pastoral counseling of women. Rather, it is necessary for ministers to deal with their attitudes and expectations regarding female and male differences, roles, and relationships. She states that the "pastoral counselor (either male or female) has been influenced by stereotyped role definitions, attitudes and expectations communicated by the predominant culture."[20]

In the problem-solving stage of crisis counseling, it is possible for a male minister to encase a woman parishioner in the strict limitations of what *he* believes women *ought* and *ought not* do, thus narrowing the range of behavioral alternatives necessary for crisis resolution.

When pastors have specific notions of what women do and don't do, and what men do and don't do, these notions find their way into their practice of pastoral care. A woman exploring with her pastor frustration with her present situation and possibilities of making a greater contribution to humanity—beyond her roles as wife, homemaker and mother—may meet with responses defined by sex roles rather than by her needs. She may be assured that her role of mother is of utmost importance and quite sufficient in God's sight and that she is accepted by God as she is. . . . For some women these may be appropriate responses. For others these suggestions would hinder fulfillment of the woman's potential and the realization of the fullness of her gifts. The expression of her gifts would be limited by sex role expectations that might have gone unchallenged.[21]

In a personal conversation with Justes, she emphasized that women ministers dealing with men parishioners can, themselves, certainly have both conscious and unconscious role biases which form impediments to effective pastoral counseling. She also indicated that it is quite possible for women ministers to miss the very real sensitivity and positive responsiveness that some men have to women's enlarging role in our society and in personal relationships, leading to a type of reverse discrimination. Abigail Carlisle's study of women pastoral counselors reports that some are aware that they are biased against certain men (physical abusers of spouse and/or children, authoritarian). In addition, some men were not able to respond well to a woman in a position of authority, and one which required competence. (It should be noted, however, that there were also therapeutic advantages for many men in their relationships with these women.)[22]

In order to reduce the limitations in pastoral care which our own sex role expectations impose upon us, it would be wise for all of us to be in some form of continuing consciousness raising.

The Facilitative Conditions

The obvious implication of what has been discussed about the person of the counselor is that no person in need can reach a higher level of functioning than that which the helping person has achieved. Therefore, that which ministers have to give in counseling is primarily themselves. This is not to say that techniques, the knowledge of what kinds of statements to respond to, at what times, and in what verbal forms, and what sorts of nonverbal interventions to make are unimportant, but these are always conveyed through the vehicle of a person in relationship with another person.

There is a growing body of evidence, growing out of research begun by Rogers, continued by Truax and Carkhuff, and elaborated in more detail with even newer data by Carkhuff, which indicates that regardless of theoretical orientation or style or technique, there are certain critical ingredients of the successful psychotherapeutic relationship. When these ingredients are present, persons in need are helped, and when these ingredients are not part of the relationship and process to an adequate degree, there are negative results.[23]

These essential ingredients, referred to as the facilitative conditions, are what the counselor introduces into the helping relationship.[24] These are just as relevant in the relationship and process of crisis intervention as they are in longer-term counseling.

The first, most important, and foundational condition that must be provided by the counselor is *accurate empathy* and its *accurate communication*. This is central from beginning to end, and without it the other conditions lose their therapeutic potency. This condition implies that the counselor is able to perceive, to understand the other person's situation, as well as the feeling or feelings which the person is experiencing. It needs to be made clear that merely *being* empathetic is not sufficient. For empathy to be effective in helping, it must be communicated in both verbal and nonverbal ways, but with an emphasis on the verbal.

As pastors, we may or may not share the particular feeling or feelings the other person is expressing. In fact, if we are human, we shall do both at different times, depending upon who we are and what the other person is talking about. It would be very unusual if we did not at times feel sadness, anger, joy, and other emotions along with the person. When we do, it is possible for us to use our own feelings to increase the depth of our empathy and assist us in communicating. On the other hand, it is possible for us to allow our feelings such free reign that they become controlling of us and therefore interfere with our undistorted communication of empathy for the other.

The point is, our feelings are not the same as our empathy. Empathy as here defined is primarily, although not exclusively, a cognitive activity, the imaginative response to what another person is describing. Both our intellectual understanding of what the person is saying and the creative use of our imagination combine to assist us in understanding what that person's situation really is, what the person's feelings are, what the intensity of them is, and then in expressing in words that we are somehow sharing this experience.

A response by the counselor that is minimally facilitative is one that is interchangeable both in cognitive content and affect with the statement of the person in need. The response becomes more facilitative as the counselor perceives and communicates how the person really feels beneath the surface, or in addition to the emotion verbally expressed, thereby enabling the person to experience and express feelings in a manner she or he was previously unable to do.

The dynamic function of the accurate communication of empathy is that it leads the other person into that very powerful experience of being understood, thus beginning to break down any sense of isolation, and contributing to the establishment of a relationship of trust within the counseling process. This, in turn, has the power to free the other person to explore herself or himself at ever-increasing levels of depth and express those self-discoveries more openly.

The second essential ingredient of all helping relationships is *respect*, the extent to which the helper genuinely cares about the other, is committed to the other's worth as a person, and is convinced of that person's potential for growth. This respect is communicated by the helper's commitment to the counseling process and in other ways in and through the relationship—initially, primarily through the accurate communication of empathy.

The third facilitative condition is *concreteness*. The counselor enables the other to be very specific, concrete, about feelings, experiences, language, meanings, not allowing the person to speak "in general," or feel "in general." The counselor assists this concreteness by a variety of means, including direct questions, suggestions, and reflections.

For example, a person might say, "I've been feeling pretty bad a lot recently." The counselor's response might be, "I can sense from the way you say this that you've been hurting and are even hurting right now. But I wonder what bad feelings you are talking about."

Rather sophisticated counselees might use popular psychological jargon: "I seem to be projecting a lot today." The counselor is obligated to respond, "I wonder if you could tell me what you mean by projecting and give me an example of how you have been doing it." The helper also assists concreteness by speaking in clear, simple, straightforward, nontechnical language.

The fourth and fifth facilitative conditions—*genuineness and self-disclosure*—are closely linked. Genuineness is to be thought of primarily in terms of self-awareness and is both means and end of counseling. To the extent that there is a correspondence between the experience, the awareness of the experience, and the communication of that awareness in the helping person, there is a tendency for the same awareness and communication to develop in the person being helped. The person who is genuine is freely and deeply his or her own self as a human being in responding to experiences of all types and has an ability to utilize internal personal responses for the helpful exploration of the relationship.

A lack of genuineness is characterized by being out of touch with one's own feelings or conflicts or motives. A high level of defensiveness is also characteristic of a low level of genuineness. An exaggerated professionalism, a rehearsed quality to one's responses, or responses growing out of one's prescribed role are reflections of a lack of genuineness. Feelings, attitudes, conflicts, and other aspects of our own being of which we are unaware inevitably express themselves both verbally and nonverbally, yet in disguised ways. These distort our consciously intended communication and thereby reduce the accuracy of our empathy, confuse the other person, and lead to greater anxiety and/or anger on that person's part.

Appropriate and helpful self-disclosure is, of course, dependent upon genuineness. Self-disclosure refers to the degree to which the counselor is willing to be known as a human being, being open to revealing herself or himself personally, either in response to questions of the person seeking help or, when the relationship has been well-established, by taking the initiative in an appropriate context to disclose important areas of his or her own life and selfhood (feelings, experiences, perceptions of reality, faith convictions) in a way constructive to the counselee.

Premature or overly detailed self-disclosure may have the effect of inhibiting the other person's self-exploration and the flow of conversation. Self-disclosure is to be distinguished from psychological exhibitionism, the uninhibited "letting it all hang out." Such undisciplined personal responses are clearly reflective of the needs of the counselor and interfere with the relationship and the process. The key to self-disclosure is the need of the other person, the perception on the part of the helper that the relationship has reached the point at which the other person is capable of listening and reflecting seriously on what the counselor shares and that the counselor's personal sharing will at this particular time assist the other person's self-exploration or decision making.

The sixth essential ingredient is *confrontation*. It should be made clear that this does not refer to verbal shock treatment, a hard-hitting interpretation of what is taking place in the person's life. Genuine confrontation is based on the assumption that a person needs and, down underneath all defenses, wants an undistorted external observation and evaluation of his or her behavior. Confrontation is simply pointing out in a clear manner, through indirect and direct questioning as well as by reflective statement, any of several forms of discrepancy in the counselee: between insights and actions, between the person's own self-concept and his or her stated ideal concept, between the person's own experience of self and the counselor's experience of the person, between what the person says and how it is said, between stated goals and actual behavior. Again, premature confrontation is often rejected.

The final facilitative condition in the helping process is *immediacy*, referring to the way both the helper and the person in need are experiencing their relationship at the present moment. The counselor recognizes the possibility that expressions by the counselee, apparently about events or relationships outside the counseling session, might in fact be referring to the relationship right then and there. This recognition is verbalized in an explicit manner, the connection is made between what the counselee has said and the meaning it may have for this present relationship, and the two persons enter into an exploration of what is taking place between them. There are two benefits of immediacy. First, it provides an intensity of experience between two persons that is seldom a part of many people's lives. Second, it provides a model to the counselee of a person who understands and acts appropriately on awareness of personal experience, who understands the impact of each on the other.

Time and further research may show additional factors at work in personal relationships which are essential to the growth of the individuals involved, but at the present time the evidence supports the conclusion that the presence of these seven are necessary for the helping process. It is upon this foundation that the crisis methodology specifically must be built if it is to produce the necessary interruption of the downward spiral of crisis and lead to positive growth.

The Process and Methods

Having considered the goal of crisis counseling, the role and the person of the minister, and the essential ingredients of the helping process, which are a function both of the minister's personhood and of training, what are the specific methods of crisis intervention that seem to be appropriate for integration into the pastoral counseling process? Gerald Jacobson, director of the Benjamin Rush Center in Los Angeles, makes clear the context of the therapeutic approach: "The advantages to be gained from crisis therapy can be maximized when the patient's crisis becomes the deliberate focus of the treatment."[25] This approach is in contrast with many traditional psychotherapeutic methods, which either allow persons in need to choose their own point of departure and route in the elaboration of their condition and situation, or move into an investigation of long-standing personality patterns, including pathology. The relevance for clergy of the focus on the contemporary issue, rather than on deep-seated psychopathology rooted in early childhood, seems obvious when one considers the role of ministers, their training, and the time they have available. To say this, though, is not to indicate that they have no need for thorough training in this approach or that they must be content with helping people in only a superficial way.

Rapoport points out that the three areas of need in crisis define the tasks of intervention. First, the distorted perceptions of the person in crisis make it necessary that the problem which leads to the call for help be clarified. As a result of identifying the external and internal events that have led to the disruption, cognitive restructuring can take place and lead toward a more rational response to the situation. Second, since strong emotions are also being experienced, these need to be discharged in appropriate ways. This task is facilitated by the counselor, who accepts the feelings and at the same time helps the person understand the source of these reactions. Finally, since there is some amount of therapeutic force built into the ordinary networks of human relationships, social structures and institutions, routines and rituals, persons in crisis need to be helped to identify and utilize those that are most appropriate for them and for their circumstances.[26] There are a number of conceptual schemes that can contain the total crisis intervention process with goals such as these.

Slaikeu discusses in detail a useful framework for conceptualizing the crisis helping process and for functioning in it. He makes a distinction between what he calls "psychological first aid" and "multimodal crisis therapy," or "first-order" and "second-order crisis intervention." Psychological first aid is given by the person or persons present when the crisis first comes to light; it is done immediately. It is accomplished in one contact, and its purpose is to provide support, to reduce lethality, and to link the person in crisis to other helping resources. These goals are accomplished by the helping person in (1) making psychological contact; (2) exploring dimensions of the problem; (3) examining possible solutions; (4) assisting the person in taking concrete action; (5) following up.[27] Without question, pastors are frequently available during the early hours and days of many crises, and to be able to function at a high level of effectiveness in this first-order crisis intervention will result in more rapid reduction of persons' distress, will help persons in crisis avoid more serious problems, will create and deepen pastoral relationships, and will be a powerful witness to the relevance of the gospel.

The goal of psychological first aid and its immediate follow-up process is restored equilibrium, and this usually seems to be accomplished in six weeks or less. Admittedly, there are a number of special situational crises in which the most intense feelings and behaviors take much longer to diminish: loss by death or divorce; reactions to heart attack, hospitalization, or severe disorders such as cancer.[28]

What Slaikeu calls crisis therapy (second-order intervention) begins where psychological first aid leaves off, which could be in the second counseling session, or even after psychological first aid has been offered in the first session. This process takes longer (usually a matter of weeks or months). It also requires evaluation, in which the counselor needs "to assess the impact of the crisis event on all five areas of the person's functioning—behavior, feelings, physical health, interpersonal relationships, and cognition." The person's precrisis and within-crisis functioning is examined according to this scheme, identifying and clarifying the person's *strengths* for use in exploration, decision making, and coping, as well as identifying particular areas of dysfunction.[29] Thus the total assessment process includes identification of the following:

1. Precipitating event(s);
2. Presenting problem(s);
3. Context of crisis;
4. Precrisis-BASIC functioning;
5. Crisis-BASIC functioning.[30]

The goal of crisis therapy is to assist the person in working through the crisis experience along the following dimensions:

1. Physically surviving the crisis and its aftermath;
2. Expressing feelings related to the crisis;
3. Gaining cognitive mastery of the entire experience;
4. Making behavioral and interpersonal adjustment required for future living.[31]

Slaikeu suggests that all of the pastor's statements during counseling sessions, as well as the congregational resources (classes to which an individual or family might be referred, pastoral care teams, and the like) be oriented to assist the individual or family in working through the crisis along these four dimensions.

An important contribution of Slaikeu's theoretical model, therefore, is the distinction between restoration of equilibrium and crisis resolution. The former will occur of its own accord in a matter of weeks, though the equilibrium which occurs may be for good (toward growth, new insights, coping skills), or ill (an ongoing retreat from relationships and life in general). The crisis may be technically over (i.e., equilibrium restored) in a few weeks, but not yet resolved (worked through so that "underlying conflicts have been resolved and will not be reactivated").[32]

Something of the nature of these conflicts may well have been revealed in the feelings and behaviors of the crisis itself and have come to light in the crisis counseling process. These feelings and behaviors may have disappeared as a result of counseling, but the underlying conflicts remain, because they can in no way be adequately resolved in a six-week period of time. It is important to discuss these conflicts or other problematic areas with the person and explore the possibility of continuing in counseling until that additional significant personal growth takes place.

Important for clergy is that Slaikeu recognizes that for some number of people, part of the task of cognitive mastery will include a theological dimension, both in terms of discovering the meaning the event has for them and in restructuring their cognitive framework. In fact, all four tasks of crisis therapy are later discussed in relation to the pastor as crisis therapist.[33]

Other writers have proposed different stages and steps of the crisis counseling process, and each of these procedural outlines can be read with profit.[34] In fact, all these I discuss here, as well as those I merely refer to in the footnotes, have very much in common, and I am not aware of any real conflict at all. One of the earliest outlines in the literature is that of Warren Jones, a psychiatrist who has had much experience and great success in training lay people for crisis counseling. He refers to the A-B-C method:

A—Achieve contact with the client.
B—Boil down the problem to its essentials.
C—Cope actively through an inventory of the client's ingenuity and resources.[35]

Taking his key words and filling in the details, the total process might look like this:

Contact	Focus	Cope
1. Establish the relationship.	5. Explore the present situation.	7. Inventory problem-solving resources.
2. Identify the presenting problem and the precipitating event.	6. Identify the threat.	8. Assist in decision making.
3. Assist catharsis.		9. Emphasize relationships with others.
4. Build hopeful expectation.		10. Summarize new learning.

It will naturally be understood that while the above outline does in general give an accurate picture of the chronological process, the individual steps themselves are not always that sharply delineated, nor do they always move smoothly and in an unbroken progression. Several steps may be in process at one given time, or movement backward to a prior stage may often take place. This should become clear as the details of the procedure emerge.

Contact

The first step is certainly the *establishment of a relationship of trust*. All counseling has already been clearly enough defined in relational terms, and it is no less important in crisis counseling than in any other type. Yet it is obvious that although this is mentioned first, it is not a step separate from several of the rest. How is relationship established in the first place? By the counselor's actively showing interest and concern. And how is this done? By encouraging the person to tell his or her story, by responsive listening, the communication of accurate empathy, the expression of warmth, the eliciting of emotional expression. As these lead to a rapid diminishing of anxiety, the person in crisis is rewarded by what is taking place and the value of the relationship is reinforced. In other words, the therapeutic relationship desired is established by accomplishing the other three steps of the process listed under Contact: identifying the presenting problem and the precipitating event, expediting catharsis, and building a hopeful expectation. This relationship then becomes the source of power the minister can utilize in assisting and supporting the person as he or she begins to move into the difficult task of behavioral change and the sense of risk it entails.[36]

An absolutely essential task of the early stage of crisis intervention is to *identify the presenting problem and the precipitating event*. What is the immediate problem? What is the source of the present distress? Relevant questions to stimulate this process are: What feelings led you to contact me (or begin to talk with me) about this? Why did you come precisely at this time? What do you want or expect me to do for you? What has been happening in your life within the past two weeks? When did you begin to feel this way (or when did you begin to feel worse)? What is new in your life situation? What persons have been involved?

This procedure is to determine *whether* there is a crisis at all, as well as a necessary early step if it is discovered that in fact there *is*.

The questions listed here and others like them are an attempt to
determine whether the person's present feeling of distress, despair,
depression, tension, anxiety, panic—whatever term or combination
of terms may be used to describe the feelings the person is now
experiencing—are of recent origin or whether they are rather
persistent, long-standing, or regularly recurring patterns in the
individual's life, and if of recent origin, whether they can be linked
with a specific precipitating event that occurred only a short time
before.

What is being described at this point is really the process of
diagnosis, or evaluation, as a part of the helping process itself.
Pruyser has made the valid point that ministers have not usually
thought of themselves as diagnosticians.[37] They have not been taught
to think consciously of themselves in that way, nor have they
ordinarily been instructed in any of the various categories of
diagnosis. Some, in fact, have had experiences that have given them
an antidiagnostic bias, and some were even taught that they should
not attempt to make diagnoses. They were encouraged only to begin
the helping process. However, consciously or unconsciously, all
ministers evaluate people we see in pastoral care (as well as other)
situations. To the extent that we do so unconsciously, we also do it
uncritically; often when we do it consciously, we do so without clear
criteria and procedures and therefore end up with confused and
inaccurate evaluations, resulting in a poorly selected approach to
helping a particular person in a particular problematic situation.

Actually, the highest level of consistent effective helping depends
upon competent assessment. The purposes are (1) to specify the
person's most important needs relevant to this particular helping
process; and (2) to assess the characteristic ways in which this person
usually functions and is functioning now, in order to determine
whether a minister is the one most capable of helping this particular
person meet these particular needs as they have been identified, or
whether some other professional person would be the most
appropriate primary helper. In the context of our discussion in this
chapter, one must decide whether the person in question is in crisis
or not. This is the logical first diagnostic determination to be made
when anyone comes to a minister for counseling or when a serious
discussion of a person's distress evolves. Crisis counseling, as
outlined and discussed in this chapter, is not effective for a person
who is *not* in a *situational* crisis, but *is* very effective for those who are.

Therefore when talking with someone who has come for

counseling, or when the conversation moves into an area of distress during a home visit, it is essential to the helping process to respond first with the accurate communication of empathy. Then, if it has not been made clear by that person's own elaboration of the story whether the distress began recently and whether there was a precipitating event, questions such as those listed above need to be raised.

If the feelings and/or behavior are discovered to be a persistent or recurring part of the person's life over a long period of time, or if no precipitating event can be found, it is assumed that there is no present crisis. The task is then to determine the type of help the person does need at this time: long-term counseling, occasional supportive counseling, referral to another professional or agency. Then that procedure should be pursued.

However, if the distress is of recent origin, if it came on rather suddenly, and if a precipitating event can be identified, then one should continue with the specified methodology of crisis intervention. It should be emphasized that even though persons in crisis are aware that something is wrong at the moment, they may or may not be able, without considerable assistance, to discover what set off this emotional response and the sense of inability to cope. It is the crisis counselor's responsibility to help them pin down the precipitating stress as precisely as possible. It is often necessary to lead them into some recognition of the defenses they are utilizing as they endeavor to cover up the nature of the crisis and the emotions surrounding it. It must be kept constantly in mind that the focus is not on what led to the preconditioning of the personality that has responded to the distress with maladaptive behavior, *but on the dynamics of the present stress itself.* Frequently the source is to be found in a disintegrating relationship, or one that is losing its power to satisfy the person's needs. Therefore specific questions concerning significant relationships are in order. In many instances, unresolved grief or other forms of separation are discovered to be the major dynamic force, although it should always be recognized that there are many situations or events to which persons can respond with a rapidly rising gradient of anxiety or a rapid onset of depression.

An illustration of the onset of crisis, its identification as such, and the discovery of the precipitating event is afforded by this conversation between a pastor and a woman who walked into his office in a church situated in a downtown section of a city. This is a common enough occurrence. She showed obvious signs of distress, nervousness, considerable confusion. The minister invited her in, introduced himself, and offered her a seat. She gave her name and sat down.

Minister:	I wonder if you could tell me what feelings you were having which led you to come by.
Woman:	Well . . . (long pause). I was just walking along the street, window shopping. I wasn't doing anything in particular, and fairly suddenly, it seemed as if everything was just unreal (her voice was quivering).
Minister:	You sound frightened.
Woman:	I saw the things in the window, and I saw people walking along and standing close to me, but (long pause) it's like they weren't really there, either.
Minister:	Were you aware of having any feelings at that time?
Woman:	Well, yes and no. Sometimes it was like I was unreal, too. But then it was just like my world was going to pieces, and I was scared.
Minister:	Everything was unreal, or falling apart, including yourself. That's extremely frightening.
Woman:	Oh yes! I began to panic and look around for something or someone to save me, and then I saw your church.
Minister:	You hoped that you could find help here.
Woman:	Yes. I walked into the chapel to pray, and I saw the sign that a minister was available, so I came into the main office.
Minister:	I'm really glad you did that, because it sounds as if you were feeling desperate.
Woman:	I was. I am. Desperate.
Minister:	Very, very frightened, right at this moment.
Woman:	Well, I guess here with you and talking, I'm feeling a little better.
Minister:	So perhaps actually talking out loud with someone is helping you experience both me and yourself as more real, and that feels safer.
Woman:	I think so.
Minister:	And therefore the fear is somewhat less, although you are still afraid.
Woman:	Yes, that's right.

The minister decided that the very first help the woman needed was assistance in expressing her present feelings of panic and sense of unreality as fully and concretely as possible, in relationship with a person who could in some sense share the terror she felt, but who was not actually afraid that the world was in fact crumbling; a person who could receive and participate in her strong emotion but was not threatened by it; who showed confidence that the world was real and could concretize this in the reality of their present relationship. So the minister encouraged her to express her emotions, to tell her story about today as he sought to communicate accurate empathy, emphasize concreteness, and take the occasion to refer to the reality of his care for her in the context of the present process.

So the questions of why she came and why she came today were clearly answered. Relationship was established as she expressed her feelings, and much catharsis was accomplished. After only ten or fifteen minutes the woman was feeling better and was clearly "coming back into the world again." This perception was stated by the minister, and she confirmed it.

The search for the precipitating event was then consciously begun, because it had not become apparent in what the woman had said up to this point. First, the minister asked if she could think of anything that might have led her to feel this way. She could think of nothing.

Then he asked, "Can you think of anything at all that has happened in the last week or two that was quite upsetting to you at the time?" Her mouth literally fell open, and she exclaimed, "How did you know?" Of course, he did not know. He was simply following procedure. The conversation then went something like this:

Minister: Could you tell me about it?
Woman: No, I really couldn't. I don't want to talk about it (silence).
Minister: Perhaps this is what you need to talk about.
Woman: Oh, I can't. It's just too painful (silence).
Minister: It's becoming clear to me that this is probably the pain that has led to this reaction of yours today, since it's so intense you feel that you can't discuss it.
Woman: I just *can't* talk about it (silence).
Minister: It seems to me that you're going to have to make the choice either to experience the pain of talking with me about it here today, and get it out and over with and really taken care of, or else you'll have to experience the panic and sense of unreality you felt earlier today, and perhaps experience it over and over again, and be uncertain about the outcome (silence).
Woman: All right. I'll try to do it. I don't know whether I can or not. It'll hurt so much.
Minister: I know it will. I'll try to help you.

It can be observed that although the minister was sensitive to the woman's pain and sought to be tender, he persistently pushed her in the direction of expressing the experience aloud in spite of the hurt. It would have been unfair to allow her pain to become a reason for not talking about it.

So she began to talk about a most meaningful and helpful relationship she had established with a counselor she had been seeing regularly over a period of some two years. This led to some recounting of her own background, one of lifelong emotional problems, a tenuous hold on reality, no friends, lonely, never married, minimally effectual in a job, a long history of therapy. But in her relationship with the counselor, she felt she had found someone who had been supportive, whom she could count on, and she had become quite dependent upon him. In their last session, however, some ten days before, she had discovered with horror that his wife had recently divorced him. She was crushed. He had been her ideal, her support, but now this terrible thing had taken place. She stated that she could never go back to him again. She had lost him. In this discussion with its additional outpouring of pain, she also saw how her discovery of this fact had initiated the feelings that had led to her present experience. The precipitating event had been identified.

This initial phase of a crisis intervention session also illustrates quite clearly how *emotional catharsis* takes place as a natural part of the process itself. It is always important for the counselor to facilitate the recognition and expression of strong emotions such as hostility, hate, anxiety, guilt, grief, and others that have distorted people's perception of themselves and their situation to such a degree that they cannot make effective decisions and perform stress-reducing actions. Catharsis can be expedited by a stated perception of a person's affective responses: "You seem to be quite sad." "You appear to be ready to cry." Or questions like "What are you feeling as you talk about this?" The purpose goes beyond the mere expression of emotions, although that in itself is necessary. Such responses assist clear and specific identification of those emotions and the person or situation toward whom they are directed. When feelings are directed toward the counselor, it is important that these be recognized, talked about, and settled before other steps are taken. As quickly as possible, though, the focus must move from emotional catharsis to an understanding of the concrete factors involved in this particular crisis and the making of decisions necessary to deal with the present situation. The counselor is not to offer primarily an opportunity merely to reduce tension or to be a target for vague emotions or distorted attitudes, although this is frequently an early part of the relationship. The job at hand is to help the person deal effectively with his or her problem.

A fourth major task of the Contact stage of the crisis intervention process is to stimulate *a sense of hopeful expectation*. There are a variety of ways this may be done, including the attitude of the counselor and occasionally specific words, as well as the crisis intervention procedure itself. Contrary to some approaches to counseling, effective crisis intervention does not allow the person to talk about just anything that comes to mind. Without making the situation tense, it is made clear that there is no time to waste. At the walk-in clinic of the Benjamin Rush Center in Los Angeles, persons who come for aid are led to understand from the very beginning that they are to have no more than six sessions and that something is really expected to happen in this time. Morley summarizes it: "On entry, plan discharge."[38] This number of sessions places a limitation on the process that tends to discourage the participants from wasting time, to reduce dependency, and to create positive expectation in the mind of the distressed person. The possibility of change, and therefore hope, is affirmed. Unfortunately, pastors are often the inheritors of what has been programmed into many psychotherapists during their training. This is the assumption that the results obtained from long-term therapy are inevitably better and longer lasting than those growing out of brief therapy.[39] To the contrary, the results of crisis intervention are clear evidence for the genuine and lasting aid given to persons by the brief method. Morley states his conviction "that this approach is not a 'second best' technique, but probably the most effective technique which can be utilized with crisis."[40]

Wolberg has discussed the suspicion of some professional psychotherapists that "symptom control" somehow does not get at the *real* underlying problem. He refers to Marmor's observation that once the symptom has disappeared there is often more consistent positive feedback from other persons, and from within the self of the person who had been in crisis, which may "serve to remove barriers to constructive shifts within the personality system." In addition, he says, there are times when motivation for *only* symptom relief may change in the course of crisis intervention into a desire for further personal growth. People begin to make the connection between issues and reactions in the time of crisis and some of those longer-standing factors in their lives, which they now understand might be changed for their own benefit.[41] This sounds very much like

Slaikeu's concept of crisis "resolution" and the movement into the necessary crisis "therapy," although Wolberg may very well be including some situations that go even beyond that.

Aldrich believes that the attitude communicated either nonverbally or verbally by the counselor in regard to the person's condition and situation may be a self-fulfilling prophecy. "When 'long-term' treatment is recommended to a patient, he is in effect told that he is not expected to be able in a short time to develop the capacity to cope with his residual problems."[42] The crisis counselor should be alert to pick up from cues in the very first interview that a person is able and willing to work on the problems. Then the counselor works with the person to capitalize on the person's motivations and strengths. While avoiding false optimism and superficial reassurance, the person's present activity in seeking help should be clearly affirmed, those present strengths pointed out and reinforced, and the expectation of change within a short period of time communicated to the counselee. Rusk states: "Hope, like confidence, is contagious." It is also an essential ingredient of the crisis counseling process, because this expectation of positive results becomes one of the prime motivators for therapeutic change.[43]

In order to systematize and thus clarify the points just discussed, it is important for the pastor and the person in crisis to discuss them, and perhaps other matters, somewhere toward the end of the first session, a procedure often referred to as contracting. This discussion includes the facts that the person is in a situational crisis (although the use of this term directly with the person ordinarily serves no useful purpose), that it is a short-term transitional state, that therefore the focus will be on this particular situation and the person's reactions to it, and that the minister and person in crisis will need to see each other, at most, only a few times over a few weeks.

Nelson and Mowrey emphasize the necessity of contracting in order to facilitate the relationship and process and to avoid confusion by either party. The contracting details are subsumed by them under "mutual party obligations" and "time limitations." The process makes explicit the decision to take action, the goals to work toward, and the probability that goals will be fulfilled. They list a number of factors to be covered in the contract.[44] I have summarized and modified these slightly but, I believe, always in keeping with their intent:

1. Definition of Role-relationships
   a. The persons in crisis are to be responsible for exploring their own situation and self and for their own decisions and behavior.
   b. The minister is to be responsible for confidentiality, and for assisting in exploration, in the formulation of the problem, in identifying resources, and in evaluation of alternatives and their consequences. The minister is also responsible for avoiding and helping the other person avoid stigmatizing labels (sick, paranoid, psychotic, etc.) and for keeping the focus on problem solving within the context of this crisis.
   c. They have a shared responsibility in arriving at a mutually agreed-upon definition and clarification of this particular crisis and in agreeing upon behavior that supports, rather than subverts this particular process: a suicide contract (see pp. 226-29), nonabuse of alcohol and drugs, contracts concerning other precipitous behavior such as running away.
2. Time Limitation. Nelson and Mowery, as do some others, state clearly that there will will be a maximum of six sessions. (Still others suggest eight.) I and others agree on their purpose, but our experience is that such goals can be accomplished without specifying an absolute maximum number. I appreciate the flexibility afforded by making it clear at the first session, after being certain that it is a situational crisis, that we will need to get together only a few times over a period of no more than a few weeks. At any point after that, when the symptoms of crisis are greatly reduced or have disappeared, the specific time of termination can be set. Often this may be fewer than six sessions—very rarely more.

The discussion of time limitation is within the framework of the model of crisis counseling presented in this book. More detailed discussion of contracting procedures would be needed if one had Slaikeu's model of crisis therapy in mind (see pp. 63-65).

It is important to determine within the first session whether a person is experiencing a situational crisis, because that assessment points to the particular procedures of helping to be used. Such a determination can usually be made within the time allotted for the first interview. It is possible, of course, that the minister has been conscientious and persistent in a detailed search of the period of time prior to the person's change in feelings and behavior but that a logical precipitating event has not become clear. It would be a mistake for ministers to allow their preoccupation with crisis counseling and their anxieties to lead them to attempt to force a focus on some external event unrelated to the person's present disturbance. If there is not a clearly identifiable event that, in the minds of the participants, can be logically related to the onset of the particular symptoms, then there is probably no situational crisis. When that is the case, most ministers would find themselves facing a situation for which they are not adequately trained, because "the very earliest evidence of an impending psychotic decompensation may be occurring."[45] The minister's most helpful course of action at such a time is to assist the person in going to a psychotherapeutic professional for evaluation and treatment.

If, on the other hand, it seems there is an accumulation of events over a somewhat longer period of time, and they appear to be logically connected to one another in terms of contributing to the person's intense sense of stress, the highest probability for effective intervention in most circumstances is to begin with the last event, treat it as *the* precipitating event, and then, if necessary, move on to the event before that, and so on. Most frequently, the successful resolution of the *last* event will reduce or eliminate the symptoms of crisis. If it does not, then work on the immediately preceding event, discuss the relationship between the two, and give some attention to the other events in the series. Occasionally, two recent events, separated from each other by a very short period of time and both logically linked with the particular feelings and behaviors of crisis, may need to be dealt with as a single, though more complex event.

Focus

The second major stage of the process is that of focusing on the present situation, the source of the stress, and attempting to identify the nature of the threat to the individual. Actually these are not two distinct and separable steps, *exploration* and *identification of threat*. They are separated in this way simply to emphasize what must be accomplished.

As a result of the intensive study of the precipitating stress of forty patients and the subsequent therapy, Kalis concluded that "a focus on the factors precipitating the *request for help* can be therapeutic" in enabling most persons to come through the period of disruption and maladaptive behavior successfully. She goes on to outline the procedure as the clear identification and isolation of factors (discussed here under "identifying the presenting problem and the precipitating event"), then moves on to a more thorough formulation of the total problem and a working through of the unique personal meaning of the precipitating stress.[46]

Hoffman and Remmel refer to this process as "discovering the precipitant." The precipitant is more than the precipitating event. It is the event plus "the special meaning this event has for [the person in crisis]." The precipitating event naturally must be clearly identified and specified in conversation, but the precipitant also includes "the thought or [I would say and] feeling aroused by the precipitating event."[47] It is clear that in many instances when that event is identified, the precipitant, by this definition, may still be unconscious. The task remains, then, to explore in detail the possible reasons this event is perceived as a threat by the person in crisis.

Basic to the entire process is the development of what Rusk calls "consensual formulation," the person in crisis and the counselor working together toward a conceptualizing of the immediate past and the present events, in order to create an understanding of the crisis to which they both agree.[48] If the distressed person has difficulty grasping some of the interaction between events, relationships, and feelings, the counselor may need to state the core of the problem as she or he sees it, in as direct and clear a way as possible. Of course, the pastor encourages feedback as to whether this makes sense to the person, and invites correction. The purpose is, of course, to make the dilemma conscious and put it into words. Only when this has been done can the distressed person become capable of moving into the later stages of the process to examine various alternative methods of dealing with the present crisis, of making decisions concerning those alternatives that seem most appropriate, and of mobilizing the ego resources that are available.

One of the major methods the crisis counselor uses in this phase of detailed exploration of the present situation is referred to as focusing, the filtering out of extraneous material, keeping the session close to the particular problem at hand. Delving into the distant past is discouraged as the counselor moves the conversation back to the present: contemporary emotions, relationships, frustrations, conflicts, losses. Clues concerning the crisis are picked up from what people say and how it is said, facial expressions, and gestures. Focusing comments are made to the persons on the basis of these clues. In this way, the counselor aids people to be honest with themselves, to select the most relevant material to deal with, and to become observers of themselves.

The process of focusing may be visualized by the following diagram:

*Past
Problems,
Relationships,
Traumatic
Experiences*

*Person
in
Crisis*

*Presenting
Problem*

Crisis Counselor

*Other Contemporary
Problems, Issues, etc.*

Persons in crisis naturally bring with them their whole past, including whatever unsolved problems might be there, as well as contemporary problems and ineffective behavior patterns that might not be related to the present crisis. The responsibility of the crisis counselor, when any issue from the past or any contemporary material not readily identifiable as being a factor in the crisis is introduced, is to seek to relate this new material to the presenting problem and its precipitating event in some way. Focusing statements and questions may be: "Your bringing up this memory of what happened to you in high school makes me wonder if you see it relating to your present experiences." Or, "I wonder if you sense some relationship between what you are describing about your problems at work and this particular situation with your wife which you came to see me about."

The counselor picks up on any material, from whatever direction it may come, and channels it back to the person in distress in terms of the clearly identified crisis problem. If, together, the two of them determine it is not related, it is dropped. It may be an issue worthy of further investigation later; it may be a problem that needs to be solved and further counseling may be indicated. But if it is not a part of the *presenting problem* at hand, time is not taken to discuss it now. The *crisis*, and it alone, is the focus. If some issue from the past is seen to be connected with the crisis in some way, then it is to be explored—not because it is past, but because it may help to clarify the present situation. The major purpose of this stage and the technique of focusing is to explore every aspect of the crisis—the total situation, contemporary relationships—in order to make it just as clear as possible to the person precisely what is taking place. An important goal of this exploration is the identification of the threat—why it is that the precipitating event stimulated this particular reaction. Rusk points to an important emphasis when he suggests, as one area of intensive exploration, that of unsatisfied needs. What changes in the contemporary life situation have resulted in formerly met needs being met no longer? Especially, what person or persons may be disappointing this individual?[49]

The woman who came into the church office seeking immediate help had now portrayed herself not only as an individual in present crisis, but as one with a history of problems. It became important then to separate the long-term personal and social maladaptive behavior from that which was crisis related only. Focusing was a major technique in making this necessary distinction.

Slaikeu's emphasis upon using the BASIC formula to compare the different aspects of the person's life at this time of crisis with the same aspects prior to crisis is a helpful guideline (see pp. 40, 64). At this point, then, the question was raised with the woman: "As you look at yourself and at the meaning of your relationship with your counselor, what connection do you see between your learning of his divorce and the experience you had this morning?"

A summary of the discussion and its conclusion led through an analysis of her needs as a person, how these needs were in some way being met in the therapeutic relationship, what it was she had imagined her counselor to be, based on what she needed to believe he was, and how the reality of who he was conflicted with her construction of what reality should be for her.

She was someone who had learned that she needed to be dependent on others. Her fantasy was that only a strong, well-adjusted (read "perfect") person was capable of sustaining her life as a person and that her counselor was such an individual. But now she had discovered he could not even take care of his own life; he was the sort of person whose wife could not live with him. Divorce was wrong. If she were dependent for the maintenance of her selfhood, her world, upon one she now perceived as not omnicompetent and all "good," what was left of her world? It was unreal; it was crumbling beneath her. Essentially, of course, it was the experience of her selfhood being unsupported and coming apart and the natural perception of threat under these circumstances. As this was discussed, she increasingly understood and could articulate what was happening to her. Her present situation was thoroughly explored, and she was able to identify why she had felt the way she did, why the event posed the threat she had felt. In addition, the phase of detailed exploration included a discussion about her unrealistic concept that only a perfect person could help her, and her fantasy of her counselor as having been perfect. This naturally extended into further conversation about what any person needs in order to help another, and a realistic appraisal of both the role and the genuine humanity, including both strengths and weaknesses, of any professional person.

At this point, the woman and the minister had accomplished the absolutely essential task of successful crisis counseling, the linking of precipitating event-threat-presenting problem. "Why is it that this *event* has been able to arouse such a degree of *threat* in this particular person at this particular time, as to produce these *feelings* and *behaviors* of crisis?" It is critical that this question be answered in concrete detail.

If the precipitating event appears to have been identified early in the process, but after several sessions the intensity of the symptoms has not significantly diminished, then the minister needs to look at two possibilities. First, the actual precipitating event may not have been identified. The minister and the other person may have been talking about some other event and therefore their consensual formulation of the problem would be seriously flawed. This particular situation needs to be discussed candidly with the person; they then move back to investigate the period of time immediately prior to the onset of the experience of crisis, in order to attempt to discover the actual precipitating event. If successful, and if a satisfactory connection between event-interpretation-threat-behavior can be made, then the symptoms of the crisis will diminish rapidly. However, if this procedure is not successful, even though the person may be in a genuine situational crisis, the precipitating event may have aroused an overt expression of a long-standing pathology with unconscious roots that have never been resolved. In this latter case, most ministers will need to inform the person of their inability to work effectively in this type of situation. Then the person should be referred to a professional psychotherapist.

Cope

The final stage of the crisis intervention process is *coping*. Decision and action, doing something about the situation, is the goal of the whole procedure.

The first phase involves making an *inventory of problem-solving resources*, seeking those strengths within the person which have been lost sight of in the midst of the distortions of the crisis, as well as those important resources outside the self: the person's usual pattern of social relationships, others who are close to the person (family, friends, co-workers), community helpers (ministers, doctors, lawyers), agencies designed to help with specific problems (vocational counseling, employment, emergency loan, housing, Alcoholics Anonymous, Al Anon, drug treatment) and, for some, the church or some particular small group within the congregation.

One way into such an inventory—and actually one that has been taking shape chronologically well before this stage in the total intervention process—is to listen very carefully for references to occasions in the person's past that were in any way similar to this present one. If none has been mentioned, the minister might ask directly, "Does this remind you of a way you have ever felt before?" This is the first time the counselor has taken the initiative to explore the past. It is done now with a specific twofold purpose. First, if persons in crisis have felt this way before, it is of some value for them to add to their perspective on their present condition the fact that they have been in crisis before, lived through it, and come out of it. This reinforces an attitude of hope toward the successful outcome of the present situation and an awareness of an inner strength that has probably been lost sight of. Second, a discussion of how the person was enabled to resolve the earlier crisis might suggest some methods of dealing with the immediate one. If methods that were effective earlier have already been tried this time without success, an analysis should be made of the reasons for their failure.

The minister's task now is to help identify those inner strengths which the person may have lost sight of under the pressure of the intense feelings of threat and helplessness of the crisis. Among these, of course, is, for some number of people, a renewal of the meaning and strength of faith, and for others, a liveliness and power of faith that may even have been only a perfunctory belief prior to this time. In addition, the participants in the process look for external resources appropriate to the person in crisis. Initial out-of-hand rejection of certain people or agencies should not be allowed without detailed discussion. Objections are to be questioned and sometimes directly challenged. People often develop a picture of agencies or community helpers not based on their own personal experience, or they may misjudge the experience of a family member or friend. To be sure, sometimes people in need have not and may not be well received or have their needs met by those we would expect to be responsive, but all possibilities for the individual must be fully and reasonably examined.

The latter part of the inventory begins to overlap with the next step, the *decision to utilize* certain of these resources (but not others). At this time, persons in crisis should be encouraged to think of every possible decision they can make and action they can perform that will change their situation and condition in some way. At times this is relatively simple, at other times extremely difficult. There are many options open to some people in most situations. With other people, a great deal of imagination and effort must be put forth in order to find the caring persons in their lives or an appropriate agency that can play a constructive role in helping this person.

Every attempt is made to encourage distressed persons to do their own planning, without inhibition or selectivity at this point. Only after they have exhausted the list of alternatives will any that have occurred to the pastor be suggested. While this procedure is obviously not nondirective, neither is it advice-giving. It is not just hearing a person out and then indicating the action to be taken—except in unusual circumstances, one of which will be illustrated later. Here, as throughout the whole crisis counseling process, persons need to be made aware again and again that the problem and the solution to it are their responsibility. The counselor is merely a process stimulator. Rusk's classic statement should be memorized: "The golden rule for the therapist in crisis intervention is to do for others that which they cannot do for themselves and no more!"[50] Therefore, after they have been encouraged, even at times pushed, to present all possible options for ways of dealing with the situation, additional alternatives are introduced by the counselor and laid alongside those made by the persons in distress: "You have mentioned this and this, but I wonder if you have thought of so-and-so." Since many people regard the pastor as an authority, care must be taken that the form and tone of these additional suggestions do not communicate a devaluing of the ideas the other person has already proposed, or imply that the pastor's will must be followed.

All the alternatives are then discussed and their significance evaluated in relationship to the crisis and its possible resolution. What is possible? What is feasible? What would be the probable results? "What could you do? How would you feel while you were doing this? What do you suppose would happen if you did that? What would be the best option to try first?" After these issues are thoroughly explored, the person is encouraged to make a decision to do something, with the pastor taking a firm stand against a do-nothing inertia. The decision, as well as the commitment to follow it through, must be that of the person in crisis. The counselor intrudes to counteract a decision only if it is clear that it could result in significant harm to the person or to someone else (murder, drug abuse, robbery, suicide), or if other possibilities of harm are so great (running away, divorce) that the action might at least be considered premature at this time and should therefore be postponed until other decisions are acted upon. After possible results are fully discussed, the decision is made, the action initiated. Even if, in some way, it is the "wrong" action (i.e., does not work to produce the predicted desired results), it usually has a positive effect in that it gets the persons off dead center. It gives them the image of themselves as being able to act, being more in charge of their own lives than they had believed they were when in the midst of crisis.

A succinct summary of these problem-solving steps is given by Hansell:

1. an energetic inventory of the elements of the predicament,
2. an innovative specification of the options,
3. a precise decision model for selecting among the options,
4. occasions to make and test the decisions,
5. assessing the outcome, and starting over when necessary.[51]

As a part of the decision-making and action-initiating process, the person in crisis must be led to see the *value of personal relationships* and to discover ways of rebuilding those that are in disrepair and establishing those that need to be developed. The frequent occurrence of disturbed, broken, or lost relationships in the onset of crisis makes this emphasis only logical, as counselor and counselee, in the midst of a meaningful relationship, seek to find the resolution of the crisis.

The step of making an inventory of problem-solving resources with the woman who had come into the church office seemed to be a dry run. She could not remember having had precisely these feelings in just such a way before. She had, of course, many times felt unhappy and thought she could not cope with her problems. On those occasions she had gone to a professional counselor, with much of her adult life being filled with short- and long-term psychotherapy. Since she could identify no other resources, she believed continued psychotherapy was the only option available to her in order to help her function.

Yet when she and the minister began to discuss what she could do about her present situation, her own feelings seemed to cancel out her only alternative.

Minister:	I wonder if you're beginning to see anything that you might do that could possibly be helpful for you in this situation.
Woman:	(long pause) No, I really don't.
Minister:	Nothing at all?
Woman:	(pause) No.
Minister:	Well, it seems to me as if you've been describing the breakdown of a relationship that's been extremely important to you. That's quite a loss. I would think that it might be worthwhile for you to try to work things out with him (the former counselor).
Woman:	I can't do that.
Minister:	I'm not sure I understand.
Woman:	I can't go back to see him. Not after what he's done.
Minister:	You're disillusioned. He was very important to you. Because of that importance, and because he did seem to care for you, you began to see him as someone who couldn't possibly have any problems of his own. But he did, and now you're rejecting him. Yet it's this loss that seems to have led you to the terrifying experience you've had this morning.
Woman:	I just can't face him.
Minister:	Yet you've made it very clear that you need to be seeing someone in counseling on a regular basis. What are you going to do about that?
Woman:	(pause) I don't know. I just can't possibly start with a new therapist. It takes so long for me to establish a relationship. And I'll have to go over so much of the same ground again. I just can't do it.
Minister:	If I understand what you've been saying, it runs something like this: you don't believe that you're ready to stop therapy; you still need that help; you can't go back to your former counselor; you can't start with a new one.
Woman:	(pause . . . then hesitantly) Yes.
Minister:	Do you see where this leaves you? You *must* do one of these.

She sat in silence. She could not make the decision. In this instance, with this type of person—one with little ego strength—the minister decided he must evaluate her situation and assist her decision making in a more direct way than usual procedure would justify. He believed she needed the continued support of therapy. He also was convinced that it would in fact be easier for her to go back to her former therapist than to begin anew. In addition, the former therapist was a part of her problem situation at this time, and the resolution of the crisis would naturally suggest that she work through her feelings *about* him *with* him.

Minister:	Which one will it be? Any one of these options will be extremely difficult for you. I share with you your sense of the importance of continued therapy, and it *is* hard to begin again with someone new. I appreciate how you feel about Dr. L, but it seems to me that you have unfinished business with him and that it's necessary for you to face him with that so that you can move all the way out of the shattering experience you've had today.
Woman:	(very hesitantly) I don't know.
Minister:	What's your alternative?
Woman:	(long pause) I'll think about it.
Minister:	All right. Take some time. But I believe it's important for you to decide before you leave here today.
Woman:	(long pause) All right. I'll go see him.
Minister:	Good! I believe you're doing something very important for yourself in this. This sounds like a good first step. After talking with him, you can decide whether to continue with him or find someone else to talk to.

A brief summary was then made by the minister as to what he understood had been happening in her life recently and what had taken place between the two of them that day, again engaging her in the summary by asking questions. She made responses that demonstrated her understanding and agreement, and she made a restatement of what she was going to do. She left the office after only an hour, no longer in the midst of the crisis with which she had entered. She still had her action to carry out, and she still carried maladaptive behavior patterns from the past. There was no personality reconstruction, no miraculous transformation of the ego. However, the crisis had been effectively resolved in one session, with the promise of at least some modest ego gains and the learning of ways to handle certain aspects of relationships.

In crisis counseling, always built into the last session, or, in this instance, the last part of the one session, is the *articulation of the new learning* that has taken place and a discussion of how it might be adapted to cope with possible future crisis. The question, "What have you learned from all this?" may be explicitly raised. Reviewing in specific terms what has taken place deposits the material in the counselee's repertoire in such a way that it will be more readily available for future reference, like data coded and filed for storage in a computer. Unsymbolized material is not retrievable and therefore not usable. The counselor, in a direct way, encourages the person to use what strength she or he does have to consolidate the gains that have just been made and to utilize that new strength and insight in solving other problems and meeting other crises that will occur in the future. Louis Paul summarizes the process: "In reversing the decompensation and restoring emotional equilibrium, we aim to strengthen the client's resources, to give him not only symptom relief, but also symptom control, social control, and some degree of insight.[52]

Among the guidelines for evaluating the process as it progresses, and for moving toward the termination of the counseling relationship in regard to a particular crisis, are the following:

Has the level of obvious anxiety decreased significantly?
Can the person describe in his own words a plan of action?
Is he explicitly hopeful regarding the immediate future?
Does he show his appreciation for the help he has received?
Is there a realistic expectation that the unmet needs which were related to the crisis itself may now be satisfied in some appropriate way?[53]

There are three termination issues to consider. This first is easy to state but not emotionally simple for many ministers to accomplish, although it is a significant ingredient to be added to the interaction with the person who has been in crisis. The latter part of the process, whether the last few minutes of one session or parts of the last two of several sessions, properly includes a discussion concerning the relationship between the minister and the person in these particular sessions, what their being together has meant to each of them, how they feel toward each other, and how they feel about bringing the session to a close. With a parishioner or someone in the community, it might touch on how their future relationship may be different than it was prior to the crisis counseling sessions and during the sessions. With other persons, as in the case presented in this chapter, the counselor and counselee clearly say good-bye. It is important that the minister serve as a model of a person who can deal with such intimacy in relationships. It can be a time of potent learning for the other person.

A second issue is that of premature termination. The person may say at the end of the first session, or at the end of any session before the pastor feels that the crisis is resolved, something like, "Well, I guess I won't be seeing you any more. I'm feeling a lot better. You've really been helpful to me. Thanks a lot. Good-bye." There may be one of at least two possible dynamics at work here. Things may indeed be going well. The crisis may be well on its way toward resolution, and the person is now making an announcement at the conclusion of the session in order to avoid the intimacy of a more complete and meaningful leavetaking. It is now the pastor's responsibility to hold the person for a few more minutes and strongly recommend one more session in order to do the necessary summarizing and accomplish the leavetaking discussed above. The pastor needs to be clear about her or his own need for such a session and give the reasons for its importance to the other. Most people will understand, will return, and will express appreciation.

However, other reasons for premature leavetaking are frustration or anger or fear, or some combination of these that the person has begun to experience in the counseling relationship. When this is the case, pastors can probably sense it from their own perception that the session or sessions have not gone well, that the symptoms of crisis are reduced only slightly, or that the whole process is moving more slowly than expected. These observations need to be shared candidly with the person, with the suggestion that together they explore any feelings that might be an impediment to the relationship and therefore to the crisis resolution. Another session is definitely called for in order to do this. If the person agrees, and if such an exploration takes place, facilitated by the accurate communication of empathy and a lack of defensiveness on the part of both participants, she or he will usually want to continue in counseling until the crisis is resolved. In fact, the relationship and process will be given a substantial boost by their having gotten over such a barrier together.

At the opposite extreme from persons who try to slip out of the office prematurely are those who do not seem to want to stop at all—ever. They flatter the pastor. They keep raising additional problems with which they need help, and with which, of course, no one but the pastor can help. Every minister knows this situation, and there are very few who are never tempted by such seduction. What the other persons' behavior appears to reflect is their dependence on the counselor. There are any number of professional psychotherapists who have not had the opportunity to learn situational crisis theory and have not had experience in crisis counseling, and who therefore raise the question of this dependence. They are aware that regression is taking place, that the persons' needs and feelings are intensified, and that they are in a state of heightened dependence and suggestibility. With the counselor taking such an active role in the helping process, with the persons being so suggestible, and with the counselor having the authority attributed to the ordained minister, does not this combination produce an increased dependence that is extremely difficult to resolve? This is a very legitimate concern, but because of other dynamic characteristics of crisis and crisis resolution, the persons' dependence does not usually interfere with a clear and constructive termination.

In the first place, the ongoing process of crisis counseling itself very quickly produces the conditions which lead to a diminishing of the anxiety and the feelings of helplessness, and thus a reversal of the regression and of the accompanying dependence produced *by the crisis*. In fact, the dependence can be utilized effectively by the skilled helper to facilitate the rapid movement into self-exploration, the expression of feeling, and the other phases of the process which lead to the reduction of dependence. Also inherent in the crisis counseling process is the emphasis throughout that it is a collaborative relationship and that the persons are going to be taking responsibility for their own decisions and the consequences of those decisions. When the persons in crisis express magical expectations of the pastor, the pastor's most helpful response is to point out the pertinent realities of the pastor's own role and capacities, and the necessity for the other persons to take significant responsibility.

Murray has proposed an enlightening analogy when he speaks of "the therapist as a transitional object . . . a secure anchor point that allows the individual a certain control at times of regression, and safeguards his newly won autonomy and growth."[54] A transitional object is a literal physical object of some kind, used by a small child in the separation/individuation phase of development to represent the mother at a time when separation from the mother is very anxiety producing. Most of us have observed a child about the age of two clinging to a blanket or teddy bear or some other object and being terribly upset if someone tries to take it away. As the individuation process continues, an increased sense of autonomy develops and the relationship with the mother, though changed somewhat, is still a reality, the transitional object is no longer needed in the same way. The child may cover up with the blanket or play with the teddy bear, but there is no longer the dependence based on separation anxiety. At times the child may give up the object completely. The particular combination of reality and illusion which creates the child's image of the transitional object is similar, Murray suggests, to the way a person in crisis relates to the counselor. When the regression of crisis is turned around, reality will come to dominance, and the counselor, like the transitional object, will be given up. With the pastor and parishioner, a meaningful relationship may continue, but it is no longer the dependency relationship of the time of crisis.

After all this is said, however, we need to remember, as we have indicated before, that *anyone* may have a crisis. Thus it is not surprising that some people in crisis are characterologically highly dependent people. This does tend to complicate things, because the minister is dealing with a situation in which the most intense symptoms of the crisis may be diminishing or even disappearing, but the persons are *not* growing less dependent. Some of the first clues may very well come during the decision-making and action phase. It is more difficult to get the persons to make decisions. They really want the minister to tell them what is best to do. At this point, still resisting the pressure to make the others' decisions for them, the pastor becomes aware that there probably is going to be a termination problem.

In such a situation, there are times when the difficulty in discontinuing the counseling sessions reflects a problem of the minister as well as of the other person. This problem is succinctly stated in terms of pastors' own need to be needed. Sometimes ministers will continue to see the person, but since the basic crisis may have been relatively well resolved, there are now very ill-defined goals in the process, and with ill-defined goals, there is usually no observable positive outcome. This leads to increasing frustration on the part of pastors. They grow angry at the other person or at themselves, or both, and they are at a loss as to how to get out of this particular interpersonal quagmire.[55]

When a person wants to continue even after the crisis is apparently resolved, the most effective action is to bring up the terms of the original contract—the agreement to see the person through this particular crisis for a specified approximate period of time and number of sessions, with the previously stated important but limited goal. The minister reminds the person of the agreement, affirms her or his caring and desire to be helpful, but indicates that if the person does· want to do serious work on some longer-term problem, the minister is not in a position to do this. If the person does not know another counselor, the minister can make recommendations, and will, of course, if the person is a parishioner, continue to function in a supportive role and as spiritual guide. Then the minister seeks to engage the person in a review of the crisis, the counseling process, and a discussion of the meaning of their mutual relationship, as described above. If the person is a basically dependent person, but the minister has been firm in concluding the sessions, the person may very well be hurt and angry. The review and summary, as it would ordinarily take place, might be very difficult, since the person will be resistant. Again, this is an interpersonal situation in which many ministers feel very uncomfortable, want to avoid making the other person angry, and are tempted to give in and continue to see the person. Ministers must be aware, however, that if they do try to continue, there is a high probability that those feelings of rejection, hurt, frustration, and anger are only being postponed. If, right at the moment in this latter phase of the crisis counseling process, ministers can be compassionate yet firm and clear, then help these persons articulate the hurt and anger, they would be playing a very constructive role in those people's lives.

Conclusion

In addition to the verbal interpersonal process of crisis counseling as described in detail in this chapter, there are other procedures and media of intervention, to which reference either was not made at all or was made only briefly. Several of these fit very closely the pattern of the usual functioning of ministers in their role as pastor, as well as some reasonably modern adaptations of the traditional functions. And some are frequently necessary or, if not necessary, certainly useful in crisis resolution. These approaches will be discussed in the next chapter.

CHAPTER 4

INTERVENTION
PROCEDURES

T he previous chapter described crisis counseling as a process between two persons in a face-to-face setting and illustrated this with an extended case. There are a number of other strategies of intervention, however, which take a variety of forms. Some of these are frequently essential for minimizing the potential dangers of a crisis and for expediting a successful outcome. Others, while not absolutely necessary, may be quite useful in many instances. The procedures to be discussed in this chapter certainly do not comprise a complete list of the possibilities. To the contrary, ministers are limited in the process of crisis intervention only by their perception of the total situation, which includes the limits of their own creative imagination. In any situation of helping, we are never bound by standard operating procedure and should be encouraged to act in any way that might seem to be productive of support and change. The interventions and methodologies to be presented here are among the rather common and important ones and are also those that seem to fit quite neatly into a minister's usual pattern of functioning. Some are self-evident and need little elaboration, some overlap with others, and some will require more detail.

Home Visits

The recommendation of the practice of home visitation will sound extremely trite to ministers who are already accustomed to going not only to homes but to offices, places of business, hospitals, and other places where people are found, as a means of fullest service to them. These visits, as we all know, are made for a number of purposes, including that of individual and family crisis. Thomas Oden has discussed the tradition of calling in homes and other places where

90

people are to be found in their usual daily activities, or where they might be in times of extremity. He has grounded this practice of the minister's own initiative-taking and response to invitation in both the Bible and the history of the church.

> As God himself came to visit and redeem his people (Luke 1:68), so we go in behalf of God's Son to visit and share that redemption in our own arena of service. As God himself becomes personally and bodily present in the incarnation, so are we called to be personally present to those in our charge, especially those in urgent need. As God the shepherd goes out to the lost sheep and leaves the ninety and nine, so at times we must leave the secured flock and pursue the lost one who is at risk (Matt. 18:12). Pastoral visitation of persons is one way of reflecting the glory of God's own visitation of humanity in Christ, seeking the lost, redeeming sin, mending pain.[1]

Oden then gives examples of Jesus' own interpersonal ministry, his going to and receiving of others, as well as his taking advantage of the moment in a number of situations. References are made also to the apostles' pattern of visitation. Finally, he points to the development of the sacrament of penance with its oral confession, and to Protestantism's recovery of "the form and style of its substitute," pastoral visitation.[2] This is a much more novel idea to other mental health professionals, some of whom are beginning to operate in this fashion with what they believe to be quite valuable results. Such a point does not need to be belabored for ministers, but it is encouraging to realize that a practice which has been standard for us is beginning to be viewed as highly important by others. One mental health professional even declares that it is "essential in crisis intervention as well as in follow-up care."[3] Another demonstrates that it may tie in with a person's need for protection and help, and provide the sense of being cared for in a way that coming to the professional's office would not. This writer goes on to warn, however, that the home visit should not be primarily a means of interveners fulfilling their own needs and that the immediate dependence established in this way should not be encouraged to persist after the peak of the crisis is over.[4] In addition to the positive effect on the rapid establishment of the therapeutic relationship, seeing persons in the setting where they experience their health and strength, as well as in the current situation of distress and sense of helplessness, may elicit more actual information, especially if other family members are present and the pastor can observe their natural interaction.[5] In some crisis intervention clinics, a home visit is standard as the first counseling session. Ministers, then, should never feel they are somehow less professional because they have gone quickly to the home of the person in distress rather than requiring an appointment in the church office. To the contrary, the pastor's role, which impels a move toward people in distress, is a clear advantage in being immediately helpful to troubled persons.

Mobilization of Interpersonal Resources

Reference has already been made to the fact that in many instances of crisis, other persons are involved in some dynamic way in its development, usually through loss, separation, alienation, disillusionment—the other's failure to meet a person's needs. It has been pointed out that even relatively modest need fulfillment on the part of others is frequently sufficient to exert a significant positive influence on the course of the crisis and that the repair and renewal of relationships may be an important part of crisis resolution. Often, however, in everyday transactions, the positive potentialities of other people are not as readily available to the person in crisis as they might be if attention to their responsibilities and possible helping roles were focused by someone who is seen as more objective and also is recognized and respected as an expert or an authority. "Typically . . . people in trouble turn to natural networks before they seek out mutual aid groups or professional help. Usually, it is only when natural helping systems have failed to avert or resolve a crisis that professionals are asked to intervene."[6]

Therefore, part of that intervention may well be the recognition that "convening key people of the troubled person's social network into the background of the counseling relationship can sometimes greatly increase its innovative power."[7] One or a combination of several factors may be at work in crisis: the real or perceived withdrawal of interpersonal need satisfactions, the person's own withdrawal, the adoption of behavior that alienates others. In any of these possible instances, the person needs the understanding and support of others in his or her social system, and while in some crises this helping may come rather naturally and easily, in others there may be resistance. It then becomes important for these others, as well as the person in crisis, to understand his or her real needs and the meaning of those tendencies to isolate oneself or to push others away in anger, fear, disgust, or some combination of these feelings. Only in such understanding will many people be able to overcome the barriers to sharing concern and helpful behavior.

Interestingly, the minister is not only the most frequent professional person consulted but, for many people, is also a part of the natural network. Therefore, for one or a combination of these reasons, the pastor may be the logical and available person to take the initiative in calling together members of the family, employer and co-workers, friends, a young person's teachers, others who seem to be related to the person—sometimes with and sometimes without the person present—for evaluating the situation. The aim is to enable these others to see how they may be helpful, to point out their responsibilities, to deal with their feelings about the person and their role in his or her life, to develop options, to make decisions. The specific persons who are called together, of course, vary with the situation. No pattern is followed rigidly in every case. The mobilizing of other persons is always done with the knowledge and, it is hoped, the consent of the person in crisis. The program for bringing others into the situation develops as a result of discussing with the distressed person all the issues involved, the relationship of these others to the person, their positive and/or negative roles in the crisis, and the importance of bringing them into the picture. Many times the person will be relieved that someone is taking the initiative to assist in bringing her or him into significant contact with these others. On occasion, of course, a person may be anxious, reluctant, or even resistant to such a meeting. That person's reasons and feelings need to be listened to with understanding and respect, and the pastor may in fact decide not to follow this course of action. If, however, there is little doubt of its importance, it is essential to communicate this very strongly to the person, and in severe crisis, insist on it, even though he or she refuses to cooperate. It must be made clear that the person asked the pastor to act in his or her best interests and that this is now being done. (Obviously, the force of this point is lost if the minister has taken the initiative in going to the person in crisis.) Nevertheless, it is essential that the pastor's conviction about what needs to be done be communicated. This is especially important in a suicidal crisis, or when there seems to be danger of a psychotic break.

In addition to obtaining more data about the person from another perspective, this process confirms to the distressed person the existence of resources which he or she may have blocked out or distorted.

It is obvious that on occasion, the appropriate persons to call together are the members of the family. Again, a family is often quite responsive, the members open to discussing how they can help, even relieved that someone is assisting them as well as the member in crisis. Occasionally there may be resistance, but the pastor needs to be quite direct in pointing out the family's responsibility for one of its own members. It is useful for ministers to keep in mind that all references to individuals and their crises hold true for the family context. (For details on family systems and family interaction, see Chapter 5). To be specific, this means that crises may take place in either healthy or unhealthy family systems. Obviously the former are easier to work with in terms of responsiveness and openness to expected constructive results in a shorter period of time. Yet just as no individual is 100 percent ill, no family is, either, and Rubenstein has pointed out that even if the family system is basically a destructive one, it may still be seen as a potential resource for the person in crisis, for the resolution of this present reaction.[8] What the family may offer in regard to support in the present crisis must be clearly distinguished from what it offers in terms of possibilities for a radical change of personality or life-style. Some care, some understanding, some active support for a family member may be found in almost any family. It is such family strength that the counselor may need to search for at this time. Rusk indicates that a family may either overestimate its own destructiveness or underestimate its competence.[9] The minister may help the members get a somewhat more balanced view of themselves and discover what resources they do have, though these admittedly may be minimal.

If the family system is not basically a sound one, the minister should take even greater care to continue to focus only on what is needed at this time to help a member with this crisis. As with an individual, the temptation to pursue other and long-standing problems must be resisted. Even if the family has other serious needs, any discussion of these and the possible modification of the destructive elements of the system must wait until *this present crisis* is taken care of. However, the impact of the crisis upon the family and the discovery that some positive strengths have been mobilized to meet a member's needs might provide initial motivation for further whole-family help.[10] Lukton summarizes this support: "It is the natural network that provides a sense of being a valued and unique human being. Restoration of that feeling can do much to alleviate crisis."[11]

Manipulation of Counseling Time

Many ministers have been quite impressed with what they have been led to believe is one of the practices of psychotherapists, specifically that of seeing persons in thirty- to sixty-minute sessions once a week; they do not realize that those therapists do utilize considerable flexibility of schedule, depending upon the person's needs, the stage of therapy, and other factors. Crisis is one of those situations where one session per week of face-to-face counseling usually is not appropriate.

Ministers are more helpful when they develop the confidence to be flexible, following their own sense of the situation in order to meet most effectively the particular needs of this unique person at this particular time. Although ministers are extremely busy, they still operate within a schedule with more possible flexibility than do many other professionals. This advantage is pointed out in a most emphatic way by a prominent mental health practitioner and teacher:

> We have been impressed in the consultation groups by the number of ministers who report not only answering an anguished phone call with a home visit within a short time, but also with the way in which, after assessing the situation, they can spend two, three, or even five hours containing a threatened explosion. After such intensive and prompt infusions of support, it is instructive to note how quickly a parishioner returns to independence and a normal functioning; whereas denying him such lavish help in a crisis often creates a need for long-term care.[12]

In addition to assigning a large block of time to an immediate emergency, the crisis counselor may decide, after the first session, to have another just two or three days in the future, rather than waiting for the sacred number of seven. There may be two interviews a week for the first two or three weeks, then no more, or they may be reduced to one per week. The time of termination may be judged by using the criteria listed for evaluating the success of crisis counseling, and by explicitly discussing with the person whether he or she has reached the point of functioning confidently without the help of the pastor.

The decision to space sessions more closely than once a week may depend on the intensity of anxiety or confusion or sense of unreality remaining after the first interview, by the presence of suicidal communication, and by the presence of identified external stress during the coming days. If the level of anxiety or other central affective symptoms have not seemed to be reduced during the first interview, or if reduced, still seem to be at a highly painful or incapacitating level, then another session would seem to be called for within a shorter interval than usual.

Certainly where there are explicit or implicit suicidal communications, it would be important to put another meeting on the schedule within two or three days. The feeling that there is no future is a part of suicidal persons' perception of themselves in their world. To assist the suicidal person in creating such a future is the immediate task of everyone in that person's life. After a reasonably good session, a specific date only a short time hence performs the function of making a gift of at least that much future, and is a breakthrough. Explicit suicidal language is self-evident: "I am thinking about killing myself." Implicit suicidal language can also be recognized: "I just don't see how I can stand all this much longer." "There's no use trying to go on." "My family would really be better off without me." "There's actually no meaning at all to life, is there?" While people may use both explicit and implicit suicidal language and not be highly lethal, it is the responsibility of the minister to check this out carefully, making the implicit explicit, examining its meaning, talking with the person about it in plain language. There is reason enough not to wait a week for the next interview to check it out further (for more details concerning the assessment of potential suicidal persons and a variety of interventions, see pp. 211-29).

Another guideline for scheduling the date of the next session is the determination of continued or additional situational stress during the days immediately following. Will there be a medical report with some probability of bad news? Are all the children going to be home from school an additional two days? Is there to be a critical interview with the boss? Might someone close to the person be dying? If so, schedule a session at the most opportune time.

In summary, pastors can be more helpful when they learn to read the person and the situation sensitively, discuss the issues, be flexible, and do what needs to be done as the total situation is examined. And remember, in crisis it will do no harm to schedule the next visit only two or three days later; it will usually be helpful and may sometimes make a critical difference in sustaining a person and turning the direction of the crisis around. The greater mistake would be to wait too long for the next time together.

The Use of the Telephone

Everyone uses the telephone, and everyone knows how to use it. So why say, "Use the telephone"? Yet in the context of the strategy of intervention in crisis, the active and creative use of this instrument of communication is often overlooked, and the differences between face-to-face and telephone counseling are frequently ignored.

When to Use the Telephone

Even with the increase in the amount of pastoral care and counseling being taught in seminary, the broadening scope and the depth of the teaching, and an increase in nonclassroom training opportunities, very little is being done to educate students in the effective use of the telephone as a pastoral care and counseling medium.

Just as little is being taught in the seminaries, a review of the professional psychotherapeutic literature reveals no more than a handful of articles dealing with the subject of the telephone in therapy. The upshot of all this is that in the face of ministers' frequent use of the phone as a therapeutic tool, and some increasing use of it by other professionals, there is a dearth of literature and very little education in regard to a reinforcement of its importance, and very few clues to its appropriate and most effective utilization. This oversight and neglect would seem to imply that it is not important to use the telephone and that when one does, it is either like any other counseling session or like any other conversation. This is a false communication.

All ministers are aware that very frequently, people in crisis will initiate their first contact by phone. If the minister is not in a position to go immediately to the person, usually the preferred response, and the person cannot soon come to the church office or the parsonage, the first session itself may take place right at that time by phone, whether it lasts only ten or fifteen minutes or an hour or more. Indeed, for a few people, because of their desire to remain anonymous or for other reasons, all the counseling they receive will be by phone.

Even when face-to-face interviews are scheduled, the phone can be used in at least three other sets of circumstances. First, there should almost always be some follow-up by the minister and "checking in" by the troubled person, especially in the early stages of the intervention process, with this procedure being explained by the minister and explicitly agreed to by the person. The rationale for this strategy will be explained in the next section.

Second, the person in crisis is encouraged to feel free to call the minister between appointments for brief talks in case of emergency, when the anxiety level rises sharply or other affective symptoms reach a frightening or seemingly hopeless point. These calls may appropriately be only a few minutes in length, although some may need to be longer. In this specific situation, the call is not considered to be a substitute for an appointment. For example, the person may be coming in the very next day, but during the afternoon or evening either feels an intense inner pressure that is unbearably painful or feels on the verge of losing control. It is possible that only five or ten minutes of expressing these feelings on the phone to the minister, hearing the minister's voice, sensing someone who cares, and reestablishing contact with reality through the relationship that is communicated voice to voice will be sufficient to sustain the person until the appointment the next day.

The minister and the person receiving help may also use the phone for the regular appointment if, for some reason such as illness, the person is unable to come to the church and it is impractical for the minister to make a visit.

The effectiveness of the telephone as a point of contact has now been proved beyond all doubt through the experience of the large numbers of suicide prevention and crisis intervention centers across this country and in many other countries of the world. In addition, many mental health clinics have begun to use it to supplement other phases of their therapy with patients.[13]

Rosenblum raises the point that while some people may be able to tolerate the pressure of a close face-to-face relationship, others may be so threatened by a personal visit that the contact may be more effectively maintained by phone. Therefore, if the caller is a person with whom the minister does not already have an established relationship, while it is certainly appropriate that a home or an office visit be suggested, the minister should not be so insistent as to close off the usefulness of telephone counseling. Rosenblum stresses that some persons may be overwhelmed by sustained personal contact, but at the same time are seeking some personal sustenance. The availability of voice contact is supremely important, for their own ventilation, for reassurance, to sustain the image that someone is there who cares. He concludes, "Telephone therapy deserves a legitimate place in the armamentarium of the therapist and the clinic. It should not be accorded second class status. It can serve as a useful adjunct to the more orthodox therapies."[14]

Differences Between Telephone and
Face-to-face Counseling

There are certain obvious differences between a counseling session conducted on the telephone and one at which the persons are physically present, yet the awareness of these differences has not always led to the conscious development of those disciplined practices that would make counselors more effective.

One of the major differences, of course, has to do with the fact that our usual perception and modes of communication with people include the visual. When a person speaks, we almost automatically turn to look as we are listening. We are seldom consciously aware that what we then hear is both added to and subtracted from by what we see. It is only when we cannot bring another person into our field of vision that we realize the sum total of the cues that are missing: the way a person cares for himself or herself physically, the posture, what the hands and eyes are doing, tenseness versus relaxation, reddening of the neck, cheeks, and around the eyes, tears, a smile or a frown, bodily movement, palpitation of the neck showing stronger and more rapid heart beat—all these indications, and others, are no longer there for us to see and interpret. And while these are of great significance when they accompany words, they are perhaps even more important to observe while we ourselves are speaking and during times of complete silence.

The lack of visual stimuli requires sensitive and perceptive listening on the part of the pastor, who must be much more aware of the tone of voice, its tremors and cracking, changes in volume and pitch, modulation, hesitation, quantity and pace of verbal production, the timing and length of pauses, sighing, choking, and other sounds, especially as these may be revelatory of feelings on the part of the caller. It may often necessitate the type of comment or specific questions that one would not typically ask in face-to-face contact because the answers would be apparent if the counselor could see the person. For example, "It sounds as if you are crying." Or, "It's difficult for me to decide whether you are laughing or crying." Or, "It seems your voice is higher than it was earlier. I wonder what you are feeling right now."

At the same time, the counselor must be just as aware that the person on the other end of the line also lacks visual perception. The physical stimuli are not available for the person in crisis, either. This demands more verbal participation by the counselor, who must confirm a meaningful presence through sound, whereas in a face-to-face setting the same things might be communicated through nodding, eye contact, a gesture of the hand, and other nonverbal signals which communicate that one is there and attentive.

The minister's use of her or his voice as a means of establishing relationship quickly and easily without visual stimuli is at least as crucial in telephone crisis intervention as in preaching or the usual pastoral care and counseling situations, although it is obviously of great importance there. The quality of the voice makes a great difference—whether it is flat and monotone or alive and flexible, whiney and shrill or well-rounded, too loud or too soft. Changes in the voice communicate a variety of feelings, including warmth and caring and assurance. In addition, on the telephone it becomes more appropriate to express concern through explicit words as well as through the tone of voice. The importance of the confirmation of presence also requires that silences on the phone not last as long as they might when persons are physically together. This should not be interpreted to mean either that the counselor seeks to force the other to talk or merely chatters away at something so there will not be silence. Rather, after a brief period, the pastor may ask, "What feelings are you having during this silence?" Or if it is obvious that the emotion is extremely powerful, "When you feel very intensely about something, it's often quite difficult to express it in words." Or occasionally, when there is no response to such questions or statements, simply, "I'm still here with you."

Another difference between telephone and face-to-face counseling is that the other person has much more control over the termination of the session. Often enough in counseling, a person's frustration and anger or fright or other feelings lead to the desire to reject or escape from the counselor and the situation. Nevertheless, when they are together in the same room, social inhibitions usually exercise pressure on the person to continue to sit there, even when he or she would prefer to leave. This provides the opportunity for the counselor to perceive feelings and facilitate their expression and a detailed discussion of them. On the phone there are far fewer social restraints, and it is very easy to hang up. The telephone counselor must be aware of the dynamics of this situation, pay close attention to rising frustration, anger, and fear, encourage the person to express these feelings, and be willing to function in a situation where some authority and control is given up to the person in need.

The Need for Discipline

One very experienced professional in the practice and supervision of telephone crisis intervention points out one of the dangers of the method. Because of our customary social conversational use of the phone, it is easy for the disciplines of crisis counseling to grow lax, allowing the verbal transaction to deteriorate into nothing but conversation. Undisciplined chitchat about crucial matters is still nothing but chitchat and is just not therapeutic. The conversational model of transaction on the phone, he believes, is worse than nothing when talking with a person in crisis.[15] Therefore, when moving from face-to-face counseling to telephone intervention, the counselor must be consciously aware of the change of modality and deliberately call into play the most disciplined methods of listening and responding. The situation demands intense concentration.

Follow-Up: Rationale and Procedures

It should now be clear that a major contribution to the life of a person in crisis is another person who genuinely cares, who seeks to understand and to help the other to understand, who brings a perspective on the problem area that is broader and more realistic than that of the distressed person, and who offers hope. Also, the more severe the crisis, the less hope and less future the person experiences. Therefore any activities that make for more frequent contact between the helping person and the person in crisis will support those goals implied by the needs that have just been stated. Closer spacing of interviews and emergency telephone calls initiated by the person experiencing stress have already been discussed.

The follow-up may take two directions. First, the minister will call back on the phone or go by to see the person, the latter being preferable and often practical from the minister's point of view. However, if a visit to the home, office, or hospital is not practical, then the phone is an extremely convenient instrument. Obviously, a minister in an extremely busy period can usually make several phone calls in the time it may take to go to a home a number of miles away. The call may be specifically scheduled and agreed to, or it may come spontaneously out of the minister's immediate caring—wondering how the person is, what is going on. The second direction is from the person in crisis to the minister, not only in emergency, but as a result of a commitment to call, following some particular action or some period of time.

For example, one outcome of a counseling session might be the agreement that the person go to the family doctor or to a particular agency, or tell a spouse or parents about his or her feelings and that a counselor is being seen. The agreement is made that this will take place within two days and that on the third day the person will report back or the minister will call. In the afternoon of the second day, however, the minister, remembering how reluctant the person was about carrying out the agreement, or that the person was still quite depressed when leaving the office, or simply having the person very much in mind, picks up the phone and calls: "I was just thinking about you. You were hurting so much the other day. I was wondering how you feel right now and how things are going with you."

Values of Follow-Up

These procedures accomplish several purposes, and several dynamics are operating at the same time. First, the minister's visit or telephone call expresses caring. A therapist states the experience of a secular setting that has been using the telephone as a follow-up support for alcoholics: "The fact that the therapist, not the patient, usually initiates the phone call helps indicate to the patient that the therapist is actively interested in his welfare and is not just a passive participant."[16] This sense that someone genuinely cares is a potent force in supporting the ego strength of the distressed person.

Second, and an alternative strategy, obtaining a commitment from the troubled person to check back supports the expectation that the person must take responsibility for his or her own life and must therefore take certain initiatives in the helping process. Additionally, when the person actually does do this, the act itself is ego strengthening.

Third, the commitment to check with each other at a specific time gives the person that much future, something positive to look forward to that the person may not have had before. As mentioned earlier, this is an absolute necessity for the person with strong suicidal thoughts and feelings.

Fourth, along the same line, the frequency of contact, the expression of caring, the doing something for oneself, the creation of even a short-term future—all create and encourage hope in the midst of crisis, the hope that action can be taken and things can change. Fifth, follow-up calls allow for further catharsis.

Sixth, the knowledge on the part of the person in crisis that there definitely will be a follow-up call is an impetus to act upon the decisions that have been made and to pursue the agreed-upon goals.

Seventh, the procedure provides a means of evaluating the results of the action taken and produces the feedback necessary for further decision making.

Referral and Transferral

The word *referral* is common enough in our usage and in our actual practice of suggesting that the persons seeing us about some personal problem or difficult situation see someone else instead, or in addition, in order that their needs might be more fully and effectively met. No minister is so out of touch with reality to believe that he or she alone can meet all the needs of all persons. Our very best service to many people is to assist them in getting to others who specialize in areas of the person's needs. Clinebell states that "properly conceived, referral is a means of using a team effort to help a troubled person. It is a *broadening* and *sharing,* not total *transfer* of responsibility. It employs the division-of-labor principle that is the basis of interprofessional cooperation."[17]

When a minister is working with a person in crisis, it would seldom mean that the minister merely shifts the person to some other professional or agency and then steps completely out of the picture. Most often the minister will remain the primary crisis counselor as secondary referrals are made for medical examination, treatment, and prescription; child care agencies; employment agencies; and many others. Even in situations where a psychiatrist or psychologist might become the primary therapist for a few weeks, the pastor often properly remains actively engaged with the person as a caring and supporting friend, as a representative of the community of faith, and as the primary professional in follow-up support and counseling after the crisis is effectively resolved.

Referral is used when it is determined that there are relevant needs of the person in crisis that cannot be met by the minister alone. The appropriate professional or agency or organization is then recommended as a part of the total therapeutic plan. The initiative to make his or her own arrangements is usually left up to the person in crisis, although in some instances the way may be made easier by advance calls from the pastor. There is also, of course, the follow-up procedure mentioned earlier which encourages and supports the person's initiative.

The term *transferral* refers to occasions of severe crisis when a person is seen to be a danger to self or someone else or is on the verge of a psychotic reaction. Not only is another professional recommended, but the crisis counselor takes whatever steps are necessary to get the person there and does not relinquish primary responsibility until the other professional or agency clearly assumes it. In severe crisis, one does not simply suggest a referral and then wait several days before determining whether the person has gone. It may then be too late.

When to Refer or Transfer

The decision to refer or transfer is determined by the person's needs relevant to the crisis and the ability of the minister to meet those needs. When the minister cannot, someone else must be found who can. In many instances, as suggested earlier, the minister will remain the primary crisis counselor and coordinates the total plan, knowing, however, when to relinquish the primary role to someone else and shift into a supportive and follow-up role only. It should be reemphasized that this is not a cop-out, nor does it suggest that the secondary and supportive function is not important. Quite to the contrary, both the referral and the continued pastoral relationship may be absolutely crucial to a successful outcome.

To repeat, transferral is indicated when there seems to be a serious threat of violence against someone else, when the person is a high suicide risk, or when behavior is reaching psychotic proportions— that is, the person's grasp on reality is being lost, and he or she is becoming mentally or emotionally unavailable to the type of counseling the minister can do.

Referral is in order when mood and emotional and behavioral changes are apparent, but a precipitating event cannot be discovered within two or three sessions. Or if the precipitating event is identified and the symptoms (a high level of anxiety, deep depression, extreme confusion, inability to take any action) remain severe after five or six sessions, particularly if the length of time from the precipitating event to the fifth or sixth session is six weeks or more, there is sufficient evidence that the usual crisis intervention procedures have not been effective. Many would also want to refer when, after two or three sessions, it is discovered that in addition to the symptoms of the crisis, there is long-term underlying pathology. Some well-trained ministers may be able to separate the crisis symptoms from the earlier symptoms and work effectively on the crisis only, but it may become quite complex.

An illustration may show the extreme needs of a person with reasonably few ego strengths when there is also a crisis reaction. A seventeen-year-old had made a mild suicide attempt and was brought to a minister by her employer. She was very depressed and felt she had nothing to live for. There had been periods of depression before, and one previous mild suicide attempt. The precipitating event for this particular feeling of worthlessness and hopelessness had been a violent argument with her mother. The home background was extremely bad and the present situation poor. The young woman had dropped out of school, had a serious drinking problem, and was sexually promiscuous. Even though her present depression fit the definition of crisis, her whole background and pattern of maladaptive and self-destructive behavior were so bad, and the present depression so severe as to prevent her being sufficiently available for counseling. Therefore the minister directly raised the question of whether it might be possible for her to handle her life in the near future. She felt totally without strength and would not promise not to try again to kill herself. The minister suggested the hospital as a place where she would be completely taken care of for a short period of time and would not have to assume responsibility for herself, which at the moment she felt incapable of doing. She agreed that she would like to be cared for in this way until she could do more for herself. The minister called the hospital to arrange for the admission procedure. He then called the employer and asked him to take her to the hospital; he also asked the employer to tell the mother to meet them there to sign the admission papers. The next day, the minister called the administrative psychiatrist and discussed the situation with him. When the young woman was discharged after a week, much of the depression gone, the minister began counseling with her.

Certainly some people overdramatize their problems, both in the degree of suicidal feelings they report or in their underestimation of their own strength. Nevertheless, when the minister has discussed these issues in a direct way with a person and has some sense that the person is reporting these feelings accurately, it is better to believe the self-description and take the necessary transferral steps than to make what might be a disastrous misjudgment in the other direction.

Naturally, referral should also always be considered after a crisis is resolved, if there are other problems the person would like to try to resolve but these are beyond the limits of the minister's training and experience or for which she or he does not have sufficient time.

It is important for the minister to keep in mind that a transferral or referral may itself be the precipitating event of a crisis. For example, people who are experiencing anxiety and confusion, or other feelings and behaviors indicative of a situational crisis, may call upon their own minister, or a pastor who is personally known in other ways, or one who has been recommended to them. This pastor is a professional or friend or neighbor whom one might expect to be understanding and helpful. The decision to call the minister or to go by the church office is an act taken to help oneself and is a constructive move in itself. With many, the positive expectation of the pastoral conversation reduces some of the anxiety, although admittedly, for others it may have the opposite effect. Then, in conversation, the minister says that one needs to go to a physician, a psychologist, a family service agency, or some other professional or agency or institution. Many persons in this situation feel rejected and frustrated, and interpret this to mean that the problem is worse than they thought. They are also being asked to change their identity from that of parishioner, friend, or neighbor to that of social service agency client or patient of a doctor or clinic. They must deal with this discontinuity between roles, the unexpectedness of the change, lack of preparation for the change, and ambivalent feelings toward the new role.[18]

In handling proposals for referral or transferral, the minister needs to be aware that in the midst of a person's crisis, an additional crisis may be precipitated. Therefore the minister must be prepared to discuss the person's reaction to the suggestion to go somewhere else and see someone else. In order to accomplish this immediate task most effectively, the minister needs certain sensitivities, information, and counseling skills.

Methods of Referral

The final issue is *how* to make a referral or transferral most effectively. The first and obvious necessity, once a person's needs have been clearly determined, is to refer to the professionals and agencies which are clearly designed to meet the specific identified needs. This will require a rather full knowledge of community resources, or at least where, with one or two phone calls, the proper ones may be found. It is also helpful to have at least some personal knowledge of professionals, both those in private practice and those who work for a variety of agencies. Referral to a place where the person's identified needs cannot be met is a particularly frustrating experience, and additional frustration, disappointment, and anger is precisely what the person in crisis does not need at this time. It can actually speed the deterioration of the situation in many instances.

The discussion thus far may be arousing some questions and even some feelings of impatience and irritation among those pastors who serve parishioners in remote and rural areas and in small towns. Where are all these psychiatrists and psychologists and social workers and social service agencies that this discussion seems to assume? In addition, it would be unfair to mislead seminary students into believing that all those wonderful additional support and primary services will be readily available in their first pastorate after graduation. There are certainly significant differences between large metropolitan areas and rural areas, and I can remember my own frustration, even dismay at times, in attempting to deal with complex persons and situations in the rural circuit I served. However, today there are relatively few parishes where at least some of these professional resources are not as available as the other sorts of activities and resources that people in those areas typically seek: shopping, entertainment, medical treatment, and so on. One of the responsibilities of a pastor who has recently arrived in a parish is to quickly search out those persons and places: the nearest town or larger town or city; the seat of the county government—not too convenient, necessarily, but not prohibitively distant, either; the creative collaboration between clergy and general- or family-practice physicians or social workers when psychiatrists are not available; and for the minister, advanced seminars or workshops in pastoral care or counseling, wherever they are being held.

Second, it is necessary that the need for referral be presented to the person in crisis in a sensitive and reassuring manner. The need that is to be met, the reasons the pastor cannot meet it adequately, and the appropriateness of the particular person or agency being suggested are all cogently explained in detail.

Third, the person is encouraged to express his or her feelings in response to the referral or transferral suggestion. These feelings are to be accepted as genuine, and there needs to be an understanding of some of the real emotional difficulties the person may have in following through on the suggestion, and of the actual inconvenience that may be involved.

Fourth, if, however, it is clear to the minister that legitimate needs have been identified, that they are related to the crisis, and that they can be met more adequately somewhere else, a summary of this is made in as convincing a manner as the minister is able. The person in crisis must not be allowed to play the "please help me but I won't let you" game by refusing to accept and act on suggestions that would facilitate the resolution of the crisis.

Fifth, it is essential that the person in crisis be reassured of the minister's deep concern and the fact that the referral or transferral does not mean the minister will no longer be involved. Many people are sensitive to any signal that the helping person might be rejecting them. No matter how well the need for referral is explained, some people still experience it as rejection. The minister might need to verbalize this in order to assist those persons to express their genuine feelings and be able to work them through: "Now I know that in suggesting that you see the psychiatrist, some people would feel that I didn't want to work with them myself. I wonder if you are having some of those feelings right now." The minister encourages the expression of whatever feelings of rejection or anxiety or anger the person might be having, then clarifies in detail that their relationship will continue, that the minister will continue to be the primary counselor, or if not, that he or she will be in touch with the person regularly to see how things are going and to help in any way possible.

Finally, it is essential to follow up on the referrals or transferrals, to see whether appointments were made and kept, what the results were, and what the next steps should be. Such continued contact is important not only for such checkup and planning, but to satisfy the natural dependency needs of any person in crisis, satisfaction of which are crucial for a person's responsiveness to the various sources of help to which he or she has been directed.[19]

Clinebell, and Oglesby, in more detail, list a number of guidelines for referral. While not all are applicable to the referral of the person in crisis, they are of value, and a minister will be much more helpful to more people by becoming familiar with them.[20]

Crisis Counseling in Groups

The placing of persons in crisis into a small group as a new modality for helping them more effectively in their distress has been described by several professionals working in the setting of crisis intervention centers and hospitals. While probably impossible in small churches and communities, and impractical in some of moderate size, it would seem to hold great promise for the minister in larger churches and in the city. It could afford some saving of the minister's own time and be a greater aid for those with whom she or he is working. Even those ministers who feel that the approach is not for them at this time should seek to understand the procedure, evaluate it fairly, and be alert for opportunities that might present themselves at a later date.

Values of the Group Approach

The group method is particularly recommended to those ministers who are serving in poverty and minority areas and are not themselves members of that particular class or racial or ethnic group. One of the difficulties encountered in a variety of forms in a traditional ministry to lower socioeconomic classes, especially blacks and Hispanics, by those who are Anglo-Saxon and middle class or above, has not usually been a lack of commitment and desire, but a massive lack of understanding, an inability to get inside the experience of the other, a failure to grasp structures of thought, and, quite simply, a different language. Many of these handicaps can be overcome when much of the personal understanding, the offering of alternatives of coping behavior, assistance with decision making, and support of the new behavior comes from an individual's own peers in a group.[21]

Confirmation of the value of crisis groups has come from two studies. One of these was in a hospital setting where immediate hospitalization was not indicated, but individual treatment was not available for six weeks. A pilot study showed that over 50 percent of the patients were definitely improved as a result of being placed immediately in a group which met for a six-week period. This led the professionals to a decision to carry on a more intensive examination of the procedure. Patients were placed in groups meeting one and a half hours each week, with up to ten persons in each group, each person attending a maximum of six sessions. New persons could come into a group at any time. Seventy-eight patients were in the experimental groups and ninety patients were in a control group receiving traditional forms of psychotherapy. At the conclusion of the study, the therapists had spent, in terms of their own time, an average of one and a half hours per individual in the experimental group and eight and a half hours per individual in the control group. In a six-month follow-up, 83 percent of the experimental group reported continued improvement, more than twice as many as those who received the usual individual treatment. The obvious conclusion is that the group method saves time and is clearly more helpful.[22]

Another study in a crisis intervention setting designated three levels of assessment of outcome, with sixteen out of the thirty clients showing maximum improvement, and nine others showing minimal or moderate improvement.[23] While this investigation does indicate that people are definitely helped by a crisis group, the report unfortunately included no reference to a control group receiving individual counseling, so no comparative judgment can be made.

A third investigation evaluated the results of crisis groups of six to eight members, meeting twice weekly for hour-and-a-half sessions for a maximum of eight sessions. The participants were asked, prior to beginning the group, upon its completion, and a year later, to complete inventories which assessed ego strength and elicited subjective feelings of anxiety, depression, and hostility. They also responded, upon completion of the group and a year later, to a rating scale of their perception of the usefulness of the group to them. Among other means of evaluation were pre- and post-treatment questionnaires which asked for the therapists' description of persons' initial problems and their clinical status upon leaving the group.[24]

> Clearly the patients studied here benefited significantly in terms of symptom change, i.e., feeling that the group had helped, feeling less anxious or depressed [hostility scores did not change], and possibly experiencing more fundamental personality changes as indicated by a generally smooth postgroup adjustment and by a decrease in defensiveness as measured by the ego strength scale. These changes appeared to last and to be augmented over time. Moreover, the benefit to the patients seemed to come from the group culture and not specifically from the therapist. . . .
> The crisis group appears surprisingly effective despite its brevity.[25]

Description of the Procedure

The first and obvious practical difficulty in beginning a crisis intervention group in the context of the local church is to have available during a single week at least four people in the early to middle stages of crisis who respond positively to the minister's suggestion that they meet together for several sessions. The other problem is that of maintaining the group with a minimum of four persons over an extended period of time. This requires that the church and/or community setting be large enough so that new persons are constantly available to come into it.

If a group is feasible from this standpoint, however, the procedures of the Benjamin Rush Clinic in Los Angeles seem directly adaptable to the minister's work. An article by Morley and Brown presents their procedures quite clearly and in detail.[26] Every person who comes into the clinic is seen individually for the first session. At that time, it is determined whether the person is in crisis. If so, a specific formulation of the crisis situation is made, the precipitating event identified, the threat explored, previous and potential coping mechanisms surveyed, and preparation made for the person to enter the group. While in the clinic's practice there are certain guidelines relating to language difficulty or to other psychiatric problems which would exclude a person from the group setting, it is not necessary to seek to have a homogeneous group—that is, all one sex, marital status, age.

In the first group session, people begin by telling one another what led them to seek help and summarizing what they discovered about themselves and their crisis reaction during their first session. The group counselor assists them in elaborating the meaning of the precipitating event, the form of the crisis, and their previous unsuccessful attempts at coping. Two or even three persons might be able to introduce themselves to a group in this way in the first session. The counselor facilitates the group, helping each person to express his or her feelings and to explore alternative coping mechanisms and courses of action which might help change the person or the situation, and encourages mutual support. As in individual crisis counseling, the group leader also directly discourages the discussion of chronic problems, explains why certain behavior that is an attempt to deal with the feelings and situations may be destructive, and rejects consideration of such behavior. All participants understand that they are to have a limited number of sessions and that their work must be done in this period of time.

Differences from Usual Therapy Groups

There are a number of differences between crisis intervention groups and most usual therapy groups, due obviously to the nature of crisis and its inherent time limits.

First, there is no focus on the development of the group as a group, with a major concern on the analysis of the group process. Rather, much more attention is given to the individual by both the counselor and the group, with group support and stimulation. This focus is designed to meet the peculiar needs of the person in crisis. It should also be obvious that the development of group feeling, in the usual therapy sense, would be made extremely difficult by the fact that a person is in the group for no more than five to eight sessions and the fact that persons are constantly leaving and new ones entering. Even so, it has been the experience of those who have been involved in crisis groups that because of the intense emotions of crisis and the need for psychosocial support, rapport and a sense of empathy are rapidly established between group members.

Second, time is of the essence. No person in the group can be allowed to sit quietly until he or she feels like participating verbally. Those who are most verbal cannot be allowed to dominate. There is much more calling on people to respond, much more going around the entire group so that all members may express themselves on an issue or respond with their feelings.

Third, obviously, the group leader is extremely active. Of course, this is true of some counselors in other groups, but it is an absolute requirement in a crisis group in order to accomplish the goals of crisis resolution in a short period of time and to maintain the process just referred to.

Differences from Individual Crisis Counseling

There are also differences, primarily in the direction of advantages, between group and individual crisis counseling. First, there is the value of group support. There can be a genuine and important offering of help, caring, and hope, both inside and outside the group, to a degree that no individual counselor alone could afford. Significant social relationships may grow out of the group association, providing sustenance between group sessions and continuing help after an individual's formal counseling is at an end.

Second, since the feelings of each member are so close to the surface, there seems to be a mutual stimulation to express feelings openly. Most of the time this is accomplished simply by being in the presence of others who are expressing their emotions. There may also often be similarities of affect that touch quite deeply those who share them, leading to a depth of affective expression and exploration which might have been more difficult under other circumstances. Some persons may also become desensitized—that is, situations or relationships or events that are highly charged emotionally in their own lives and which cause them distress may become less painful or threatening when the person hears the same matters mentioned again and again by others.

Third, the way an individual functions in a group often reveals the type of faulty response to persons or situations that is very much a part of the present problem. The counselor is alert to these styles of relating, makes certain the group is aware of what the person is doing, and asks the other members to comment on this behavior and discuss other ways the person might respond to others.[27]

Finally, in a group, there is additional input for alternative coping mechanisms and feedback on decision making. No matter how intelligent and creative the counselor, it is self-evident that several people can think of more things and provide a greater variety of feedback than can one. Often these suggestions and positive and negative criticisms might be accepted more readily from peers than from the professional.

Difficulties of Group Crisis Counseling

One of the major difficulties in group crisis counseling is the additional burden on the counselor, who must be fully aware at all times of all the needs of all the individuals and also of the group process. It is not easy to keep a focus on the crisis of *every* individual in the group, especially while several members are responding to the crisis of one. Yet no one's crisis must ever stray from the counselor's attention.

In the second place, the first crisis a person presents may, upon further investigation, turn out not to be the primary or most potent one. A crisis covered by another crisis is more difficult to identify in a group setting, where the demands on the counselor's attention are so great.

Finally, the counselor must be much more alert to potentially destructive coping behavior suggested by members of the group. He or she needs to hear and evaluate quickly, ask for feedback by other members, explain the potential destructiveness and why it cannot be considered, and use this situation as effective teaching, not only for the person to whom the suggestion was directed but also for the person making it and for the group as a whole.

It is clear, in spite of these difficulties, that where the formation of a crisis group is feasible in terms of the number of persons available to start and continue it, it is a preferred method of helping persons significantly in a brief period of time.

Conclusion

This chapter has sought to present some of the important and sometimes essential intervention procedures for assisting persons toward the resolution of their crises. Many of these are methods which many clergy are already utilizing, combining in some form a number of the traditional pastoral functions, their genuine concern for persons, some procedures borrowed from other professionals which seem appropriate to the minister's own functioning, and their own creativity.

Probably the final emphasis of this discussion should be on the matter of the minister's creative imagination in developing a program of help, styled for a particular person with a particular problem in a particular life context. The pastoral counselor should be free to use flexibly, in a manner appropriate to the unique situation which every person in crisis provides, the means and procedures of helping that are available. Any creative impulses to respond to the person's need in ways that are not among the standard procedures should not be inhibited initially just because they are new. They should be encouraged to spring fully forth into consciousness, and only then tested to see if they are within the bounds of what the minister understands the goals of crisis counseling to be and within the disciplines of the total procedure as previously outlined in Chapter 3. If they are judged to be potentially helpful, then they should be attempted.

Ministers should never forget that they have available the valuable resources of the community of faith as a whole community, its worship, its various subgroups and programs and activities, its individual members, the faith itself, the authority of the ministerial office, the tendency of many persons both inside and outside the church (although obviously not all, and pastors should certainly be prepared for this) to respond positively to ministers' initiative in the attempt to be helpful. Clergy need to be imaginative in the use of these and other resources in the service of persons who are suffering emotionally.

CHAPTER 5

INTERVENING IN

FAMILY CRISES

One night in my fourth year as a pastor, I had been visiting prospective members of the church. One more call and I would go home. I started up the sidewalk to the home of a woman who had attended our worship service several times. I had never met her husband, but he had made it clear through mutual friends that he was not at all interested. As I approached the door, I could hear loud voices inside. Standing with finger poised on the doorbell, I froze as I heard the furious obscenities the man was shouting and the loud mocking responses of the woman. I could tell they were walking from room to room during that horrible battle.

Clearly a family crisis! Also a *pastoral* crisis! What is a minister to do? Should I push the button? Then what would I say when one of them came to the door? Should I beat a hasty retreat and cross them off the prospect list? Or pray for guidance, leave, phone the next day to set up a visit, then play it by ear? I chose the last. But when I walked into my home some fifteen minutes later, the phone was ringing. The woman I had heard shouting only a few minutes before was asking me if I could come over right then and talk with them. Her husband also wanted me to come. I went, heard them out, and planned some additional conversations. At that time I did not know much about marriage counseling, but everything turned out all right.

Ministers can be involved not only in the lives of individuals but whole families, two or more people at the same time, people who live in the same household or are related to one another. Such involvement may flow naturally out of a developing situation while a minister is present. Or a couple or family may invite a minister to work with them in a crisis. Or a minister sometimes may go ahead and push the doorbell. A pastor's effective work with a family in crisis is usually considerably more complex and challenging than with an individual, but the situation also provides an opportunity to widen the sphere of pastoral influence. There is an additional value if there are children in the family: Then we hope to create a climate in which their growth toward maturity as human beings is greatly increased—by our direct recognition of them and help to them, by the modeling effects of our behavior on the older persons in the family, and by the direct and explicit conversations with parents concerning the needs of the children in that particular situation. This chapter will discuss all this in detail.

References to the family have already been made: the family as a context of crisis; the importance of the family as a resource for an individual in crisis, with the pastor often needing to take the initiative in bringing the family together to clarify the crisis and to help family members respond in the most constructive ways to the person (pp. 93-94). Later, the discussion of grief will make clear the need to consider the whole family—not only the responses of each individual, but the family interaction itself. The importance of the explicit expression of empathy to one another will be emphasized, along with the need to assist family members to understand and respect the differences between them and the reassignment of family roles (pp. 146, 161-62).

Certainly there are many occasions of individual crisis. Yet many of these occur to individuals who live in the same household with others or are otherwise related to a family in such a way that the rest of the family is affected, sometimes quite profoundly. Sometimes family members may be involved in the triggering of another member's crisis. Often the helpful responses of some or all family members may assist in the positive outcome of the individual's crisis. These situations may not be family crises as such, but periods of distress or conflict, calling for problem solving and help within the family.

In the family crisis, by contrast, there is a *direct* line of impact between a precipitating event and the family *as a whole,* in addition to the event's impact upon each individual in the family. The loss of a family member by death or some other means is a good example. So also is divorce, where each family member loses in some sense the family *as a whole* as it was. Other events include moving from one location to another, a new person coming to live in the household, the destruction of a home by fire.

A number of situations usually referred to as family crisis, however, will not be discussed here: domestic violence, battered spouses and children, and incest. In addition to the usual situational crisis dynamics, these usually involve persistent patterns of behavior and personality dynamics unique to each form of behavior, which call for specific and specially tailored approaches to effective intervention. An excellent presentation of these (as well as other types of emergencies, including psychiatric emergency and violent or potentially violent behavior) has been made by Diana Sullivan Everstine and Louis Everstine.[1]

The Family as a System

In order to define a family crisis with more precision and to develop guidelines for intervention, it is essential to understand the family as a system. It is self-evident that a family is made up of separate individuals, but in a sense, it is also a single organism just as each of us is a single organism. Each one of us has a variety of individual organs, which are linked together. Generally when we are functioning well, these organs work together for our benefit within our particular system. If one part of a person's system malfunctions, then the whole organism is affected in some way. Certain other parts of the physiological system seek to adjust to compensate for the malfunction or to correct it, with different organs in the whole body constantly operating in an attempt to maintain a relatively stable physiochemical balance (homeostasis) for that person's health and most effective functioning. Obviously, we realize that in the extreme case, either the requisite organs of the body cannot make sufficient adjustment to produce the needed homeostasis, or the adjustment itself is so radical that it becomes dangerous to the life of the whole.

Something of the same holds true for families. Though families may differ from one another in many ways, each family develops its own internal operations (a family self-image, characteristic modes of thinking, ways members relate to one another, forms of communication, etc.) which seek to maintain the family as a unit while trying to meet as well as possible the needs of each individual member. Unfortunately, some families do this very poorly, to the detriment of the individual members, while some families accomplish this dual function (maintaining itself as a unit *and* meeting the needs of its members as individuals) quite well.

An obvious assumption, when viewing the family as a system, is that any behavior on the part of one person affects the entire system and therefore each individual within it. Thus, as a result of any new learning on the part of any member, the introduction of new behavior into the family, a new family member or the loss of a family member, or any other change in the system as it is, the members initiate behavior toward one another which they have learned in the past as the proper way to meet the needs of the entire system. The difficulty is that in the face of radical threat to the system, the old modes of family functioning may not be effective. In such a case, family crisis will result.

A major function of the family is to provide self-defining experiences for each family member. That is, within the family interaction, each person provides and is provided with those sorts of experiences which encourage the development of a clearcut sense of one's self as a human being, the ability to know oneself as oneself, in relationship with but still separate from others. In the family we are also provided with experiences that lead to effective and meaningful or ineffective and self-defeating styles of interacting with one another. As we begin to discuss the family system in these terms, we can readily begin to see that some families will be more vulnerable to more types of precipitating events than others, more families will be particularly vulnerable at certain times than others, and families will have differing quantities and qualities of resources with which to meet their crises.

Beavers places families on a continuum between what he calls entropic and negentropic. *Entropic* refers to a closed system where little or no energy input is received from the outside. An entropic family may be chaotic, with insufficient structures in its system to be able to receive and assimilate and utilize new learning on behalf of the family and its individuals. Other such families tend to exhibit rigid structures of interaction; energy is expended more and more on maintaining the structures themselves, leaving less for growing or for dealing with crises. The *negentropic* system, on the other hand, is open to energy from the outside. There are obviously certain clearly delineated patterns of interaction within the family, but these are characterized by flexibility, and there is input on the part of every family member of new learning gained outside the family. Thus the family receives new energies, and its members are capable of testing new ways of relating to one another.[2]

Criteria for the Evaluation of Families

Reference has been made to the twofold purpose of families and, in general terms, the fact that some families accomplish that purpose quite well, others poorly, and, we can assume, still others are somewhere along the middle of the continuum. Through a systematic observation of families by perceptive persons, these families can be differentiated. However, the critical question has to do with the specific criteria by which family systems can be evaluated. What are the particular behaviors identified in families which then can be consistently related to the highest quality of self-defining experiences—those experiences which contribute to the development of human competence, mental and emotional health, and satisfying relationships? These behaviors have been identified and arranged in a number of categories by a team of researchers in an extensive and sophisticated study which took several years to complete.[3] Ministers' awareness of these criteria, their knowledge of the specific behaviors which characterize each one, and their ability to evaluate the strengths and weaknesses of a family according to these dimensions, are essential to the approaches used in working with individual families in crisis. This assessment guides the selection of the types of interventions that will have the highest probability of being facilitative to resolving a particular family's crisis. Beavers lists and describes these criteria of family evaluation.[4]

A Family's Own Systems Orientation. Members of these families are aware that people do not prosper in a vacuum. Human needs are satisfied within an interpersonal system. A second characteristic is that the most effective families are aware that within the system, certain behaviors elicit certain reactions and these reactions in turn may stimulate additional reactions. By contrast, dysfunctional families do not seem to be able to make such connections between their successive behaviors. The third assumption of the family systems perspective is that human behavior results from a complex interaction of a number of variables; there is no simple cause-and-effect process in human life and interaction. Finally, a systems orientation includes the awareness that human beings are finite, that they are limited in power, and that self-esteem lies in relative competence, rather than omnipotence.

Boundary Issues. Optimal family members have clear boundaries between themselves in the context of a family structure in which there is commitment to one another. In the research, it was easy to determine, for example, how a mother felt as compared and contrasted with a father, or how one child viewed a specific situation as compared with another child or a parent. These differences were accepted and respected. Individuality was encouraged. Even though the family was distinguishable by its members' commitment to one another, there were also whole-family permeable boundaries to the outside world, allowing for an effective interchange of information, interests, and energies through the different members' participation in relationships and activities outside the family.

Contextual Clarity. Contextual clarity begins with a strong parental coalition, in both function and affection. In the healthy family there was a relatively equal parental overt power, with the parents holding the balance of power over the children. These generational boundaries are necessary for meeting the needs of both parents and children. Children did not threaten parents, and the parents met one another's needs well enough so that neither tried to exploit the children in the service of his or her own adult needs.

Power Issues. The fourth criterion seems to overlap in some ways with the third. Here, however, it has to do with *how* power is expressed, the power of a noncoercive loving relationship with a meaningful other, versus the power of coercive control over others. The clear generational line, referred to in the preceding paragraph dealing with contextual clarity, expresses itself through the parents' own egalitarian coalition, with the children being less overtly powerful, but with the parents being open to the childrens' contributions and these contributions actually being a part of the material of decision making.

Encouragement of Dependence Versus Encouragement of Autonomy. Autonomous persons are aware of what they feel and think. They take responsibility for their own behavior. They are able to think of themselves as unique individuals, no matter how closely intertwined their lives are with the lives of others. Encouragement of autonomy is a function with several specific characteristics: the ability of family members to take responsibility for their own individual thoughts, feelings, and behavior; openness to communication from others; respect for the unique and different subjective views of reality found within and outside of the family. In the optimal family, in contrast with those that functioned at a lower level, there was a striking absence of blaming, personal attack, and scapegoating. Initiative is encouraged and failures well tolerated. If we can assume that movement toward autonomy is facilitated by an amount of risktaking reasonably appropriate to the individual's age and abilities, and if failure is not reasonably well tolerated, it can readily be seen that a child will soon learn that initiative taking is too dangerous. In addition, there is, on the part of the optimal family, a whole-family awareness that children grow up and leave home under what usually are ordered circumstances, in contrast with those families which seek to bind children tightly to the family of origin and make leavetaking extremely difficult, or those chaotic families in which children leave home prematurely and impulsively.

Affective Issues. It is important to observe the characteristic family mood or feeling tone. Of course, any family on a given occasion may be sad or angry or euphoric, according to situational factors, but each family also has a basic, underlying, persistent characteristic mood. It is of critical significance also to determine whether individuals are allowed to have their own feelings and to express those feelings openly and clearly to one another, and whether empathy is openly and clearly expressed.

Effectiveness of Negotiation and Task Performance. Can individuals and the whole family hear and accept directions, organize themselves to respond to a task, develop input received from other members, negotiate differences, and provide some coherent and effective response to a challange?

Transcendent Values. This study also pointed to the power of a family's underlying, supporting, guiding set of values, philosophy of life, and/or religious faith, as seen in the family's actual behavior. There may be considerable or very little congruence between the values certain members explicitly state and those by which they seem to live. Every family truly needs, according to Beavers, such transcendent values. These provide a perspective from which to judge one's own behavior, as well as to view and adapt to the inevitable changes involved in growth, development, aging, and losses when family members leave home or die.

> People must view a day's reality in the light of a conceptual and relationship system broader than themselves or their families in order to make sense of events, to accept losses of loved ones, and live with huuan consciousness encased in a finite, aging body which must die. Without investing in such a transcendent belief system, no human exists without hopelessness and despair.[5]

Beavers goes on to say,

> This is one of the most significant of the lessons taught by optimal families—accepting loss is related to possessing a system of transcendent values that provides hope, trust, and meaning when human helplessness is overwhelming.[6]

These criteria, with their specific attitudes and behaviors, can assist ministers in their evaluation of the strengths and shortcomings of the different families with which they carry on pastoral care and counseling, including crisis intervention.

Levels of Family Functioning

Using scales which were developed in order to evaluate family functioning in regard to the criteria just discussed, the Timberlawn researchers identified three major levels of families as defined by their observable functioning. In general ways these levels have already been referred to and some of the behaviors characteristic of different levels have already been stated. It remains merely to define these three levels somewhat more sharply, recognizing that there are even different levels of functioning within each category, and at times a family within any level may exhibit some of the behaviors of another level. A detailed description of each of the following may be found in several other references.[7]

The Severely Dysfunctional Family. These families produce a larger percentage of persons with serious psychiatric problems than do other families. The families have very little structure, tend to be chaotic, and the individuals are poorly differentiated from one another within the family. There is little respect for individual perceptions and feelings and little tolerance for differences. Because of disconnected thought patterns, there is little ability to perceive the results of one's own behavior. There are very inadequate and confusing patterns of communication. Family members do not take responsibility for their own thoughts, feelings, and behavior. Responsibility to others and shared meanings with others are very infrequent. This lack of capacity to assume responsibility for one's own behavior leads inevitably to the blaming of others. Parents do not work well together and there may be either no stable coalitions within the family or a coalition between one parent and one child which excludes the other parent and children. Thus children grow up without learning about relationships of mutuality and are confused about the appropriate roles of parents and children. There is much "mind reading" and speaking for the other(s). Some children are, in fact, taught to be responsible for one or both parents' well-being and grow up carrying an intolerable burden, a responsibility they are totally incapable of fulfilling. The result is unrealistic guilt, a chronic sense of failure, and low self-esteem. Such families are quite inefficient in setting goals, planning tasks, and solving problems because of the low tolerance of differences, the scattered thinking, the ineffective communication, and the lack of genuine respect for one another which is necessary for successful negotiation.

Over the long term of the family's life, it is easy to see how difficult it would be for a child to grow up with any sense of self-worth (or much of an individuated self at all) or with adequate social skills. The implications of this collection of family attitudes and behaviors for resolving family crises are also quite clear, and the difficulties a pastor faces in assisting such a family are sharply pointed up.

Beavers also speaks of two types of dysfunctional families, differentiated by two major patterns of functioning which produce different forms of adolescents' departure from the family. These are designated centripetal and centrifugal (described originally by Stierlin et al.)[8]

Centripetal families teach, through their attitudes and behavior, that the world outside the family is mysterious, dangerous, not to be trusted, and that one's only hope is within the family itself. The difficulty of an attempt to separate is obvious. Children are bound to the nuclear family by unrealistic forces and are incapable of investing much of themselves in people or in significant ongoing activities in the larger community. When there is psychiatric disorder, it probably will take some pattern of schizophrenic or borderline symptoms.

Centrifugal families, on the other hand, produce so few need satisfactions within the home that children feel their hope is *only* in the world beyond; therefore when a family member is frustrated or angry or has unmet needs or there is conflict, the drive is literally to leave. The family member leaves home with the expectation that needs will be met "out there," but without sufficient self-esteem and social skills to increase that possibility. To the contrary, much of the behavior is self-defeating. Premature and impulsive leavetaking is characteristic. Children, when quite disturbed, are likely to exhibit their disturbance in sociopathic forms.

The Midrange Family. In contrast to the severely disturbed family, the midrange family contributes substantially to the development of identity on the part of the children but does so in such a way as to build in a considerable amount of pain and limit certain human possibilities. Family members can be more clearly distinguished from one another than in the severely disturbed family, and they do take more responsibility for their own thoughts and feelings and behavior. There is still, however, a noticeable limitation on such personal responsibility. Anger and sexual feelings are disapproved of, not always explicitly and openly, but clearly enough by parental attitudes and the form and nature of rule setting. Ambivalence, the simultaneous experiencing of conflicting feelings, is found intolerable. Within such a family, a person either loves *or* hates (and, of course, hate is disapproved of); one is not *supposed* to, thus cannot do both at the same time. Behaviors tend to be seen as only right or wrong, not ambiguous. A type of human perfection is assumed to be possible, and we fail to achieve it not because we are merely human, but because we are human and thus willfully bad. Therefore thoughts and feelings, as well as behavior, must be inhibited and finally denied or repressed. An omnipresent and all-seeing referee develops within the family and is a constant controlling force. This referee may be abstract or personified. Because of the rigid rule system, one finds that it is dangerous to do something "wrong"; therefore the blaming of others is readily learned. The family structure is quite rigid, communication is highly controlled and tends to be nonaffective in nature, and the family operates on an authoritarian basis. Such behavior produces a dominance-submission pattern of relationships. Because of this, there is anger and conflict, but since these are disapproved of they are kept under wraps, expressing themselves in subtle but no less hurtful ways, or occasionally erupting with some severity only to be followed by guilt. The anger and sense of opposition are then put under wraps again.

The family reluctantly allows the children to grow up and leave home. This leavetaking occurs with more regularity and order than in the dysfunctional families. However, emotional separation is extremely difficult. The dependence-anger ambivalence continues. The family referee follows the children wherever they go. Products of the midrange family are often competent in their work and usually have a number of social skills, but in their new relationships, they tend to seek to reproduce the forms of their family of origin. The midrange family has particular difficulty in handling loss in a constructive manner.

The observation of the Timberlawn researchers is that most American families fall into the midrange category. And even though the original research dealt with middle-class white families, investigations of black working-class families, surprisingly in certain ways, but not so surprisingly when other factors are considered, tend to support the findings of the original research project. In the attitudes and behaviors studied, the two groups tend to be more alike than different.[9] An analysis of the data resulting from a study of one-parent families is still in process.

In more complex discussions, Beavers distinguishes between centripetal midrange families, which tend to produce neurotic offspring, and centrifugal families, out of which character disorders are more likely to come. He also describes family patterns in which marriage partners have differing neurotic tendencies.[10]

The Healthy Family. The healthy family is the most adaptable, most flexible, and thus most capable of assimilating new learning and handling crises. There are differing levels of functioning within this category, just as in the others, the highest level being referred to by researchers as the optimal family. There are, they believe, relatively few of these.

A good picture of healthy families can be gained by looking at many of the attitudes and behaviors mentioned under each of the eight criteria of evaluation. To summarize, these families are the least authoritarian, exhibit the least scapegoating, are the least threatened, are most open and receptive, give and receive and consider information within the family, allow for and respect individual differences, are tolerant of failure, are allowed to have feelings and to express them in appropriate ways, have and clearly express empathy, have a strong parental coalition, accomplish family goals effectively, and, in short, have a lot more fun. There are, of course, structure and order and family rules. A functional transcendent value system contributes to the development of individual identity, stimulates commitment to the family yet makes it relatively easy to leave home at an appropriate time, and guides personal and social behavior.

These families may certainly experience situational crises: anxiety and anger and hurt and confusion and other crisis behaviors. But it seems to be quite clear that the pastor's primary task in pastoral care and crisis counseling with them is simply to be there as a representative of the community of faith, to be a catalyst in assisting such families to draw on their own strengths, and at times to help them identify events related to the precipitation of the crisis when these events are not immediately apparent to them.

Definition of Family Crisis

Even though the term *family crisis* was briefly defined in the introduction to this chapter, the detailed discussion of the family as a system made up of two or more subsystems (the individual members and the stable and transient coalitions) makes it possible to delineate more precisely the occasion of *family* crisis as distinguished from the crisis of an individual which also affects the other family members in some way.

As defined previously, an individual situational crisis is the reaction of an individual to an external event perceived as a threat—an event which, because of its novel character in the life of a person and/or its links to earlier unresolved traumatic events, is not adequately resolved by the person's usual coping behaviors. The reaction includes confusion, the narrowing of one's perspective, intense feelings, and maladaptive behavior. "A family crisis refers to the same process, but focuses on the family as the locus of the problem. In a family crisis, then, the interactional patterns are in a temporary state of disequilibrium or flux caused by a stimulus that is novel to the family."[11]

Not only is the event novel, but it is so much so that the family's usual problem-solving skills are not sufficient and its trial-and-error attempts are not successful within the brief period prior to the onset of greater confusion, intensity of emotions, and breakdown of communication within the family. It is not just separate individuals, but the whole family system that is threatened and disrupted. Family homeostasis has broken down.

Just as in individual crises, the intensity of the disruption and threat is not usually primarily inherent within the event itself. Therefore the helping person must examine this question in detail: "What kinds of precipitating events will interact with what kinds of families, under what kinds of circumstances, to effect a crisis?"[12] The various events will call for the family to reevaluate itself, reassess its interpretation of the events, change in some ways its members' forms of relating to one another. The members will be challenged to attempt a more open affective communication with one another, reassign and assume new roles in the family, work together in new ways to solve problems. The challenge to the family in crisis can be best understood in light of the various individual and family self-concepts and behaviors discussed in connection with the eight criteria of family evaluation and the levels of family functioning. Just as any individual, no matter where that person is located at a given time on the continuum of dysfunctional to healthy, may experience situational crisis, so may any level of family have a crisis. However, in the light of the identification of levels of family functioning, it can be better understood that these different types of families will interpret the many events differently, and differing families will have more or fewer resources with which to attempt to resolve the crisis.

For example, a healthy family that has sought to support certain moral standards may be hurt and dismayed, not knowing immediately precisely what to do when an unmarried teenage daughter becomes pregnant, or when a child's use of illegal drugs is discovered, or when a child announces that he or she is homosexual. Family members' declared convictions are challenged; they have feelings of hurt, guilt, anger, and other reactions to deal with; they have to do something. But their family mythology or value system or philosophy of life or faith or love or commitment to one another is not necessarily destroyed. They are accustomed to expressing themselves openly to one another in love and with respect and are capable of entering into negotiation with one another and working with one another to solve problems. They have flexibility in thought and behavior; they do not ostracize family members for being different; they assume responsibility for their own behavior without scapegoating others or unrealistically blaming themselves. An event may pose a challenge to the family, a family problem, but it is not necessarily a crisis.

A midrange family, on the other hand, while the members very well love one another, may experience one of these events as truly shattering to the family image and may tend to respond by attempting to make the rigid family self-concept and system even more rigid. Clear, straightforward effective communication with one another is minimal, and so the strong feelings are unexpressed and become barriers to problem solving, which may probably be attempted in authoritarian ways without understanding, ways that are likely to stimulate additional hostility. It is a genuine family crisis.

It should be emphasized that the concept of family homeostasis does not preclude the introduction of new learning into the system, or the sharing of new relationships among the members. Almost all families have some capacity to assimilate new experiences in some way that does not alter the members' patterns of relating to one another more quickly than they can handle. All families go through some changes. We have seen, however, that families are considerably different in their levels of tolerance toward change and their capacity for adjustment. Most changes undergone by both individuals and families come about in very small increments. We do not see, for example, a child's growth from one day to the next, though it is taking place. There are certain periods in life, however, when a child changes considerably within a designated period. These are times of stress in the family and are usually considered to be developmental crises. Other changes are more radical and do demand radical readjustment, usually within a very short period of time. These are what we have defined as situational crises. All families make changes to accommodate differences occasioned by these events, but some have extreme difficulty.

We see some of that extremity in a family where there is a deeply emotionally disturbed person. The whole family system may in some way have been involved in the production of the disorder, with members of the family being in unspoken and often unconscious collusion with one another to keep one person sick as a method of maintaining the whole family homeostasis in the best way they know how. If that designated "ill person" becomes well, and the family itself has not been undergoing significant change during the same period of time, the "becoming well" is experienced by the rest of the members as a threat to their system—a threat to the way they have learned to assign and to take roles, to assume responsibility or shift blame within the family, to the forms of relationships they seem able to tolerate better than others.

Such a reaction is also observed many times in the family where there is an alcoholic person. The alcoholic stops drinking and the family, without additional help, begins to collapse. The husband or wife, for example, has *needed* for something to be wrong with the spouse or has needed the spouse to be dependent on him or her or on the children, to look to that person alone for their sustenance. The nonalcoholic spouse has gained some type of satisfaction or reward from "being in charge." So many different things have to change if the husband and father, or wife and mother, stops drinking. Or a mother or father or child comes back from the psychiatric hospital and seems to be doing relatively well. Again, the family members must relearn how to relate to one another, to reassign the roles and functions, and the whole system is changed by this event. Or a family member dies and the homeostasis of the family system is dependent upon the successful reassignment of roles and the developing of new forms of relationships. Again, some families handle this task rather effectively, but others fall into a trap. Some may tend unconsciously to assign the total need-fulfilling role of the deceased to one individual member, rather than allotting the functions more appropriately to those persons most capable of meeting those particular needs. Other families may contain an individual who unconsciously identifies with the deceased to such a degree that she or he needs to seek to assume the total role. The former system has been broken and a new system of relationships must be learned. This is a time of family crisis.

The Process of Intervention in Family Crisis

The process of intervention in family crisis requires the same grasp of the dynamics of situational crisis and crisis counseling procedures as those already discussed. In addition, it is necessary to be aware of the whole family as a system, to be able to use some set of criteria, such as the scales developed by the Timberlawn researchers, to evaluate a particular family, and to be skilled in some of the processes of family therapy. If this is beginning to sound complex, it is because it *is* complex. In addition to what a minister may have learned up to this point, it is important to obtain some training in conjoint marital and family therapy. At the very least, there are additional books which give attention to the procedures and dynamics of a psychotherapist's (and the minister's) assisting in family interaction.[13]

The function of a family therapist is to attempt to put all parts of the family system in touch with one another in such a manner that the feelings, empathy, and information interchange can take place more fully and clearly and be received and understood. The assumption is that if this task is accomplished, the members of most families can gain a clearer perspective on what has been and is happening within their particular family, identify the central issue or issues to be dealt with, have a greater understanding of one another and one another's needs, and increase their ability as a family to evaluate alternatives as a family, make decisions, and effect action in response to the relevant issue(s).

The family therapist tries, through the process of facilitating communication within the family, to demonstrate that each family member is a person of worth, regardless of age and role in the family, has needs to be met, feelings to be identified and expressed, and a point of view to be considered. The process helps the members know one another better than they did before. Through the verbal expression of the facilitative conditions, the therapist is constantly modeling to the family the personal characteristics and the types of communication that are essential for the members to assimilate in their interaction with one another.

In counseling with one individual, we not only pay very close attention to what that person is saying at both a cognitive and an affective level, make the choice as to the most facilitative response, and observe the other person while also observing ourselves, but we learn to look at our relationship as it is progressing and, at a certain point, begin to talk explicitly about what is going on between us. When a third person is added to the process—the spouse of the other, for example—we do all that we have learned is useful in individual counseling, but we become acutely aware that what we say to one of the persons is being heard by the other as well. Also, we observe not only the two individuals and the relationship between ourself and each of them, but we are attentive to their interaction with each other, to their relationship itself. Thus the *relationship* becomes a major, though not always an exclusive, focus of our responses. What is happening *between* the two of them? The counselor helps them begin to observe their relationship and talk to each other in clearer, more constructive ways.

Minister:	Sharon, when Bob said that, I noticed that you grimaced. What did you understand him to be saying?
Sharon:	He said that . . .
Minister:	Just a minute. Say it directly to him.
Sharon:	You said that you don't want me to get angry any more, and I think that's unrealistic. (silence)
Minister:	Sharon, what do you make of the silence?
Sharon:	It seems as if he's mad at me now. (Bob begins to shake his head) Then what *is* it?
Bob:	I'm not mad. It's just that I'm not sure that I can explain it any differently.
Minister:	Would you try?
Bob:	I don't know why, but when Sharon . . .
Minister:	Wait. Say it directly to her.
Bob:	When you get so mad when I mess up in some way, I really get scared. *Very* scared. I don't know how to answer. I don't know what to do. That's why I retreat—just go to another room. I guess I get mad at you for getting mad, but I think that must be because I can't handle it. I leave more because I'm scared.
Minister:	So you're not demanding that she not *be* mad, but that she understand that, as you are now, it scares you.
Bob:	Yes. (turning to Sharon) I know that there are things that are going to make you mad. I wish you wouldn't, but I know you will.
Minister:	So what's important for you is that you get to the place that you don't get so frightened as a result of her anger. The need is for you to be able to hang in there and talk it out.

The process is the same, but more complex, when there are three, four, five, or more people in a family. The counselor not only will focus on several persons and the relationship between each pair of them, but also will be attentive to the dyads and triads within the family interaction. There will be direct communication with each individual, trying to assist each one in expressing herself or himself as fully and clearly as possible, trying to help the others understand each person and communicate that understanding, and eliciting the communication of empathy to each one.

It has already been pointed out that the pastor who is assisting an individual in crisis needs to be more verbally active than in other traditional approaches to counseling. It can now be said that this same pastor will need to be even more active when intervening in family crises, since the usual tasks of identifying the precipitating problem and precipitating event, facilitating catharsis, exploring the present situation, identifying the threat, and so on, will involve taking the initiative and eliciting responses from several persons, not just one. In addition, it entails the types of statements and questions that will help family members talk to one another in the ways discussed briefly above. Furthermore, the problem-solving stage usually will require considerable negotiation between the family members in an attempt to reach some reasonable consensus concerning the decisions to make and the actions to take. In the midst of it all, the minister is seeking to evaluate the family and help them identify their strengths, isolating for discussion those that seem to be relevant to the resolution of this particular crisis. Because of the intense concentration and verbal activity needed, and the fact that several people need to make their contribution, the sessions may frequently take an hour and a half or more. Therefore family crisis intervention can be both an exhilarating and an extremely exhausting activity.

Although family crisis intervention draws upon family-systems theory and on many of the forms of verbal facilitation and intervention of traditional family psychotherapy, its goals remain those of crisis counseling, not those of long-term family therapy. These goals are the restoration of the family to its usual level of functioning while the painful and maladaptive behaviors of the crisis are reduced and disappear. The purpose is not to attempt to correct any longer-term family dysfunction and raise the whole family to a higher level of functioning, although some families, like some individuals, may learn something about ways to cope more effectively with an impending family crisis in the future.

Although the following incident does not portray a family that had reached the point of crisis, it does illustrate how a family situational crisis may begin and how a pastor may function with the family. In this instance, an event had disrupted the family system and most certainly posed a threat. Confusion was increasing and anxiety was present, but the crisis itself was prevented by father's immediate awareness of the need for outside help. He called his minister, explained that his wife's emotional disorder had been getting worse, that early that morning she had been taken to the psychiatric hospital. He asked whether the minister would be able to help him and their six children, ages five to eighteen, understand what was happening and reorganize themselves in some way. The minister made special arrangements to go to the home that very night, where he, all six children, and the father sat down together in their living room.

The minister asked each individual to express how he or she felt about their mother's increasing withdrawal from them and the things she had been saying that seemed so strange. The minister asked that no one be interrupted; after each had spoken, with the minister helping with the fullest and clearest possible expression, the others could ask that person anything or say anything they wanted. They all seemed confused. There were feelings of fear and some anger. The minister assisted them to understand that it was to be expected that they would all have similar reactions, but that each person would also have some reactions that differed from those of other family members. Then the minister asked how each felt about the mother being away for a fairly long period of time. Again, each person had an opportunity to respond.

Next the minister asked whether they understood what had been going on and why their mother was now in a hospital. He gave as adequate information as he could to help each one better comprehend, at his or her own level, the nature of the mother's illness and stressed the point that she really did love each of them and did not want to be separated from them, but that she had to go to the hospital in order to get better. It was also stressed that no one in the family was responsible for her being in that condition or had caused her to go away.

Finally, they talked about how they were going to handle school and household responsibilities and the particular role of the three older children in assisting the three younger ones, while the father continued to work at his job, and also took on some new tasks in the home and new responsibilities with the children. Each was asked what he or she could do that would help. Each person's emotional needs were taken into account as tasks were parceled out and clearly accepted, in order to try to minimize resentment and confusion and not to overload any one person. Everyone had additional tasks and some understanding of the reasons these changes were necessary. No one had a responsibility beyond his or her level of maturity, and no one was truly overloaded with work. The father, who had felt overwhelmed with the overall responsibility, got things back in perspective, and the chaos that had begun to develop started to disappear.

In the following weeks, all did not always go smoothly. As in every family, sometimes a job was not done adequately or on schedule, someone was a bit neglected, irritations arose. But these situations were handled, and over the long haul, things went fairly well. A true family situational crisis had been *prevented* by the early and helpful *inter*vention. The minister, of course, continued to make approximately weekly visits to the home. He also visited the mother at the hospital and was able to effect some information interchange between the mother and the rest of the family.

The situation just described illustrates the value of gathering together as many of the family members as possible for group discussion. At times, one or more of the persons cannot be present, as in this particular instance the mother was absent. The minister, understanding the potential usefulness of the family meeting, will need to make this value clear and help in any way to bring them all together at one time. Often, of course, it will also be important to talk to one or more family members individually, the parents apart from the children, or the children apart from the parents. The ingenuity of the minister will be challenged again and again in assessing the family, the members' level of functioning, their specific relationships with one another, and the particular situation of crisis. Out of this the minister will develop a strategy of working with the family in a way that has the greatest possibility of being effective.

In contrast with the procedure of getting family members together, there are occasions where they very definitely need to be separated. Most often these are during times of intense anger. There is no basic principle stating that we do not talk with people while they are angry with each other. The point is that it may be important to separate persons by going with one into another room when there has been physical violence, when such violence seems possible, or even when there seems to be no reasonable possibility of reducing the verbal attacks. In the incident with which this chapter began, had I gone ahead and pushed the doorbell and been allowed to come into that home, it might have been more effective to break their escalating circle of verbal attack and counterattack by talking with each spouse separately for awhile, draining off some of the intensity and readiness to attack, and then follow that by talking with the two of them together. The way it actually turned out, that particular man and woman still had the commitments and perspective and ego control to cool down by themselves, but the separation strategy would need to have been considered in an earlier intervention.

At another time, I was called to the home of a woman who had left her house in order to phone me. She reported that her husband and their twenty-four-year-old son were physically fighting. Even though the violence had stopped by the time I arrived later, the two men were not at the point of being able to talk to each other. Each was quite willing to talk with me, however, and did so very productively. It was then possible for the three of us to talk together.

Another occasion for separating family members rather than getting or keeping them together will be discussed under intervention in the crisis of the severely disturbed family.

Intervening in Families of Different Levels of Functioning

Some brief references have already been made to the relative ease versus the relative difficulty of assisting families at different levels of functioning. It would be a mistake to carry the same set of exact procedures and styles of relating and responding into different types of families in different situations. Clues to each approach are given by some combination of the type of family system, the particular crisis, and our own personal strengths and limitations.

Longitudinal follow-up studies of individual psychiatric patients have produced findings that are hardly startling for anyone who might have thought the matter through and made a reasonable prediction. Those who improve most readily and maintain their improvement over a long period of time are those who were healthier prior to the time of their emotional disorder, while those who are most difficult to work with successfully and are most likely after some improvement to have a recurrence of serious disorder, are those who tended to have been more unstable and have poorer emotional adjustment over the prior years. Experience shows that some of the same results occur in individual and family crisis counseling.

The Healthy Family. The healthy, and especially the optimal family, has resources both within and outside the family which usually lead to a rapid resolution of a crisis. Here the role of the minister is primarily that of being the living symbol of the faith, which itself may touch reservoirs of strength, and to be the catalyst in the family's using its own strengths to help itself. The characteristics of the healthy family, as presented earlier, are precisely those which assist fairly rapid and effective crisis resolution. Usually, most of these families could handle family crises without any minister at all, and certainly without any other professional helper. Yet when we refer to a family's resources, the church and its pastor may already be a part of the usual social network of which the family is a part, so a call to the minister or the ready response when she or he drops by are natural parts of the family identity, functioning, and problem solving. In this situation, it is more as though the minister is a temporary part of the family, merely assisting the members in their conversations with one another. Of course, the members of any family in crisis may be undergoing intense emotions, have some confusion, and because of their usual patterns of spontaneity in conversation, interrupt one another and perhaps may not be pursuing a single theme logically. Even so, the pastor will not have a serious problem of control. He or she can use questions or suggestions to call attention to what someone has said, to help a particular person finish an interrupted communication, and to keep a focus in the conversation.

The Midrange Family. A useful statement concerning the minister's participation in the crisis of the midrange family has been made by W. Robert Beavers.[14] One central point is that this family imbues certain words with a magical quality—especially certain types of verbal expressions understood as substituting for genuine, open, direct, communication of needs. Courtesy, cognitive statements of understanding, well-developed rationalizations, promises, and other forms of speech are taken to be sufficient. Many ministers feel relatively comfortable with these families, because the members tend to have the intensity of their feelings somewhat more under control; besides, these families are just like those in which many of us grew up. The power the members attribute to their words and our words draws us into the trap, because we are in the "word" business ourselves. We begin to attribute unusual power to words. We are somewhat like the people in this system. Yet often within these families, a crisis does not seem to move as quickly toward resolution as we had hoped and expected, and we wonder about the reason for this. There are several possibilities or combinations of possibilities.

In addition to the tendency to repress and inhibit the expression of feelings, to rationalize the situation, to fall back upon the system's rigidity as a way of controlling behavior and the sense that the words equal the act, there is the tendency to view the pastor as the family referee, the authority who represents right and wrong. Of course, right and wrong is defined by the family in its own terms rather than in terms of the minister's understanding of himself or herself as a person and as pastor in this particular situation. Therefore the minister is often confused by the way the family members respond—they continue to expect some authoritarian solution in spite of the pastor's attempts to assist them in the necessary process of taking responsibility for themselves. All the more confusing, the usual family referee requires the family to have the attitude that the members ought to be able to handle the situation all by themselves, even while they communicate to the minister that they expect the minister to solve it.

If this is interpreted as being extremely discouraging, the major point is being missed. These families do often have considerable strengths, and the pastor can help them identify these and use them in coming through the crisis in a positive manner. Persistence can elicit some amount of emotional expression; the members can be guided in talking to one another more clearly; the true caring they have for one another can be drawn upon to elicit expressions of empathy; some new behaviors can be attempted. The major thrust of this description of the midrange family is given so that the minister will not be lured into any of the several traps along the way. The minister will need to keep in mind that talking *about* feelings is not necessarily the same as expressing them; rationalizations are not explanations; the family's desire to be told what to do does not mean the members will not have resistance to what they are told if the minister is seduced into doing so; their desire to be told what to do does not relieve them of their responsibility to make their own decisions and take the potentially constructive action; resistance to the helping process does not mean that the family does not really want help.

The Severely Disturbed Family. Crisis intervention with a severely disturbed family offers the pastor quite another challenge; the sense of "I can't handle this family" may arise fairly quickly. Family members may be explosive in their emotional expression. Communication is chaotic. People go off on tangents. Several subjects are being introduced by several people at the same time, and several conversations (including statements that seem to be made to nobody in particular) may be going on all at once. If we have the experience of being in Bedlam, beginning to feel confused and somewhat powerless to affect anything and therefore anxious, then we have some idea of what it is like to be a member of that family.

How, then, is the pastor to function? Rule number one: Become a General Patton. Take charge! This family needs a referee, so become their temporary referee. Here the drawback of passivity in pastoral counseling is most apparent. It is important to be assertive, active, in control.[15] The family will profit from the order brought into their lives, even from an outside source and even if only temporary. This is not to suggest that the pastor be dictatorial and harsh, but rather clear and direct, with persistent exercise of control. Insist that only one person speak at a time, and stay with that rule. Even though some amount of talking is necessary, words have less impact upon this level of family than upon others. Some families will be suspicious of words; therefore, a variety of actions appropriate to the nature of this particular crisis need to be suggested.

In a large family, if the communication is so chaotic, with constant interruptions, unrelated comments, several conversations at once, then we would do well to call time out, briefly explain the difficulty, and develop a new strategy based on talking with individuals in smaller units, designing these as far as possible according to some combination of who talks better with whom, where the power lies, and who seems to be affected most by this crisis. Perhaps some outstanding experts can handle all the members of such a family at one time (General Patton trained as a family therapist), but when we discover we cannot, rather than persisting in a course of action that is supposed to be correct but is frustrating to all of us, we must break it down into units we can handle more effectively. Once that is done, the usual crisis counseling procedures and problem solving with an action orientation is pursued, along with additional attempts to bring some of the individuals in the smaller units back in touch with one another to gain some reasonable consensus, often with the pastor-referee's encouragement concerning decisions and actions.

Unfortunately, it is easy for ministers, with their desire to be helpful, to be seduced into an attempt to lead such a family into some new and significant and permanent change. However, if for even a moment we lose sight of the focus and limited goals of crisis counseling—the reduction of the symptoms of crisis—we are lost. We cannot be the primary therapists in changing this family system to one that is more effective and competent and with which we would feel more comfortable. This family will usually be less capable of assimilating new learning from crisis resolution, which might then become part of more effective family functioning on a consistent basis. To pursue every new subject family members raise, or to give in to the temptation to try to change their fixed patterns of interaction, is to waste our time and theirs and will fail to assist them in resolving the present crisis.

Naturally, as the crisis is reaching some resolution, if any one or several family members express some continuing distress about their relationships with one another, this provides an opportunity for the minister to suggest family therapy with a competent professional.

Helping the Alcoholic: Creating a Crisis

One cannot be a parish minister long without being called upon to respond to the request for help by an alcoholic person or by a member of such a person's family. If the minister seems at all open to talking with people about such problems, and this begins to be known, requests for help will escalate. Certainly the problem itself is widespread, with an estimated ten million alcoholic persons in this country,[16] and with anywhere from *at least* six to ten more lives *directly* affected by the person's uncontrolled drinking. Probably this problem is brought to a pastor's attention most frequently by a woman who comes by or calls to talk about the disruption and distress produced in the family by the husband's abuse of alcohol—he stays out late, disappears for days, physically and verbally abuses the wife and/or the children, wastes needed money, loses a job or successive jobs. The wife suffers strain from dealing with the abuse and from the pressure of covering up for the husband. The pattern of approach to the minister seems to be changing somewhat, with men beginning to be more willing to ask for help with their wives, parents at their wits' end in regard to their children. There is particularly some increase in the number of men and women taking the first step toward help for themselves, although this last group is still a minority. Since one of the predominant symptoms of the illness is the denial that anything is wrong, the illness itself stands in the way of the sufferer's asking for help and creates unbelievable resistance in the form of discounting other persons' concern, minimizing the seriousness of the drinking, reacting angrily and defensively, refusing pleas by family members or work associates to seek help.

Although awareness of the impact of alcohol abuse upon members of the family has always been widespread, the concept of alcoholism as a family illness—the family itself being ill—is relatively new in terms of its increasing acceptance among professional workers in the alcohol-abuse field.

Many situational crises are triggered in families when a member is alcoholic. Time and again ministers are called upon to help put out the fires. Usually they respond, and very frequently they are helpful in terms of the immediate crisis. Yet the frustration increases as the usual talks with family members, and even with the chemically dependent person, reach a dead end. The problem drinking continues and new crises occur.

More effective approaches have now been attempted and have been found to be more helpful in at least two ways. The minister may use the occasion of a drinking-precipitated crisis to share these new understandings with those whom some professionals in the field are now calling the co-alcoholics, the non-alcohol-abusing members of the family. These approaches are based upon the helper's understanding of the family as a system and of the existence of the "alcoholically ill" family. Most earlier helping attempts were based upon the assumption, still held by practically all family members of an alcoholic person and by some professionals (happily, fewer and fewer), that if the "sick" (or even "bad") person will only stop drinking, the problems of the family will be taken care of. Earlier in this chapter, reference has been made to the fact that often the family suffers considerably when the person in fact does stop drinking. This takes us back to the family as a system.

Not only will the family situation not necessarily become better when the person no longer drinks, it sometimes becomes worse. In addition, very often the chemically dependent person will not consider stopping until the family itself first begins to change. When others in the family, essentially the spouse, but others also, change their attitudes toward themselves, toward one another, and toward the alcohol abuser, and as a result change their behavior within the family, the *system* is no longer the same. It has changed, and the chemically dependent person is forced to try to accommodate those changes in some way: to try to understand the new attitudes and behavior and the impact on him or her, to look at herself or himself differently, to struggle to deal with his or her own behavior in the new system. This is not to predict that the drinker will always quickly volunteer for treatment and/or stop drinking, but the whole situation is different, and the possibility that the alcoholic person will seek help increases. It must be said very candidly that sometimes the drinking becomes worse; the alcohol abuser may even leave the family. There are risks.

But even if the alcoholic person does not stop drinking, the rest of the family members have begun their own process of growth. They have stopped playing their characteristic roles in the family, roles which served them well neither within nor outside the family relationships. Although roles such as the enabler, the hero, the scapegoat, the lost child, and the mascot are understandable in terms of the way they are defined and/or learned in the alcoholic family, "there is no healthy way to adapt to alcoholism."[17] These habitual and often unconscious ways of perceiving one's self and the particular behaviors growing out of them in this form of dysfunctional family are themselves not quickly changed. However, family members can learn to behave differently, and as they do, the new forms of family interaction can become rewarding in themselves.

Basically, the nonchemically dependent family members need to make two crucial decisions and support one another in carrying them out. First, it is essential that they decide to stop organizing family life around the impossible goal of trying to keep the alcoholic person from drinking. The false underlying assumption is that *they* are responsible for the other's misuse of alcohol. That assumption is not true. The drinking person alone is responsible for the first drink. The uncontrollable continuation of drinking regardless of consequences is a result of the disorder of alcoholism.

The family's second necessary decision is that it will no longer, except in actual life-threatening circumstances, contribute to the person's drinking behavior by covering up—lying to employers and others—and trying to rescue the person from other consequences of drug abuse.

Families may be assisted in these decisions by a minister and continually supported not only by the minister and possibly a congregation, but also by Al-Anon, Ala-Teen, and by what at this time is a slowly increasing number of special groups for younger children of alcoholic families.

Once these two decisions are made and acted upon, a series of crises are precipitated for the chemically dependent person. It is useful for family members to tell the person in a straightforward and unemotional way the steps they are now beginning to take, both in order to take care of themselves and to produce a healthier family life. They should be quite open about the fact that they are going to Al-Anon and Ala-Teen and state their reasons for doing so. The alcohol abuser will almost always be bewildered by this straightforward manner of speaking and threatened by potential changes, and will also often be angry. This person's habitual response to any type of unpleasantness or stress is to escape, which often means more drinking. In the face of negative reaction by the abuser, family members may call their decision into question and be tempted to regress to their former behavior. They have not chosen an easy course for themselves, but it is the only way to health as a family and as individuals.

Often it is necessary to take a further step, intentionally precipitating a crisis so that the chemically dependent person might experience sufficient pressure to enter a treatment program. More and more families are planning family intervention sessions.[18] The pastor inexperienced in these procedures would do well not only to read about them in detail, but to call upon the services of an alcoholism counselor who has arranged and participated in such sessions before. All the persons most directly affected by the alcohol abuser's behavior will need to agree that there is a drinking problem, that it is affecting family life, work life, and perhaps other important areas. They agree to meet with the alcohol abuser in order that they may tell the person how the behavior is affecting each of them, that arrangements have been made for the person's treatment, and that they all want the person to enter this treatment program immediately. Participants may include family members, an employer or supervisor or business or professional partner, a colleague at work, a best friend or two, perhaps the pastor, and often, very helpfully, an alcoholism counselor.

Considerable ingenuity may be required to get this group together with the alcoholic person at a time and place where there will be no interruptions and the person cannot easily walk out. It can be seen that a number of planning sessions may need to be held. At the appointed time and place, each person is to make a statement of concern and care, then go on to a very specific and detailed account of the alcoholic person's behavior and how that behavior has an impact on others. There is to be no blame or recrimination. There is to be no response to the alcoholic person's rationalizing, angry, blaming, or attacking language. Anger is to be expected, whether or not it is overtly expressed. Participants are not to take cues from the alcohol abuser's responses to discuss anything other than the observed drinking behavior and how it has an impact upon those present. Nor is the family to crumple in the face of promises to do better and that there is therefore no need for treatment. There is to be no argument and no retreat.

Again, such a procedure is fraught with potential unpleasantness and danger. A few alcoholic persons will respond with cooperation, but most will go through their whole bag of evasive and/or attacking tricks. Remember that this person's style of life is now being severely threatened. The person is suddenly being thrust into the midst of a situational crisis. The drinking of some will get worse. Many will continue to be hostile toward those who have taken part, at least for some period of time; some of these will eventually change their attitude and be grateful for the fact that the family has responded and the way in which it was done. Some will not. The family must be convinced that the crisis precipitated by the intervention is still the best possibility for the chemically dependent member and that regardless of what that person does, the family members must take care of themselves as best they can. Whatever the alcohol abuser's response may be, the pastor continues to be available to the whole family.

Summary

In a family crisis, the basic definition and the dynamics of the situational crisis remain the same, but instead of the threat being perceived by an individual person, it is experienced by a whole family as a system. Just as individuals can be evaluated in order to work with them more effectively, so can families.

Eight areas of thinking patterns, attitudes, feelings, and habitual forms of communication have been identified as a useful scheme, both for the assessment of the level of overall family competence and as guidelines for discovering specific family strengths to be used by them for their benefit in the midst of crisis. These evaluations guide the pastor in crisis intervention with a particular family.

Forms of the minister's verbal helping responses are the same as in working with individuals, but attention to the relationship between individual family members, and between coalitions within the family, require even more active and directive statements and questions as the pastor helps them express themselves more clearly and fully, listen to one another attentively, strive to understand one another, identify their resources, and then negotiate their decisions and problem-solving activities.

When there is chemical dependence in a family, there is a variation on the crisis intervention theme. It is observed that when a family has an alcoholic member, and the other members begin to change their forms of relating to one another and to the alcoholic person, these changes precipitate a series of crises for the chemically dependent person. An even more intense crisis is precipitated for an alcohol abuser when the family plans a formal intervention procedure. Here the alcoholic person is confronted with a full description of his or her behavior and the impact of that behavior on other members of the family and other persons outside the family, with the attempt to get the person into a treatment program.

CHAPTER 6

THE MINISTER'S ROLE AND FUNCTIONING IN THE CRISIS OF GRIEF

It would be extremely difficult to determine precisely the most serious and demanding instances of human distress for ministers who seek to engage hurting persons in helpful ways, for the demands are not always inherently resident in the destructive power of certain situations, but are more dependent upon what types of problems produce a higher degree of anxiety within the individual minister. One minister may become quite anxious and upset over situations that another can handle with genuine confidence and poise, and those that elicit inappropriate and unhelpful responses from the latter may not threaten the first at all.

Nevertheless, almost any minister who has been involved with dying persons and with persons immediately following the death of someone close to them would probably agree that these entail considerable emotional involvement and demand a high degree of sensitivity. The crisis of grief is one in which ministers must participate frequently and is probably the crisis with which we are most often involved. There is no escape from it. It is both a burden and an opportunity. If our own feelings in regard to death have not been worked through, we will inevitably be handicapped in this particular ministry. On the one hand, we may allow ourselves to be pulled into an overinvolvement, an overidentification in which we feel the pain so intensely that it incapacitates us. We become anxious, shaky, depressed. On the other hand, to protect ourselves from the pain, we may insulate ourselves emotionally to the extent that we are not fully present for the other person. We become incapable of genuinely communicating empathy, producing a situation in which all our responses are distorted by our self-protective efforts. We ministers must in some way prepare ourselves emotionally for the experiences of death, dying, and grief. This means, of course, that we must be prepared to look openly at the reality of our own death and accept the full emotional impact of this experience into our own present being.

A beginning checkpoint would be to engage in a detailed fantasy of one's own dying and death, then seek to imagine what it would be like not to be, to picture in one's mind the world simply going on without one. If one finds oneself totally unable to go through such a fantasy in some detail, with some degree of reality and emotional response, it may well be that one's own feelings about death, one's own awareness of oneself as a mortal human being, have been too well repressed. An opposite reaction is also possible: In the midst of such fantasy one might begin to find oneself overwhelmed by emotion; anxiety rises too strongly; the feelings block the progress of the fantasy or linger on well after the fantasy is concluded or one cannot get one's mind off death. In either instance, a minister would be well served as a person and as a professional if he or she were to talk this over in detail with a competent and sensitive colleague or with some other professional counselor.

The Minister and the Grief Crisis

From the point of view of the Christian faith, there are three important motivations for ministry to the grief-stricken. First, it is the responsibility of the faith to speak to all issues concerning the meaning of life and death; questions of meaning are raised in a particularly potent way in the experience of grief. Second, the faith itself stimulates the compassion that impels the minister to seek to engage every person in the moment of suffering. Third, an effective ministry to persons at the very time of their grief will save many from much distress at a later time.

Unresolved Grief Related to Physical and Emotional Disorder

A summary of the material elaborating this third point is of significance in establishing ministers as the number one, frontline preventive mental health professionals in our society and should give them a proper sense of the extreme importance of their ministry with the bereaved. An increasing mass of research data points to the central motivating force of unresolved grief in a variety of emotional and behavioral disorders.

Physical Illness. A number of studies relate inadequately expressed grief to the onset of illnesses characterized by physiological symptoms and physical complaints. In a study of forty-one patients with colitis, Lindemann noted that thirty-three of them had developed the disorder shortly after the loss of an emotionally significant person.[1] Parkes, a British research psychiatrist, has made extensive studies of the medical records of forty-four widows, comparing the postbereavement period with a time two years prior to the death of the spouse. The investigation showed a 63 percent increase in the number of visits to the doctor in the first six months after bereavement, and a continued higher rate for the rest of the time studied. This is not at all surprising, however, in light of the uncomfortable physical symptoms of grief itself, with a six-month period easily including the peak of the grief reaction. In addition, there was a significant increase in the number of consultations for physical disorders of the arthritic and rheumatoid variety. This in and of itself does not mean an *actual* increase of the pathology, as Parkes recognizes. He does reason, however, that the secondary consequences of grief, such as dietary change and the modification of autonomic functioning, may well produce other physiological changes that are conditions for the onset of illness, either in terms of general poor health or, in some instances, specific pathology.[2]

Taking a further step beyond the investigation just discussed, Parkes made a study of 4,486 widowers. "Of these, 213 died during the first six months of bereavement, 40% above the expected rate for married men of the same age." This confirms earlier reports on the higher mortality rate of bereaved persons and makes the judgment conclusive that the loss of a mate by death leads to a greater probability of one's own death. Parkes found the greatest increase in the cause of death in the group diagnosed as "coronary thrombosis and other arteriosclerotic and degenerative heart disease," with the next highest group diagnosed as "other heart and circulatory disease." Of the deaths, 22.5 percent were in the same diagnostic category as the cause of death of the spouses, 23.9 percent higher than the number expected by chance.[3]

Mental Illness. There is also evidence of a causative relationship between an experience of grief that is not fully worked through and the development of mental illness. Moriarty, in *Loss of Loved Ones*, states, "It is the thesis of this book that the loss of loved ones, especially through death, is one of the most important causes of major mental illness."[4] He demonstrates that one of the factors in adult mental illness is the damage to the development of the child by the death of parents or siblings and that, in addition, in the adult, the death of a loved one may actually precipitate an emotional disorder. Detailed data collected and analyzed by Parkes sustain Moriarty's findings. Parkes discovered in his investivation that the number of mental hospital patients whose illness followed the loss of a spouse was six times greater than expected when compared with a nonbereaved population, suggesting bereavement as a precipitating factor in the illness.[5]

Family Disorder. Norman Paul, a psychiatrist specializing in family therapy, states that he has never seen a family in which there was a seriously emotionally disturbed member where there had not been discovered a maladaptive response to object loss by one or more members of the family. Contributing to the emotional disturbance of the mentally ill family member was a pattern of inflexible interaction within the family system, the presumption being that such forms of interaction were originally denial responses to the earlier object loss.[6] Assuming the dynamic priority of inadequately expressed grief, Paul developed a treatment modality that sought to bring the grief out into the open where it could be fully experienced by the grief-stricken person and shared by the whole family, with each member of the family brought into the process of empathizing with the grieving family member.[7] This treatment modality for disturbed families has proved to be successful, thus tending to confirm Paul's original thesis that unresolved grief was the root problem, and suggesting an approach to families in grief that might be utilized to advantage by the minister.

Suicide. Several studies of suicide also point to unresolved grief as being a significant motivating factor. One of these reported that 95 percent of the seriously suicidal patients studied had suffered the death or loss, under dramatic circumstances, of individuals closely related to them. This percentage is contrasted with the control group of patients who were judged not to be seriously suicidal, among whom only 40 percent had suffered comparable loss.[8] Another study compared persons who had attempted suicide with those who had actually succeeded. The type of loss seemed to make a difference, with 26 of the 71 attempted suicides having experienced the divorce of parents and 20 of 44 of the completed suicides having undergone the death of a parent. When the investigators looked at the increase in seriousness of the suicidal impulses, they found an increasing incidence of loss of a parent by death: suicidal gestures—21 percent; serious attempts—30 percent; completed suicides—45 percent.[9]

The total impact of these findings is that there are a number of areas of possible pathological response as a result of unsuccessfully resolved grief crises. In other words, there is a massive amount of extreme human suffering that takes place over an extended period of time and from which many persons might be saved by timely and effective grief counseling. The minister is the only professional who has the combination of social expectation, professional freedom, and professional training to be of significant help to the greatest percentage of persons in our society in their time of grief. Here, as in a number of other instances, the pastor is the frontline professional; the first (or among the first) to identify and engage persons in distress, working with them in the early stages of crisis with the possibility of preventing greater breakdown of personal emotional life and interpersonal relations.

The effective meeting of the needs of persons in grief, not only as an immediate humanitarian activity but also as a contribution to the total increase of the mental health of a community and the avoidance of later maladaptive behavior, has begun to be seen by other mental health professionals as an important phase of their work.

In a pilot study, one community service took the initiative in contacting 20 bereaved families, 8 days after the death of a family member, to offer their counseling services. The stated assumption of the agency was that the persons' usual sources of support would be inadequate at this particular time. The fact that 18 of the 20 families accepted the offer is probably some kind of judgment upon the ministry of the area. A follow-up questionnaire revealed that 24 of the 26 family members who responded rated the service as either helpful or very helpful.[10]

We ministers should feel no jealousy toward anyone who performs such an obviously helpful service. Nevertheless, we should take this as some criticism of our own failure to perform our traditional and expected functions at the time of death.

Needs of the Minister
in Working with Those in Grief

In order to work in the alleviation of the pain of grief in the most effective manner, there are several prerequisites for ministers. First, as has already been stated, they must have come to terms with their own feelings concerning death and dying—more precisely, their *own* death and dying—and have assimilated these feelings into their own present living. Second, they must have a dedication toward persons in pain that compels them to go to suffering persons, using their pastoral initiative courageously, creatively, and sensitively. One aspect of this is the social expectation, the assignment of the social role to the ordained ministry as those who should go to people in grief. While placing demands upon us, this role has been given to us as a great gift. The other aspect of the act of going is ministers' own dedication and courage, and only their own personal faith can lead them to that point. Third, they must have an understanding of the dynamics of grief itself, the course of grieving, and the needs of the bereaved persons. Finally, ministers must have some knowledge of the procedures that will enable them to utilize their relationship with grief sufferers in the most healing way. It is these last two areas that will be discussed here.

Grief and the Bereaved Person

The Dynamics of Grief

A detailed analysis of the dynamics of grief is to be found in an earlier work.[11] In brief summary, the working definition of grief is that it is comparable to a severe attack of anxiety which has as its external stimulus the death of a person with whom one has been closely related. There are three things to note about this proposition.

First, grief is like some of our other experiences. Second, the crucial question to be answered is, "Why does something that happens outside us cause such a severe painful reaction within us?" Third, the form in which the relationship is stated implies that there are many emotions involved in our intimate relationships with one another, only one of which is love. Even where there is love, even when love is clearly the predominant emotion, there are always other emotions at work also, and these are either intensified or complicated, or both, at the time of that person's death. This anxiety of grief is conceived of primarily as a separation anxiety, the prototype of which is the first learning on the part of the small infant that the absence of significant adults inevitably means pain, physical discomfort. The first learning concerning relationships is that the presence of significant other persons means the meeting of personal needs, the sustenance of life, and that the absence of that other is a threat to one's self. The other person is the major value in any person's life. The loss of the other equals the loss of one's self. Separation from the person *out there* causes a sense of threat to the self *inside.*

Based upon separation anxiety, but usually discussed under another name, is guilt or moral anxiety. There are few if any close relationships in which persons are always capable of fulfilling all the needs of each other. Therefore even in the finest relationships, there are at least moments of need frustration, with the attendant feelings of resistance, hostility, or hurt, producing behavior toward each other that is perceived as threatening to the relationship. The experiencing of this threat is the experience of anxiety, but anxiety which in some sense is related to our own behavior, and which is therefore called guilt.

Finally, there is in grief what we term existential anxiety. These are fears arising out of our own existence as human beings, universally shared. They grow out of our freedom, our responsibility for decision, the search for meaning, an awareness of our own finitude, the certainty of our own death. The death of an emotionally significant person serves as a stimulus to bring to the surface this anxiety which is constantly with us but which usually lies well under the surface of our awareness. In the ordinary course of daily life in our society, we have devised ways of depersonalizing death and separating ourselves from it. But when someone emotionally close to us dies, these social defenses break down. *This* death has reference to our own life. In a sense, it is as close as we can come to experiencing our own death, while still being able to observe, reflect, and respond to it. This response inevitably contains some fear.

There are several other excellent books which discuss in detail the dynamics of grief, none of which are directly contradictory to the ideas presented here. They do, however, utilize different conceptual frameworks, such as psychoanalysis and some of its later refinements, as well as ethology and investigations of infant behavior, since both these fields of study make suggestions concerning the source and meaning of the human experiences of attachment and separation.[12]

The Needs of the Bereaved

It is self-evident that the complex interplay of anxiety with the other emotional reactions of grief produces an intense sense of need in a person who, in fact, at this point is in a state of crisis. It is helpful to the minister to be able to identify the precise needs of the bereaved in order to assist more effectively in the process of crisis resolution. Reference has already been made to the role of words in the counseling process. The needs of the bereaved and the procedures of the helping person are best understood in light of that discussion. Therefore, the major, though not the only method the pastor uses, is to facilitate the verbal expression of the grief sufferer in regard to the deceased, the relationship that existed between them, and the death itself.

The first need is to identify and express feelings: sadness, hostility, guilt, fear. The need is for catharsis. Speech is a substitute form of the emotionally charged acts that need to be performed, understood, and accepted in the context of relationship with the deceased.

A second need is the affirmation of the self. Feelings of self-blame and self-depreciation need to be expressed. Lowered feelings of self-esteem need to be raised. Words to another person can be a means of reestablishing a threatened and disrupted selfhood, since they are the vehicles for reinforcing the attitudes of love and protection toward one's self that were the attitudes of the one in relationship with whom words were first learned.

The third need is that of breaking the ties with the deceased. This is not as harsh as it may sound at first. It certainly does not mean forgetting the deceased person or not loving that person any longer. Rather, it means a transformation of the act of love. If we continue to try to love in the same way we did when the person was physically present, directing the emotion outward toward that person, then we work ourselves into an emotional trap, for in reality there is no person *out there* to receive it in the same sense that there once was. The need is to direct such love for the deceased inward toward the images of that person that remain within us, with the outward expression being directed toward others. This last statement introduces the next two needs.

The fourth need is the resurrection of the deceased within the self. To the extent that persons have been emotionally involved with each other, to that degree they have identified their lives with each other. This means that one's self has certain aspects of the life of the other as a living component. Yet this life of the other within us need not die along with the other's physical body, although this is the first emotional reaction to the death. As we move past this first response, there can be revival of the other's life within one's self. Therefore, the self becomes whole and fully alive once again, though not without pain, not as if the loss had not occurred or as though it were not real. The language that had been the communicating link with the other, in being heard by the speaker as he or she talks of the person and their relationship, carries with it some emotional power of that relationship and reinforces the internalized living presence of the other.

Once this is done, the next need is to direct one's emotions outward in the renewal and deepening of old relationships and the establishing of new ones. In the midst of the sense of deadness and threat we feel when someone close to us dies, we need an added portion of this high quality of interpersonal sharing.

Finally, there is a need for the rediscovery of meaning. This is not the introduction of an entirely new element, but the use of another set of terms to refer to the process of meeting these first five needs. The basic meaning in one's life is essentially emotional and relational. This is precisely what the first five needs refer to. Nevertheless, and this is the second level of meaning, the human being naturally seeks to express perceptions of experiences in some coherent way that makes sense to that person and enables expression of the meaning of that experience to others. It is a human necessity to put our experiences into meaningful symbols, which then become reinforcing to the entire process. This is accomplished largely through the use of language.[13]

An understanding of these needs as the tasks to be accomplished in pastoral care of the bereaved, and an awareness of the relationship of the words of the bereaved to the fulfilling of these needs, clarify the specific goals that are important for the grieving person to attain and point to important aspects of the pastor's procedures.

The Stages of Grief

Other important guidance is offered the minister in the understanding of grief as a process and in the knowledge of the stages of grief, their characteristics, and the duration of the normal grief reaction. Parkes has observed that

> grief is a process and not a state. Grief is not a set of symptoms which start after a loss and then gradually fade away. It involves a succession of clinical pictures which blend into and replace one another. . . .
> Each of these stages of grieving has its own characteristics and there are considerable differences from one person to another as regards both the duration and the form of each stage. Nevertheless there is a common pattern whose features can be observed without difficulty in nearly ever case.[14]

There are a number of ways to view these stages of the process that takes place from the time one learns of a loss to the time of resolution or reorganization of one's life. Oates, Spiegel, and Gerkin have proposed outlines that can contribute significantly to the minister's understanding of what is taking place with a grieving person.[15] Unfortunately, one of the most useful books ministers can place directly in the hands of bereaved persons, that of Westberg, is somewhat misleading when it comes to the issue of stages.[16] Each of ten chapter headings is referred to as a "stage," although some are stages and some seem to be other reactions or behaviors *within* stages. The identification and discussion of each is quite helpful to most people, but it is necessary for the pastor to explain that all the elements mentioned are not technically stages, with one merging into and then being replaced by another and so on through the process. It would be more edifying to think of these as "The Common Elements of Grief," as Mitchell and Anderson refer to their analysis of various feelings and behaviors following a significant loss, or *The Many Faces of Grief*, as Edgar Jackson does in his presentation.[17]

Ministers also need to beware of those who, in speaking and writing, refer to the stages of *grief* as described by Kübler-Ross.[18] She has certainly made no such claim for her development of the stages of *dying*. While there are some similarities (especially with *anticipatory* grief), there are some very real differences also. "Bargaining" is different in its dynamics from the wish and the attempt to keep the lost person alive or to bring the person back to life. The long period in grief of trying to live without the lost person and to reconstruct one's life is not at all the same as "depression" as a stage of dying. Most certainly what she describes as "acceptance" is quite different from an adequate reorganization, resolution, or adaptation, the continuing of one's life without the one who is no longer physically present.

To seek to force Kübler-Ross' scheme onto the reactions of a person who is grieving *following* a loss, or to carry her understanding of some of the reactions of a dying person into our pastoral relationship with a person in grief could very well seriously interfere with our understanding of the person with whom we are engaged. The result could be confusion and frustration on both our parts and therefore impede the grieving process of that person.

The discussion of stages of grief that has been most enlightening and helpful to me is that of Parkes, based upon the organization of data derived from extensive personal interviews with twenty-two widows at the end of the first, third, sixth, ninth, and thirteenth months after the loss by death of their husbands.[19]

The first phase is that of *numbness and denial.* A feeling of numbness was described by ten of the widows and lasted anywhere from one day to more than a month, with five to seven days being the most common. Sixteen of the widows reported difficulty in accepting the fact that their husbands were really dead. Even though numbness is a relatively transient phenomenon, some form of denial of the full reality of what had happened tended to persist. Even after a year, thirteen of the widows said that there were still times when they had difficulty believing their husbands were dead.

The second phase is that of *yearning.* In this stage are noted the sense of intense longing and the preoccupation with thoughts of the deceased person. The widows often had haunting memories of the final illness or the death. Much attention was directed toward places and objects associated with the lost person. Ten of the widows thought they had heard or seen their husbands, and sixteen reported a sense of the presence of their husbands near them during the first month after the death. This sense was still present in twelve widows a year later. Twelve widows reported attacks of panic. As might be expected, there were a variety of physiological disturbances during this time, as well as self-reproach, general irritability or bitterness, a disruption of social relationships, restlessness, and tension. Methods of the mitigation of or defense against loss were varied: partial disbelief in the reality of external events; the inhibition of painful thoughts; selective forgetting; identification, as shown in the tendency to behave or think more as their husbands did; dreams of the husband, with happy dreams of interaction being far more common than unpleasant ones. This phase begins with diminishing of the numbness of the first stage and an increase in the intensity of affect, and usually lasts several weeks.

The third phase is that of *disorganization and despair.* This phase is less clearly delineated than the first two because its features are less dramatic. It seems to be introduced as the intensity of yearning and sharpness of emotion diminish, and some degree of apathy and aimlessness begins to take over. Even one year after bereavement, fifteen of the twenty-two widows declared they still preferred not to think about the future, and five more regarded their future as distinctly unpleasant. This "no future" orientation seems to characterize the phase.

The final phase is that of the *reorganization of behavior,* characterized by a greatly diminished symptomatology, the opening up of the future, a sense that life tastes good again. However, this does not come about as rapidly as has been commonly thought. A summary of the situation after thirteen months showed loneliness still to be a very common problem. Social adjustment was rated by the interviewer as good in five instances, fair in nine, poor in eight. Six widows had definitely worse health than before the death of their husbands, and none was healthier. Six reported themselves as happy, seven as sad, two as neutral, and seven as having moods that fluctuated between happiness and sadness. In terms of overall adjustment, the interviewer made the judgment that three were very poorly adjusted, depressed, and grieving a great deal, nine were intermittently disturbed and depressed, six showed a tenuous adjustment which might be easily upset, and four had made a good adjustment. The conclusion is that even after thirteen months, the process of grieving was still going on, and although all the principle features were past their peak, there was no sense in which grief could be said to have finished.

One of the important observations made as a result of the study had to do with differences in the degree of the overt expression of emotional distress immediately following the loss and the longer-term outcome with regard to emotional adjustment.[20] The group of widows with the mildest forms of emotional expression during the first week of bereavement grew to be the most disturbed in the third month. During the period of six to nine months it was impossible to distinguish them from the two groups who were moderately and severely disturbed initially.

However, toward the end of the year the first group again became more disturbed, and after the end of the year, three out of the five widows in this group were now moderately or severely disturbed. In contrast, only one of the eight widows who were in the initial moderate-affect group and three of the nine in the initial severe-affect group were similarly disturbed. *It is difficult to avoid the conclusion that early full grieving, the overt exhibiting of emotional behavior, produces a reduction in later symptoms of disturbance, while the repression or covering up of initial affect leads to a greater severity of those feelings when they finally do emerge.*

Practical Implications for the Minister

Parkes' findings make several contributions to the minister concerned with the practical aspects of pastoral care of the bereaved.

First, they confirm that rather severe emotional disturbance and behavioral problems, which under other circumstances might be judged as severe to an abnormal degree, are actually normal in the grief reaction. Knowing this will, first, reduce the minister's own anxiety in the pastoral relationship with the grieving person whose emotions are being quite strongly expressed or whose behavior seems unusual. In addition, this knowledge will enable the pastor to help the grieving person accept his or her own feelings and behaviors, since one of the initial fears of many grieving persons is that they are abnormal or are losing their minds.

Second, the findings of this study confirm that the earlier full grieving takes place, the more likely it is that there will be a significant reduction in later symptoms of disturbance. This not only gives permission but actually encourages the minister to seek, from the very beginning, to facilitate in an active manner the emotional expressions of bereaved persons.

Third, the findings demonstrate very clearly that even after thirteen months the process of grieving will still be going on, and although the principle features usually will be past their peak, there is no sense in which grief could be said to be concluded. Overall, the evidence seems to support the hypothesis that early and regular pastoral care and counseling would, in fact, other factors being equal, enable a person to move through the stages of grief more rapidly and with less severe persisting symptoms of disturbance.

Fourth, since grief is a process with stages, it is essential for a person to go through each of the stages completely in order to reach a positive resolution of the whole grief reaction. To continue to repress and suppress the feelings involved in grief, to go about one's usual business as if there had been no loss, to attempt to skip stages, or not to do what needs to be done to work out the internal psychological and external social tasks, is to thwart the process, to impede and perhaps finally block resolution or reorganization. If there are impediments to moving through the stages, the result is what may be termed morbid, or pathological, or unresolved grief, in which there is a fixation on a particular symptom or a particular segment of a specific stage of the normal grief process (usually either Stage 2 or Stage 3 of Parkes' scheme), with the adoption in a rigid and inflexible manner of one or a small select number of the mechanisms or behaviors of that stage. This fixation is in contrast to the usual grief process, during which there is experimental testing of the various behaviors over a period of time, discarding those that are not functional in the maintenance and structure of the self, then going on to utilize in a constructive and adaptive way several of those that facilitate self-maintenance and growth.

This fixation may, of course, be a sign to the minister that the person is not dealing constructively with some aspect of his or her response to the loss. The pastor is then in a position to discuss that person's pain with him or her, observe that even after six or so months the grief does not seem to be progressing, and suggest that the person talk with some other professional in addition to the pastor, if such a professional is available. The pastoral counseling of a person severely affected by loss and making no progress is discussed in the next chapter.

An additional study points up other factors to be aware of in the process of grief work when the loss takes place within a family setting. The importance for the family of a death has been recognized and was the basis of a research project in which crisis intervention teams of mental health professionals visited families no later than twelve hours after the death of a member, then sought to see them as whole families for two to six sessions, over a period of one to ten weeks. "This short-term intervention is aimed at increasing the effectiveness of the family in coping with feelings, decisions and subsequent adjustment related to the death."[21] For research purposes nonintervention crisis and noncrisis control groups were selected. The results support the importance of viewing the family as a single whole system, an organism in and of itself, and the successful reassignment of roles within the system as being of major significance in the health of the family and its individual members.[22] This task of assisting the family in the redistribution of roles becomes a self-conscious focus of intervention in grief. It should not be overlooked that children are very much a part of the family, and while their roles are not usually as instrumental and task-oriented as those of adults, their social-emotional roles are of crucial influence in the life of the family.[23] The whole family, including the children, profit from being assisted in a realignment of roles as a necessary adjustment to loss.

The functions of the minister in the grief situation, then, are based on the data presented up to this point:

1. the need for immediate initiation of the facilitation of the grieving process;
2. the overall long-term needs of the bereaved and an understanding, not only of how the person's crying and other

nonverbal emotional expressions may be elicited, but also of how extensive talking within the pastoral relationship enables those needs to be met more quickly and more fully;

3. the concept of crisis derived originally from a study of grief, and the effectiveness of crisis intervention as an active, frequently guided form of counseling, in contrast to a more passive, nondirective modality;

4. the duration of time in the course of normal grieving;

5. the needs of children who have lost someone significant in their lives and the importance of attention to their grieving;

6. the values of an interaction approach to grief which takes place in a family matrix, the effectiveness of shared empathy in the healing of grief within the family, and the need to work consciously at the reassignment of roles within the family.

The Practical Functioning of the Minister

The Schedule of Pastoral Care

A schedule of pastoral care in the crisis of grief might resemble that which follows, recognizing some considerable variation because of different external circumstances and differences in individual needs and responses. The minister should contact the family or grief-stricken person just as soon as notified of the death. If at all possible, a personal visit is most effective. What takes place in this call will vary considerably. It may, under some circumstances, be quite brief. The significant thing is that, on a personal level and also as the representative of the Christian community, the minister has been there and has come as quickly as possible, communicating to the bereaved the priority of the event in the mind of the minister and in the life of the community. If during this visit there is no reasonable period of time for conversation or no substantial amount of overt expression of emotion or no opportunity to talk about the death, the dead person, the relationship, or the funeral, then a second prefuneral call is absolutely necessary, scheduled so that sufficient time may be given to these tasks.

Therefore, at the second call prior to the funeral, the minister would inquire about and encourage the bereaved person or persons to talk about the death and its circumstances. The minister needs to be prepared to receive anything the bereaved want to say about the dead person and their relationship. Finally, at some point it is essential that there be a focus on the funeral. This discussion appropriately deals with a number of details, which at first glance may seem to be irrelevant to the grieving process and may even be experienced by some ministers as a jarring note and a distasteful duty. However, not only is this necessary for the mechanical details themselves, but important opportunities arise out of such a discussion.

First, talking about the funeral in any concrete and detailed way may be an important reinforcement of the reality of the finality of the death that has occurred. Second, by the way the minister introduces the discussion, there may be the direct facilitation of talking about the dead person. For example, questions may be asked concerning the form and elements of the service, from the point of view of who the dead person was. Did he or she have any specific instructions concerning the service? Did you ever hear the person express views concerning death or funerals? Were there any favorite passages of Scripture or hymns or other music? What sorts of things do you (the grieving person or persons) feel are important about the dead person that I (the minister) should consider in the preparation of the funeral and a short sermon? Third, the discussion of the funeral with the members of the family provides the context for a declaration of a sustaining and hope-stimulating faith, as the funeral is interpreted and developed with them as a service of worship to God, not just as a religiously oriented memorial ceremony.

A third step in the schedule of pastoral care is the funeral itself. Putting it in this way indicates clearly that the funeral should not be conceived of by the minister apart from pastoral relationships, nor should counseling be separated from the funeral in some formal way. The funeral becomes an outmoded, meaningless, distasteful custom *only* if ministers and congregations allow it to become so. It may be, indeed *must* be and *can* be, a vital element in the grieving process. The guidelines contained in Irion's superb book for evaluating a funeral contain ten highly significant criteria arranged under social, psychological, and theological needs to be met, all relating to the effective healing of grief and the maintenance of community. These are important, and every minister should have them at hand during the preparation for a funeral. Other useful perspectives and guidelines are discussed by Mitchell and Anderson.[24]

The fourth step, which is critical in order to facilitate the grieving process, is a postfuneral call within two or three days following the service. This is frequently the first occasion offering sufficient time for an extended conversation in some reasonably quiet setting without many interruptions. That conversation will often reflect back on the funeral and the bereaved's responses to it, and this may be the springboard into more detailed talking about the dead person and the relationship, and more overt expression of emotion. Remember that most funerals take place during the stage of shock.

Finally, for the most effective facilitation of the process of grieving, there should be continued regular pastoral conversations, approximately weekly during the first six weeks or so, moving to perhaps every ten days to two weeks for approximately another six weeks, then tapering off into less frequent contacts as grief work seems to be in the process of being accomplished, the pain diminishes somewhat, and activities and relationships are being renewed. If there seems to be absolutely no or relatively little diminishing of grief behavior after about three months, then serious consideration should be given to bringing a professional counselor into the picture, and if after six months there still seems to be no change, a referral definitely needs to be made.

While on the basis of the data clarifying the needs of the bereaved few pastors would disagree that a schedule something like this would be useful to follow, the issue of time raises its ubiquitous ugly head. If you are the only pastor in a church where there are several deaths each month, or on the staff of a large church which includes an aging membership, especially in a city where there are many funerals of persons who are not members of your congregation, how can such a schedule possibly be followed? One or a combination of three ways can be considered. (1) Where there is a church staff, responsibility for grief counseling might be relatively evenly shared by all staff members, or one staff member with particular sensitivities and skills might be relieved of some other responsibilities in order to pursue this one most effectively. (2) Lay people may also be trained in grief counseling and assigned to visit persons or families regularly throughout the mourning period. (3) The minister may bring those grieving persons who are willing into a grief work group, not only saving some of his or her own time, but in fact rendering a different and in some ways a higher quality service to those in distress.

The Methodology of Pastoral Care

The final section of this chapter will seek to deal in an even more concrete manner with the specific methodology of the minister's grief counseling, the actual functioning with the bereaved. First, recognizing the particular nature of the event of death, it should be declared that the broad methodological base out of which the minister's grief counseling activities arise is provided by the several essential ingredients for all effective helping relationships and for crisis intervention. Of these, those most relevant to the early stages of grief counseling are accurate empathy, respect, genuineness, and concreteness. Most people in grief will initially be sufficiently expressive of affect, so the pastor's responses, reflecting accurate empathy and respect, will cement the relationship for further dimensions of counseling and assist continued and deeper emotional expression. The minister should, of course, be prepared to receive great amounts of painful emotion. The primary methodology, then, especially in these early stages of pastoral care, although certainly not the exclusive one, is the attempt to reflect back to the person in an accurate way the verbal meaning and the specific affect and the degree of intensity of affect of that person's communications. This type of response is facilitative of further and fuller affective expression and of increased depth of self-exploration. If there is not such free flow of emotion on the part of the bereaved person, the minister should move on into the more directive procedures of crisis intervention.

At this point, there is more verbal activity on the part of the counselor, with more initiative taken in questioning. The particular questions grow out of the value to the bereaved person of focusing on the memories, images, and emotions surrounding the death of the person: the illness, the accident; the way the person looked and sounded; what took place, what was said; the death itself. The bereaved person should be encouraged to talk as much about all this as she or he is willing. The person may need to be assisted in a review of his or her emotional and behavioral reactions at that time. Direct and forceful questioning usually will not be needed, since grieving persons often offer just such material as this. If they do not, however, they will ordinarily respond to soft and gentle suggestions, particularly elicited by the minister's warm and sincere interest and concern about what has taken place. In those relatively few instances where the bereaved persons are only minimally responsive (at this point we are talking about pastoral visits that follow the first postfuneral call), more direct questions and suggestions that lead into a review of memories, images, and emotions surrounding the death may be used. This should certainly not be interpreted to mean insensitivity to a person's proper privacy. It does not refer to harshness or hard confrontation, but to the combination of genuine interest, an openness to receive even negative and strong emotion, and whatever persistent leading may be necessary.

As minister and bereaved move past the events surrounding the death and the funeral, they properly enter into a phase of reviewing the relationship between the bereaved and the dead person. The grief sufferer should be assisted in recounting everything he or she possibly can concerning the relationship. The minister will need to persist in asking for concreteness, for specific examples, for details of remembered events, scenes, encounters. A full elaboration should be encouraged. At all times it is crucial to attend to affect and facilitate its full expression. It is important that ministers not allow their own feelings of anxiety and uneasiness in the presence of painful experiences and emotions to produce behavior on their part that would reinforce the telling about only the good aspects of the relationship, forcing the person to squelch the feelings experienced as negative, the conflicts, the unpleasant and unfulfilling aspects, with the effect of stimulating even more guilt about having such feelings. This does not mean that pastors are robots without feeling. Many times our own sadness is stimulated, and at times appropriate to helping the other person, our feelings may be shared. The point is that the strength of our own feelings, whatever they may be, must not lead us into behaviors that would inhibit the expression of the other person.

The minister should always be prepared to be patient with repetition. Frequently the repetition of events or certain aspects of the relationship will be necessary in order for strong feelings to be identified and come out fully, and for the ties to be broken. All these procedures will be elaborated and illustrated in the next chapter.

Finally, when the bereaved person has reached the point of readiness, movements toward giving up the physical presence of the deceased (the giving away of clothes or books or other possessions, the changing of a room) are to be affirmed and assisted. So also are any movements toward reentry into old groups and activities and occasionally the taking up of new ones, the reestablishing and deepening of friendships and occasionally the establishment of new relationships.

As suggested earlier, special attention needs to be given to the children in a family where there has been a loss, both when they are with the rest of the family and when they are alone. Work with the entire family should be emphasized, using, as much as possible, something of the schedule and procedures already described, but recognizing that there will be numerous practical barriers in the way of any ideal accomplishment of this goal. One procedure growing out of the work of Paul suggests that we encourage the family members to share their grief fully with one another. As each does so, the others are assisted in expressing their empathy with that person (see p. 146). After feelings are fully expressed, the realignment of family roles will need to be discussed and the family members assisted in the decision making necessary to accomplish this. While some families handle this very important group task rather effectively, some may fall into a trap, tending unconsciously to enter into collusion in seeking to assign the total need-fulfilling role of the deceased to one individual member, rather than allotting the functions more appropriately to those persons most capable of meeting the particular needs. Other families may contain an individual who unconsciously identifies with the deceased to such a degree that he or she seeks to assume the total role.[25] For some families, a simple open discussion of their need to relate to one another in somewhat different ways, now that one of them has died, will be sufficient to head off this potential problem. For some it will be more complex, and it may be that some professional other than the minister will need to be consulted. But the conscientious minister has a crucial function to play in perceiving the new family interaction and guiding the members toward the help they need.

An especially important aspect of the minister's grief counseling is the utilization of an understanding of the inter- and intrapersonal dynamics of leave-taking. This involves the strategy for breaking away from such an intensive relationship with the bereaved with whom he or she has been working during the period of grief and its resolution. The self-conscious use of the termination of the counseling relationship, with its dimensions of interpersonal depth, is an important contribution to the mourning process itself and one which most ministers probably have overlooked, although undoubtedly many sensitive pastors have in fact functioned in very helpful ways at this end stage of grief counseling, without always being fully aware of the double significance of what was taking place.

The understanding of the relationship of bereavement itself and the termination of counseling has been developed in a very lucid and helpful way by Loewald in psychoanalytic terms. In any leave-taking or separation, he states that

> an attempt is made to deny loss: either we try to deny that the other person still exists or did exist, or we try to deny that we have to leave

the beloved person and venture out on our own. . . . In true mourning, the loss of the beloved person is perhaps temporarily denied but gradually is accepted and worked out by way of a complex inner process.[26]

This has already been discussed to some extent in relationship to loss by death. What takes place in counseling of any depth is that a relationship of considerable meaning and intense emotion is established, and when the counseling ceases, the relationship either comes to an end or at least changes radically. Leave-taking must be accomplished. There is a loss of a significant other person. As pastor and counselee move into the last few sessions, such loss begins to be anticipated, and anxious feelings similar to those of grief (in this case, anticipatory grief) begin to be experienced. "The extended leave-taking at the end phase of analysis is a replica of the process of mourning."[27] This last statement is the key to understanding how an effective termination of counseling assists the process of mourning for which the counseling was taking place.

It is absolutely essential that the parting be made explicit in words, that the emotions be expressed, the meaning of the relationship articulated, the good-bye said in a clear and appropriate way. When this is done, "then neither the existence of the person from whom we part nor the anticipated life without him can be denied."[28]

Due to the quality of relationship a pastor establishes with a bereaved person, especially if she or he carries through with the full course of grief work suggested, it is not uncommon for that pastor to be placed unconsciously by the bereaved in some aspect of the role of the dead person. To the extent that the pastoral counselor recognizes this behavior, it provides the opportunity to help the bereaved person understand that he or she is seeking to deny the death by externalizing aspects of the dead person that are actually living parts of the bereaved's own self. In other words, the reaction of denial, which to some degree is a part of every grief, like all repression, is never fully effective. That which is directly denied begins to express itself in some way in overt behavior. In the grief counseling relationship the repressed elements of the lost person begin to be externalized, expressed in some form of the contemporary transactions taking place between the pastor and the grief sufferer. These are recognized by the pastor, discussed with the person in terms of their meaning in this present relationship, and thus it becomes possible for the bereaved person to accept them as a part of herself or himself in a new form. Denied aspects of the deceased's life are gotten out, recognized for what they are, then taken back into one's self. "It seems that emancipation as a process of separation from external objects . . . goes hand in hand with the work of internalization which reduces or abolishes the sense of external deprivation and loss."[29]

Effective mourning involves not only certain aspects of *relinquishing* the lost person, but also of allowing those aspects of the other person, which through identification have become a part of the very selfhood of the bereaved, to become fully alive, of *receiving* the lost person in a new way. When this begins to happen, grief work is moving toward its conclusion. Yet the end of counseling is something of a replica of this process, and can be consciously utilized by the pastoral counselor as a repetition of the loss by death. A conscious leave-taking between the pastor and the bereaved can begin to take place in the form of an explicit discussion of the way they feel about the cessation of the counseling relationship itself. As this is done, the original grief for which the counseling has been taking place may be more adequately healed.

Now this sounds rather complex, but it only refers to the fact that certain unconscious elements of one's own self in relationship to the deceased have now become conscious in relationship to the pastoral counselor. By experiencing them consciously, expressing one's feelings concerning them, and recognizing them for what they are, they become transformed into living sources of meaning and strength which may be consciously incorporated by the person into the present behavior and relationships.

It would seem that the minister's strategy with the grief-stricken might be to make the somewhat frequent visits to which reference has already been made, beginning in the midst of the crisis itself, when a person is both highly vulnerable and in need of support as well as open to influence by another caring person. Because of the heightened emotions of the grief crisis, a relationship of meaning and depth is rapidly established. Into this relationship elements of the bereaved's relations with other significant persons, often including the deceased, are introduced, making this material available for further discussion, with a dual focus on the relationship with the deceased and the present relationship with the pastor. As the number and frequency of the visits decrease, the minister begins to refer to the eventual ending of this form of their relationship. This makes possible a reliving of a leave-taking, with the minister being attentive to all the important aspects of such a separation, encouraging a full expression of all the feelings involved, including his or her own. Such a process enables the mourner to assimilate in something of the same way, and as a part of her or his own being, aspects of this present relationship with the pastor, as well as to complete the mourning process initiated by the death of an emotionally significant person. The minister, of course, realizes that more often than not during pastoral care with a bereaved person, they are moving toward a transformation of their relationship rather than the total termination of it. Nevertheless, when it has been as intense and meaningful as it has been in grief counseling, even such transformation entails the anticipation of object loss from the perspective of the counselee.

When the minister engages in grief counseling, she or he must always be aware of the fact that it is done in the context of a faith-stance toward life which has a dynamic meaning. The psalmist says, "As for [human beings], [their] days are like grass; [they] flourish . . . like a flower of the field; for the wind passes over it, and it is gone, and its place knows it no more" (103:15-16). This is certainly a description of each of us. We are here and then we are gone. And gone also, in a physical sense, are those we love and with whom we have had conflict and with whom we have shared many aspects of our lives. Yet this is not the whole of the psalmist's message. These words are set in the midst of an affirmation of faith in the Lord who "knows our frame, [who] remembers that we are dust." Then the psalm goes on to proclaim, "The steadfast love of the Lord is from everlasting to everlasting upon those who fear [God]" (103:14, 17). It seems to be the nature of human existence that a person is never left totally without possibilities. There may be other ways of saying it—in fact there *are*—but a person of faith can declare with the psalmist that the continual existence of possibilities is a reflection of faith in God as active love, and our possibilities in any situation, as God's gift. The anxiety of grief not only has potential destructive powers, but like any anxiety, may have a primary function to produce growth in human life, including growth in faith. It can be the painful stimulus that leads a person to resources that can not only heal but make new. Ministers of God are given the opportunity to be servants in this process of healing and renewal in the central crisis of human existence, death and grief.

CHAPTER 7

INTERVENING IN A PATHOLOGICAL GRIEF REACTION

A Case Study

This chapter attempts to illustrate how a counseling strategy might be developed and applied by a minister in a specific situation of grief.[1] This case material presented here has both the advantages and disadvantages of an extreme reaction. It demonstrates that even in quite difficult instances progress in the alleviation of maladaptive behavior may be achieved, even though in a number of respects the case is not typical of that with which the minister usually deals. Nevertheless, once given a particular situation, in light of the needs of all bereaved persons and the suggested possible methods of intervention, the minister must make a series of decisions as to the most intense needs, those that may be met most readily, and his or her own means of relating helpfully to that person or family. The following case study illustrates how some of these decisions are made and what procedures may be followed. We would do well to keep in mind, too, that although the pastoral counselor involved in this case came into the situation of morbid grief reaction several months after the funeral, parish ministers themselves do in fact sometimes deal with extreme behavior in response to bereavement, and often have not been involved with the persons in a pastoral relationship prior to the time they are called into the situation.

The operation of the mechanisms of denial and the repression of affect, and even of memory surrounding the death of a person with whom one has been closely tied emotionally, has been observed by almost every person who is frequently involved with the bereaved. Therefore, it should be clear that the purpose of this report of the losses of a twenty-year-old female psychiatric patient is not to demonstrate that such repression *can* happen, but, first, to portray a rather unique combination of such repressions, producing an almost total amnesia as to the details of a relationship that had existed since the patient's birth. A second purpose, however, is even more important to the parish minister. This is to introduce a methodology for the facilitation of grief work which can be utilized not only in such severe cases, but is adaptable to the counseling procedures in dealing with "normal" grief, beginning at the time of the loss, in the hope of preventing "morbid" grief reactions.

This young woman was admitted to a psychiatric hospital on the basis of about five months of moderate depression reactive to a series of events: anticipatory grief during the several-month terminal illness of her grandfather, with whom she had an unusually close emotional relationship, her boyfriend's breaking off of their romance, and the death of her grandfather about a month later.

The patient was the first child of her parents. A congenital disorder required rather constant attention, continued because of parental anxiety even after the disorder was corrected. This attention was drastically and suddenly curtailed by the birth of the next sibling when the patient was about three, then further diminished by a third child. One can presume the sense of deprivation this small child must have felt as that exclusive and intense care was now shared with others.

When she was fifteen, she left her own home to live with her maternal grandparents in the same city, due to the availability in another high school of a better department in the field of her major interest. In this home she was once again the exclusive center of attention, reproducing the situation of the first three years of her life. The grandfather became the focal point of her affection.

The contemporary events of loss began when, in the patient's second year of college, the grandfather was hospitalized with cancer. Although the patient knew of this, she was not informed of its critical nature until several weeks after his admission, when she was actually in the car going to visit him for the first time. This tardy statement did not prepare her for the shock of his debilitated body and his inability even to recognize her. She remained in the room only briefly, recoiling in horror, and never returned.

Within several weeks the young man with whom she was in love simply stopped calling her. When the impact of this broken relationship hit, she made a mild suicide attempt, rather obviously communicative-manipulative in nature, reflective of her genuine feelings of abandonment and despair. She reported later that there was the equally genuine feeling of not wanting to kill herself *dead*.

Within another few weeks the grandfather died. The precise

beginning point of her depression could not be identified. It had apparently been in the process of development during his hospitalization, prior to the breaking of her relationship with the young man, and had never lifted, although she was never totally nonfunctional. After about three more months, during which she saw a psychiatrist several times, she was admitted to the hospital.

It was judged that although there was an underlying long-term deep emotional need that would call for continued treatment, a noticeable raising of mood and mobilization of ego resources might be accomplished by means of intensive crisis therapy focusing on her recent experiences of loss, since, with the exception of the acting out of the suicide attempt, they had never been openly expressed—certainly not in a direct manner. It was hypothesized that the loss of the grandfather was primary, first, chronologically, because it in fact dated from her experience in the hospital room, and second, because of the lifelong relationship. It was not implausible to consider the hypothesis that her anticipatory grief reactions were of such a nature as to have played some role in the withdrawal of the boyfriend, although no data were obtained to substantiate such a presupposition.

A minister was available to talk with her in the hospital. His decision was to see her twice a week, forty-five minutes to an hour, for three weeks, with an exclusive focus on her grief reaction to the loss of her grandfather; then, if progress were made, to move to the loss of the boyfriend and the suicide gesture. The therapeutic relationship and the methodology employed were planned in accordance with the needs of bereaved persons, as previously discussed, and the rationale for stimulating the grief sufferer to talk as soon as possible and as fully as possible about the dead person, the relationship, and the death events. With this patient, a clear contract was made concerning the focus of the talks and the number of sessions. Such a contract would not usually be made in the "normal," or nonpathological grief reaction, when one presumes that a person's grief work will be done in the company of several other persons, of whom the minister is only one, in several structured and nonstructured social settings, and over a period of several months.

A very strong distrust of and anger at the hospital on the part of the patient was evident at the beginning and continued throughout the interviews. However, the minister was not officially related to the hospital, and the young woman was genuinely responsive to the attempt of someone to talk with her about her grandfather, something she had avoided but felt was important. One must not overlook, however, her hidden agenda which became apparent a bit later: the search for an ally to help her in her struggle against the hospital staff and in her attempt to be discharged.

The first task was to seek to elicit the effect that one would normally expect during the time of anticipatory grief and the initial grief reaction itself, through the exploration of the grandfather's illness, his death, and the immediate postdeath experiences, including the funeral. This beginning point was based upon the rather well-established evidence that the shock and denial, the usual first reaction to the death of an emotionally related person, is the attempt to deal with the intense anxiety of loss and its threat to the self. In most instances, shock and denial are not capable of handling the combined power of the internal feelings and the external reality of the death. The next normal phase of grief, then, is an outpouring of emotion, the feeling and the expression of pain, the variety of emotions not always clearly differentiated and identified at this point. Yet this rather uninhibited cathartic expression is initially tension relieving and opens the door to more specific exploration. When this has not taken place, as it had not with this patient, further stages of grief work cannot be accomplished. Therefore, the methodology of the counselor is to ask the grief sufferer to recount as much detail as possible about the death and the events surrounding it, always seeking more detail and for the expression of the feelings the person might have been experiencing at the time. This is a very directive, sensitively persistent lancing of a psychic wound that is still festering. The use of a term like *directive* is not at all in conflict with the central role of the accurate communication of empathy, seen by Carkhuff and others as the absolutely essential ingredient of all effective helping relationships, as discussed earlier.

Following this cathartic expression, inevitably including the beginning of self-exploration concerning the relationship between the grieved person and the deceased, one's feelings about one's self and the other, a complete review of the relationship is the next appropriate phase. Again, the procedure was to take an active role in asking the bereaved person about the deceased as a person, about their relationship, asking again in detail for all the possibly significant memories, what they did together, what they said, what the bereaved person felt at the time, the meaning of all this for her.

With the young woman suffering from depression, an unexpected barrier was discovered almost from the very beginning. Not only could she not presently respond with the appropriate affect, not only had she repressed the actual feelings, but she had repressed even the memory of having had feelings at all. Indeed, she had little memory of most of the events surrounding her grandfather's death, and had lost *almost all memory of the events of her lifelong relationship with him.* The selective nature of this memory loss must be emphasized, because memory loss in general was not a part of her clinical picture.

She did recall the shock of seeing in the hospital what she reported as the wasted body of what had been her grandfather: "It was not really him" (denial). She remembered his inability to recognize her, and leaving the room to vent her anger at her family for not having prepared her for this and for their present open discussion of his impending death (her response to what was seen as a challenge to her denial). She could remember her father telling her of the grandfather's death, but could not feel presently or recall her feelings at the time. She had gone to the funeral home alone, refusing to go with any of the family, reporting that she would not put herself in the position of being with anyone else when she was feeling deeply and might have to express her emotions in their presence: "It's a sign of weakness." When questioned persistently about what she experienced when she stood alone before his body, it was interesting to note that she responded fairly readily that her only memory was that of anger: "I was mad at him because he had left my grandmother alone." It was only in a later session that she was able to say that she was angry at him for leaving *her.* As far as the funeral was concerned, the patient remembered attending, but details of the event and her feelings before, during, and after were not available to her.

This type of directive attempt to stimulate her self-exploration was carried out through persistent and specific questioning, reflective responses attentive to affect, and statements which were intended to be invitational to affect: "I think if I were in such a situation I would feel . . ."; "That would make me feel . . . ." These types of statements would tend to have the effect of giving permission to feel and express loss, guilt, sadness, anger.

Three aspects of the patient's behavior during this first session need to be noted. First, she was not without feeling, apathetic. Several times feelings would begin to rise to the surface in the direction of expression and would be cut off. To the extent that these were attempts to *remember* and *relive* feelings at the time of the grandfather's illness and death, the mechanism seemed to be that of repression. When the affect was genuinely contemporary, at the moment she spoke, there was much more conscious suppression, prior conditioning to fight one's own feelings and not to let them out for others, or even for one's own self to see and experience fully. Second, she herself seemed genuinely astonished and baffled by her inability to remember what had gone on and how she had felt, as if, until now, she had even put out of her mind the idea that she *should* try to remember. Third, positive transference toward the minister began to develop quite rapidly.

In the second session, the minister made the decision to move on to the second phase of grief counseling, that of reviewing the whole relationship between the grief sufferer and the dead person, even though obviously phase one was incomplete. It was judged that further direct confrontation with the events of the death would meet with continued unconscious resistance and, since time was limited, that the approach to the painful emotions might be made by withdrawing to earlier, more pleasant memories. Then the counselor could lead the patient chronologically back to the illness and death, with the ego now being strengthened by some reinforcement of earlier "good objects," earlier relationships and experiences and responses of significant other persons which one has taken into oneself as a part of one's own self image. Also during this second phase, the relationship between the patient and the minister could continue to develop and perhaps aid in facilitating the exploration of the repressed painful affect.

The grandfather was spoken of in quite idealistic terms. According to the patient, the relationship with him had been a most meaningful one all her life. When she was a child they had done many things. He was always there. He was available, but *he did not bother her or make demands of her*. Following the principle of concreteness as a necessary facilitative condition for effective psychotherapy, the patient was asked to describe specifically and in detail events in her relationship with her grandfather. What did they do together? What did they talk about? Recount times together, activities, conversations. The first response, with some amazement to herself, was, "I don't know. I can't. I can't remember." After persistent asking by the minister for memories and images, only four could be produced. One, when the patient was small, he occasionally took her to the carnival. Two, he took her fishing a few times, but in fact, she did not like to go fishing. Three, she could remember him in his chair watching television. Four, she talked with him about her problems, but pressing for detail revealed that it was actually her grand*mother* who talked with her. No more information was forthcoming concerning what had taken place between them, except that she was quite clear that at no time, even when she was small, did they express their affection for one another in any physical way. Time and again throughout the interview, the young woman's reply was, "I don't remember. I just can't."

This degree of memory repression is considerably more than ordinary, extending beyond just the affect and painful events of the death itself to the patient's entire lifetime of relationship with her grandfather, but which, except for a few small fragments, she was unable to document in concrete terms. One might begin to speculate that in addition to the rather obvious repression operating, much of the relationship between the two was one of fantasy and idealization on the part of the patient—not new fantasy and idealization as a part of the grief reaction, which, of course, does happen, but extending from her childhood days, as she sought available love (i.e., need-fulfilling) objects in response to perceived rejection by her parents. A picture of the grandfather began to emerge, as much as the minister could piece together the reality of it—a man who was rather passive and undemonstrative, who placed no demands on his granddaughter, who could then be viewed in contrast with the parents and idealized. In addition, her own emotional life seemed to be patterned very much after his—the suppression of affect, not allowing the "weakness" of feeling and its expression: identification with partial aspects of the real man as well as the idealized man.

The young woman's rather rapid positive transference seemed to be in terms of her feelings toward her grandfather, assisted by the actual role of the minister as not related administratively to the hospital, the negative transference already having been directed at the hospital as personified by her administrative psychiatrist. This double transference was rather strongly demonstrated when she sought to maneuver the minister into the position of taking her side against the hospital, saving her by aiding in her discharge, an apparent reenactment of the utilization of grandparent against parent. The maneuvering ended when the minister proposed this interpretation of the behavior he was observing, and pointed out that the reality of the present situation was such that he could not fulfill this role and that this would not fit their original contract. The full import of the interpretation did not gain immediate full acceptance, but both the comparison of the relationships and the present reality were understood, and it was possible to move on with the grief work.

It became apparent because of the rapid development of the relationship between the patient and the minister that he had the opportunity to use the potency of the relationship and the necessity of a clearcut termination to seek to produce for the patient a model of what separation or object loss in a healthy form might mean. Referring back to Loewald's comparison of the psychodynamics of mourning and termination of therapy, it was felt that one way of breaking through the patient's strong denial of so much of the relationship with her grandfather, and the accompanying repression of affect, would be to move with her through an emotionally intense but verbally explicit separation.

At this point in the fourth session, there was the beginning of a breakthrough in the expression of feeling when the minister clearly reminded the patient that they would have only two more sessions, and then he, too, would leave her, a repetition of loss. This focus on what was happening at the present moment is the introduction of immediacy as defined by Carkhuff.[2] It produced a series of affective responses, beginning with tears and the statement, "Everyone I really care about leaves me." She was able to say that she was hurting over the anticipated separation from the counselor. In this context, she began to discuss how difficult it was for her to say good-bye. This was followed by the first realization that she had not told her grandfather good-bye, knowing now that she could have visited him earlier in the hospital, that she did not because of her own need to deny what was taking place, accepting her responsibilty, and beginning to feel her guilt about it. Once again she reflected upon seeing his body at the funeral home and feeling anger "because he had left *me* alone," the *me* replacing the *grandmother* of her earlier statement. It was suggested that she might well have feelings of anger at the minister at the present time because he was leaving her, but she reported not experiencing this.

The fifth session picked up on the separation theme, and how people separate from one another. An attempt was made by the counselor to enable her to say good-bye to her grandfather *now*, both by asking, "What would you like to tell him now?" ("I don't know") and then asking her to see the minister as the grandfather and talk directly to him ("I can't do it"). Finally the minister asked, "How are you going to say good-bye to me?" Again, "I don't know," but her deep expression of hurt and her tears began to show that she was opening up to the possibility of *feeling* her emotions and expressing them openly and directly. The next procedural steps in the last session would have been to attempt to link this present relationship, the separation, the experiencing and expression of this loss and its good-bye—including its hurt, threat, and anger—with what went on at the loss of her grandfather and of her boyfriend.

However, before the final session her parents came to the hospital, requested her discharge, and took her home. She and the minister never said good-bye. Nevertheless, the progress made during the sessions points to the efficacy of the methodology used by the minister, combining in short-term crisis counseling the essential ingredients Carkhuff has pointed out as necessary for any helping process, the directive and active aspects of crisis intervention in general as applied to the specific needs of the bereaved person as stated earlier, and finally drawing upon the explicit termination of the counseling relationship as a means of enabling a person to fully experience a contemporary separation in a manner that might facilitate moving toward a resolution of the original grief.

A more detailed discussion of the nature and dynamics of persons' unresolved grief, the value of identifying such persons, the role of the parish pastor, and the counseling and intervention procedures may be found elsewhere.[3]

CHAPTER 8

THE MINISTER
AND DIVORCE CRISES
Richard A. Hunt, Ph.D.

A crisis includes three basic elements. First, a major, often sudden change has occurred that makes an intensive impact upon the usual life-style of an individual or family. Second, the individuals involved feel anxious, overwhelmed, and to some extent unable to cope constructively with the changed circumstances. Third, a revised solution to the situation is required in a relatively short period of time.

Whether divorce can be considered a crisis or a series of crises depends upon the perspectives of the individuals involved. The crises relating to divorce will be different for each partner, for any children involved, and for relatives and friends. Effects may also carry over into one's work, leisure pursuits, drinking, and health, in both obvious and subtle ways.

Even when a divorcing or divorced person asserts that he or she is not experiencing a crisis, a sensitive pastor may see signs that the participants are exhibiting "crisis" responses as described in this volume.

Some Theoretical Perspectives on Divorce

Before considering the actual work of pastoral care and counseling with persons in a divorce crisis, it will be helpful to consider the minister's own approach to divorce. There are at least six perspectives that should be examined by the minister as bases for counseling with persons in a divorce crisis. These perspectives are demographic, sociological, legal, theological, personal, and psychological.

Demographic

Compared to twenty or thirty years ago, the incidence of divorce has increased. Measuring this increase, however, is difficult. The

175

ratio of marriages registered to divorces granted in a particular year and in a specific geographical area does not give a true picture of current marriage and divorce rates. A pastor who has just seen three of the supposedly stable couples in the congregation obtain divorces, or who has had five of the eight most recent couples with whom she or he counseled finally divorce, may be tempted to assume that we have a crisis of divorce in the entire society. This is not the case.

A more useful statistic is the ratio of divorces per one-thousand population. Except for the post-World War II peak in 1946, the rate has risen only very sightly since 1920, fluctuating between six and ten divorces per one thousand married females fifteen years of age and older in the U. S. population. This means that each year, approximately one to two percent of all existing marriages end in divorce. Of these divorces, approximately three-fourths of the men and more than half the women marry again.[1]

The improvement of accurate reporting of divorce statistics and the trend toward easier legal proceedings for obtaining divorces probably constitute two primary reasons for the increase in divorce rates over the past fifty years. Other sociological factors will be discussed below.

Although an overall average divorce rate may be calculated, this represents a combination of rates, which vary considerably in different parts of the United States, in different age groups, and with many other factors. The percentage of marriages that end in divorce is highest (a peak of approximately 6 to 8 percent) during the first three years of marriage and shows a gradual decline from about four percent to less than one percent between the fifth and thirtieth years of marriage.

Those who have divorced previously are two to three times more likely to divorce again. From 50 to 75 percent of marriages which occur when one or both partners are under age eighteen end in divorce. Those persons with similar backgrounds, to some extent expressed in religious similarity, have divorce rates much lower than those in religiously mixed marriages or with no religious background.

Approximately 18 percent of all households with children are single-parent households. Although fathers are increasingly obtaining primary custody of children, some 85 percent of single parents with children in the home are mothers. In addition, income in these families is much lower. By 1980, among white children, 5 percent of households with income over $20,000 were one-parent homes, while some 60 percent of households with income under $6,000 were one-parent homes. Among black children, the corresponding percentages were 10 percent and 80 percent.

Sociological

In most segments of U. S. society, divorce is now more acceptable than it was even ten years ago. Several factors have influenced this trend. Some 60 percent of all married women are now working in paid employment outside the home. The emphasis upon nondiscrimination in employment, the increase in the number and types of jobs available to women, improvement of contraceptives, and the general urbanization and mobility of our society make it easier for either spouse to exit an unhappy marriage.

Most religious denominations have also contributed to this trend by either openly or indirectly permitting divorced persons to remarry. With divorced persons seeking another marriage, pastors are usually required to give attention to the factors in the previous divorce. How well this is done, however, depends upon the training of the pastor and the resources available.

The advent of no-fault divorce in the mid-1970s reflected these and other factors, emphasized the concept that both partners contribute to the demise of a marriage, and provided an alternative to the traditional adversarial approach in which the attorney for the "innocent" spouse attempted to prove the other spouse "guilty" and therefore owing some type of restitution as well as divorce.

Legal

Technically, *divorce* is a legal term that refers to the termination of a marriage contract. In these terms, marriage is a civil contract between two individuals, differing from ordinary contracts in several ways. The marriage contract does not specify details of the responsibilities of the participants. Instead, assumptions from common law guide the determination of duties, privileges, and divorce, except in those occasional instances where a couple has established an alternative legally binding marriage contract prior to their marriage.

The process of the dissolution of the marriage contract may be relatively simple if there is no court contest, and if children or property settlements are not involved. Where divorce proceedings are complicated by legal charges and countercharges, battles about child custody or monetary settlements, then the litigation may itself produce secondary crises in addition to the primary emotional reactions to the divorce. In addition to a variety of approaches to divorce by attorneys, divorce mediation, based upon the arbitration principles of the American Arbitration Association, is now available to a divorcing couple as an alternative to formal divorce court trials.[2]

Theological

There is a rather wide range of theological interpretations of divorce, which in turn depend upon one's theological and philosophical assumptions about marriage. Hobbs has summarized some of the biblical materials, although one might disagree with his suggested style of marriage.[3] Perhaps the primary Scripture passages which specifically mention divorce are Mark 10:2-12 and its parallels in Matthew 5:31-32 and 19:3-11, set in juxtaposition to Deuteronomy 24:1-4 as one test of the relation between the old Mosaic legalism and Jesus' teachings about the higher righteousness of grace and love, as applied in the context of the early Gentile Christians in the Roman Empire. Brief and insightful analyses of Jesus' teachings on marriage and the family are provided by both Branscomb and Bailey.[4]

It seems clear that the intention of Jesus regarding marriage was that the two persons are to remain together for life. In this sense marriage is considered an unconditional heterosexual union, and divorce is absolutely out of the question. Although some Christian traditions have applied this teaching literally, thus refusing to recognize divorce (except for adultery), other interpretations assume that the original purpose of Jesus' teaching was to illustrate again that human beings are already sinners who do what they want, not what God intends, and therefore salvation must come by God's grace, not by reason of the way one has lived.[5]

As a couple enters marriage, the typical Christian wedding ceremony attempts to clarify the intention of each partner to continue with the mate, regardless of the circumstances or consequences. This is clearly a commitment to continue together in the marriage without any reservations. It has the possibility of being the solid foundation upon which a couple can give and receive care and acceptability, and share, examine, and utilize, in mutual growth and fulfillment, all types of feelings, both positive and negative.

What is the theological understanding, then, of the couple who, regardless of their intentions, now after months or years of married life together are seriously considering divorce, or perhaps are divorced?

In the New Testament there is abundant emphasis upon grace, forgiveness, restoration, and the possibility of a new decision and commitment to life, available to every person. In a couple's initial approach to marriage, the emphasis is upon complete commitment to make the marriage work in the achievement of growth for both spouses as individuals and to share this fullness with others. When a couple is involved in some aspect of divorce, the changed perspective is based upon what is, not what ought to have been. There may be some marriage situations in which, given only two alternatives— continued quarreling and misery, or divorce—divorce is the better of the two decisions.

From the perspective of grace, God continues to accept the persons involved, whether they continue in the marriage, divorce, separate, or remarry. Therefore the crisis of divorce can be accepted as an opportunity for renewal, in which each participant learns anew of the pervasiveness of human sin in relation to God and the ways in which individuals are accepted by God. On the basis of God's unconditional acceptance of each person, each is then freed to examine his or her own patterns of behavior and interaction, learn from them, and utilize this information for growth and the resolving of the divorce crises in the best ways possible.

Personal

Your approach as a minister to the crisis of divorce depends partly upon your own personal experiences in your childhood family, your marriage, and your current family life-style. If neither you nor any of your relatives have ever personally experienced divorce, you may find it difficult to allow an individual whom you are counseling to make that decision. You may think the couple just has not tried hard enough to resolve the issues (since you have been successful in similar problems), or that one or both spouses now have the opportunity to escape from each other (which you at times would like to have had, were it not for being a clergyperson).

Consider your own personal feelings about divorce. Among possible emotional responses you may experience are feelings of resentment, hostility, or perhaps anxiety which the presence of divorce may elicit in you as a person. How do you really, down deep, feel about your own marriage and family? How do you personally look at divorce? To be effective in the crisis of divorce with counselees, you must examine carefully your own very personal, sometimes suppressed feelings about your own family situation.

If you have experienced divorce, either personally or through a close relative, you may bring other types of personal feelings to the divorce situation of persons with whom you work as a pastoral counselor. You may encourage an easy divorce prematurely, thus preventing the counselees from finding for themselves their own decision concerning their marriage. It may be possible that your own guilt about a divorce in your past may combine with your parishioners' divorce crisis to produce anxiety in you and prevent your functioning at maximum levels with the couple. On the other hand, having experienced a divorce and worked through the attendant feelings in a satisfactory manner, you may be more sensitive to the dilemmas and uncertainties that the divorce process can bring to individuals who seem relatively mature and stable.

Whatever your personal situation, it is important that you examine your own positive and negative thoughts and feelings concerning divorce. Only in this way can you become flexible and free to interact constructively with the individuals in a divorce crisis. The possibilities of counselee growth depend heavily upon the level of your own personal empathy, respect, genuineness, and concreteness in relation to the individuals in a divorce crisis.

Psychological

There is little if any relation between the legal grounds for divorce and the psychological dynamics that lead two mates to go their separate ways. The no-fault divorce action, stating that the marriage is "insupportable" or "not functioning well," actually reports nothing about the spouses interactions with each other. In the minority of cases in which some ground for divorce is given, it is usually mental cruelty, neglect, and indignities; neither do these reasons say much about what is actually happening in the marriage.

Often behind these stated legal grounds are financial tensions, dissatisfaction, alcoholism, adultery, or other forms of dysfunctional behavior. Underlying these conscious and rather specific reasons are motivational and emotional factors, which are expressed in these behavioral forms. The demographic, sociological, legal, theological, and personal perspectives form the context within which the psychological aspects of divorce are set.[6]

The Psychological Process of Divorce

Divorce is not a one-time decision. It is a process that begins months before the initiation of the legal process and continues far beyond the final decree. In one study of 425 couples, only about 20 percent had secured their divorce decree within 11 months or less from the time they first seriously considered the action, while over 50 percent had seriously considered divorce for one to three years prior to the granting of the decree.[7]

The process of divorce can be considered as a series of six stages, or steps. At each step the minister has unique tasks to accomplish with the persons involved. The progression is not inevitable, since at any crisis point the individuals may be able to resolve their problems and continue together.[8]

Stage One

The first step toward divorce occurs when one or both spouses have vague feelings that everything is not quite right or happy in the marriage. For some individuals this awareness itself may constitute a preliminary crisis relating to divorce. Although a spouse may not clearly identify specific instances of failure, there is a general feeling of discomfort. Initially individuals do not express these feelings but continue to hold them within themselves, thus creating secondary or additional anxiety about whether the mate knows that something is wrong. This discomfort may be related to the real but consciously suppressed expectations of parents, mate, or self.[9]

Due to these feelings of anxiety, a variety of defense reactions may occur, such as disturbances of sexual functioning or psychosomatic disorders. Some persons may return to behavior patterns that were appropriate at an earlier age (regression), refuse to talk about their feelings (withdrawal), or explain them away (rationalization). Some individuals may respond to these vague feelings with mild depression, loss of energy, sporadic bursts of work or recreational activities, or romantic interest in another person.

The minister is not likely to see many persons during this first stage of the divorce process. Those who do seek counseling will probably come with complaints that seem unrelated to any consideration of divorce. The minister can be most effective at this point by assisting the individual, or perhaps the couple, to give expression to the uneasiness and ambiguities, and thus clarify the situation. In some instances the most active step the pastor can take at this point is to make his or her counseling services available and known to these individuals. A sensitive pastor can help an individual identify and name the feelings involved and learn about options, among which divorce may be mentioned. For some parishioners, reading resources may be quite helpful.[10]

Stage Two

One spouse decides that the discrepancy between overt behavior and underlying feelings is too great to be ignored. At this point divorce as one solution may first be considered. Other possible solutions, such as changing oneself or the mate, changing jobs, residence, or other external factors may also be attempted, to reduce the apparent discrepancy between what one desires (expectations) and what seems to be happening (the perceived situation). A definite decision about divorce has not yet been made, but the individual may suggest that "things can't go on as they are."

This feeling may be expressed to the mate, or perhaps to friends or relatives or to the minister. Recent research suggests that women who consider separation are most likely to talk about it with their relatives (especially their mothers) and friends.[11] One inference from this is that church leaders can minister indirectly by training members to be able to respond in therapeutic ways to relatives and friends who talk with them about divorce.

The individual's awareness of her or his own judgment that things "cannot continue as they are" may precipitate a variety of secondary reactive feelings—guilt, panic, anxiety, anger, depression, withdrawal. If at this time the individual comes to the minister-counselor, the pastor's primary task is to allow the individual freedom to explore these basic feelings and thoughts about possible termination of the marriage, the alternatives to termination, and the secondary feelings relating to this decision.

It is at this point that the individual first begins to consider the *details* of divorce. The counselee may be asking questions: Who will have custody of the children? How can I explain the breakup to my relatives and friends? How will I support myself financially? What will others think of me? What are the relative advantages and disadvantages of divorce, as compared to the difficulty and pain of staying together? Even these questions may precipitate panic, depending upon the individual's ego strength and sense of self-sufficiency.

The person who is no longer closely tied to relatives may worry very little about their reactions, while one who has several close relatives who have divorced may almost expect that divorce is the typical way marriage ends. The woman with no job or career experience may be quite fearful that she cannot survive as a divorced person. The man whose career success and possible promotion may depend in part upon maintaining the appearance of a successful marriage (a minister, for example), may also be anxious about the negative consequences of divorce. These are the beginnings of what might be called secondary crises, which often spin off from the central divorce decision.

Stage Three

In this stage there may be superficial or genuine efforts at reconciliation by one or perhaps both spouses. One of two primary courses will develop at this point. If through marriage therapy or other aids reconciliation efforts are successful, the consideration of divorce is either eliminated, or at least pushed into the background as long as things continue to improve between the spouses. If efforts toward marriage improvement are not successful, then the decision to divorce becomes clearer and more definite, with both spouses aware of the decision. Typically, the decision is then announced to close friends and relatives, and to the minister.

The action the minister takes at this step will depend upon his or her relation to the couple and upon the type of reconciliation efforts they are making. If the minister hears of their decision from others but not from the persons involved, then as one aspect of active pastoral care, she or he may approach one or both spouses with an expression of concern and an offer of the availability of counseling. For example, in a visit to one or both spouses, the pastor may say, "I have heard that you are considering divorce. For most persons, this is a difficult time. I do not assume that you should either stay married or divorce, but I am available for you to discuss with me any matters that might help you arrive at a satisfying solution. If you prefer, I can suggest other counselors who could also provide an opportunity for you to explore the issues without telling you what you should do.

That will be your decision." If one or both individuals accept the pastor's invitation, then the situation becomes one in which the pastor has been told of the decision.

When individuals come to the minister to discuss divorce, general principles of counseling are basic. If a couple is sufficiently motivated to attempt reconciliation efforts, then the situation develops into a marriage counseling process, requiring specialized skills. If these efforts to improve the marriage are successful, then divorce is avoided, and the marriage may become a successful one. Many helpful references for the minister are available.[12]

If divorce seems to be the most satisfactory solution to marriage difficulties, then it is important for the minister to accept the freedom of the spouses to make this decision, without in any way condemning or otherwise rejecting them for it. It is assumed that at some point in the process the minister and the person or persons have discussed whatever problems or questions may have arisen, in light of the relevant biblical passages and/or Christian tradition. The pastor may now assist in confronting the crisis aspects of the divorce. As in premarital counseling, predivorce counseling should enable the spouse or spouses to (1) express feelings of ambivalence and hostility which may surround the decision; (2) separate real from imagined or misinformed problems; and (3) find solutions to practical problems relating to the divorce decision.

Decisions on some of these practical issues—when the individuals intend to separate (if still together), how family income and property will be divided, who will care for children, how living arrangements will be changed—may be final, and others may be temporary with further review at a later time, usually after the divorce becomes final.

There is also the matter of the legal aspects of divorce. The minister's predivorce counseling will focus upon the individuals' feelings and upon securing appropriate expert help in areas that are not within his or her own competence. Legal technicalities are properly the responsibility of an attorney, but the minister may provide assistance in securing qualified counsel for questions and information.

Stage Four

After the decision to divorce, an attorney is contacted and legal proceedings begun. During this interim of several weeks or months between initiation of the legal process and the final decree, usually one or both parties continue to examine further their personal reasons for divorce and plan for postdivorce arrangements.

In many areas it is now possible to find attorneys with marriage and family counseling training who will work with both spouses in a no-fault (or equivalent) divorce action. This will usually reduce the expense and can aid the couple in making mutually acceptable decisions about divorce arrangements. In cases where spouses still have unresolved conflicts, divorce mediation and arbitration is increasingly a helpful alternative to an adversarial court trial.

Some spouses may entertain hope that a last minute breakthrough may occur, making the divorce unnecessary. During this time the first impact of the reality and finality of divorce will strike the individuals involved. The pastor needs at least to remain in contact with both spouses, and with the children, in order to provide the opportunity to express these anxieties and to discuss other matters relating to the action. Some persons will experience a major crisis when they recognize the reality of the divorce action.

If the pastor is sought for counseling, the basic principles of crisis counseling will apply. The pastor can explore the following issues (clarification is important): What resources and strengths does each individual have? What hidden feelings and anxieties have been brought into consciousness as a result of anticipating divorce? What current conflicts and perhaps bitterness are developing between the spouses? Regardless of the date for the legal termination of the marriage, the psychological divorce usually occurs earlier and precipitates the need to work through feelings of rejection, depression, anxiety, guilt, hostility, loss of self-esteem, and perhaps increased meaninglessness of life.

In other instances, however, the psychological divorce may bring feelings of relief, renewal, and increased self-esteem as a person experiences release from a miserable or intolerable marriage situation. These may be an individual's primary responses, but sometimes they may be a defensive denial of the reality of the loss.

In most persons a mixture of pain and relief will result from this psychological realization. Even if all details of postdivorce plans seem appropriate and in order, crisis aspects may emerge. Dependency needs of the individual may increase, which means that person may want the pastor to be available at any time to do special favors. Without unwittingly becoming caught in this web, the pastor can be available to the individuals to provide steady support in the inner reorientation process of subjective acceptance of the divorce.

Stage Five

In this stage, the final divorce decree has been granted by the court. In some states and in some cases, an interlocutory (temporary) decree provides a waiting period before the divorced persons may remarry. As part of this decree, postdivorce living arrangements, income distribution, property settlements and related conditions become final.

Although the change of status from married to divorced is commonly considered effective as of this date, its psychological meaning depends upon the extent to which the individuals have become emotionally divorced before the issuance of the final decree. If they have worked through the crisis of psychological divorce itself, as described in stage four, then the next step (stage six) of readjustment to being single begins immediately. If the psychological reality first strikes an individual with the final formal decree, then the crisis intervention and counseling work described in stage four should be done at this time, before the individuals can begin the readjustment phase.

Stage Six

After divorce, the initial period of adjustment to being single again must be faced. This may have begun earlier, but often may have been prevented by legal complexities. In a contested divorce, the spouse who is seeking the divorce may have had to live in a carefully prescribed manner to avoid giving possible evidence to the accusing mate that would prevent the divorce action. In other instances, the individuals may have assumed they were already single again and could begin dating before the divorce was complete and final. The actual date of the decree may make little additional change in their daily routines. In every case, however, there will be adjustments to new living conditions, possible renewed dating, and other changes that result from a divorce.

Try as one may, there is no way an individual can return to the same type of single status that existed prior to marriage. Even if all legal and community distinctions were eliminated, the divorced person is psychologically in a different situation from the single, married, or widowed person. The readjustments will typically take the form of either bereavement and grief processes or feelings of genuine relief from tensions, although both these trends may be present in the same individual. Overtones of these feelings will continue throughout life, although the primary divorce readjustment will typically require approximately one to three years.

The exact combination of feelings about postdivorce adjustments will depend upon an individual's perception and evaluation of the marriage situation. If the marriage was filled with tension, uncertainty, fear, and other hurtful (ego-deflating) feelings, the postdivorce adjustment period will probably be seen as a welcome relief and an opportunity to begin living again. Even with this more positive view, a person may still seek to understand what went wrong in the marriage, to what extent he or she contributed to the problems, and how to avoid another similar situation. The return to dating may also bring feelings of uncertainty and intensified caution, to avoid becoming enmeshed in another painful relationship.

Probably most persons with this positive evaluation of their divorce will be unlikely to seek counseling. In those instances when these persons do seek counseling, the primary focus will probably be upon the actual adjustment to current situations in the context of having had an unhappy marriage experience.

Among helpful questions to consider are these: To what extent does the individual realize that the miserable marriage was a product of the two persons' interactions? In what ways is the individual now changing behavior patterns in order to attract a different type person, if remarriage is the goal? With what groups does the individual associate? Are these groups likely to provide wholesome and genuine sources of self-esteem for the individual? What generalized attitudes toward men and women does the individual have that may distort his or her perspective concerning involvement with the other sex? These and related specialized areas need to be explored as part of the readjustment counseling.

At some point there must be a fully conscious psychological acceptance of the reality of the changes related to divorce. In some persons, this occurs before the divorce decree; in others, within the first few months afterward; in still others, several months later. If not before or soon after the decree, the individual who seems overly accepting, elated, and unrealistically happy (euphoric) about the new freedom may be covering up (suppressing) painful feelings. The facing of these deeper feelings may be prevented if the individual should remarry shortly after divorce. Individuals who experience the deeper shocks of divorce several months after the decree may have had difficulty in meeting new friends, resolving financial problems, or handling other aspects of the postdivorce life-style.

In some individuals, the delayed impact of the crisis may precipitate more serious defensive patterns. Some persons may begin to act as they did at earlier stages of life, responding in ways that would have been appropriate then, but now are not (regression). These might include inappropriate humor or giddiness, disorganized planning, treating the pastor as a parent, and expecting others to take all the responsibility for any unpleasant situation that arises. Other persons may act out sexual or aggressive feelings. For example, a woman may dress and talk seductively in her contacts with a male pastor, or a man may become angry at the pastor for supposed minor injustices or failures. Depression is another way in which individuals may respond to the crisis. Usually depression is hostility turned inward because the individual is afraid to express it openly toward the original target of the anger. In other instances, individuals may displace hostility by becoming angry with an innocent person. For example, persons may exhibit hostile behavior toward a child who in some way reminds them of the ex-mate with whom they are angry, but toward whom they cannot express that anger directly.

Frequently, grief processes will be a part of the postdivorce adjustment. These may follow typical patterns, the major difference being that the mate is lost, but not actually gone. The ex-spouses may continue to see each other because of visitation rights for children, financial involvements, mutual friends, or even accidental meeting.

The spouse who did not want the marriage to end may feel considerable hostility toward the ex-mate, and the ex-mate's friends and possible romantic acquaintances. This hostility may often be displaced onto others (family, children, friends) or turned inward to appear in the form of guilt and depression. One task in the counseling situation is to allow the individual to acknowledge this hostility and dispose of it in a healthy manner through forgiveness, through changing the situation, and through changing his or her own self-evaluation.

Grief in divorce results from the sense of losing a very valuable and important person in one's life. To compound the grief further, the loss was not due to physical death. Physical death often is interpreted to mean that there was really nothing more the surviving spouse could have done to prevent the loss. If the divorce is interpreted by the individual in this way—that is, as a real event that cannot be changed in any way (thus that the divorce is as final as death)—then grief over the loss may be expressed and the loss acknowledged openly. The individual can then move on to reconstruct life from this point. To the extent that a person interprets the divorce as inevitable, the pastor would only be stirring up trouble unnecessarily if she or he sought to change this interpretation (though the minister may not consider any divorce to be inevitable).

The most difficult grief, however, is the situation in which the bereaved person continues to have unrealistic hope that the loss is not final, that the ex-spouse will return. Thus the individual's unresolved dependency needs may lead to continuous neurotic attempts to entice, harass, cajole, or otherwise seek the return of the ex-spouse. Another form of this grief may occur in the individual's effort to find a new spouse who is either identical to or quite the opposite of the former mate. In either instance, the adjustment behavior is being controlled by unresolved grief relating to the lost partner.

If the individual at this point comes for counseling, the task is to assist the person to identify these hostility and grief reactions and to examine how they are related to loss situations that happened to the person earlier (such as moving away from a childhood home, loss of relatives, failure at one's job or education or other goals). In this way the painful edge of the crisis is blunted and the individual can then proceed toward more realistic postdivorce adjustments.

If a divorcing person displays these grief reactions, yet does not come for counseling, the minister may take the initiative through a pastoral contact of some type. For example, the possibility of counseling may be suggested: "It has been several weeks (or months) since your divorce. This is sometimes the most difficult time, since others probably assume you are no longer bothered by it or that you do not want to discuss it. You may even feel confused about what your real feelings were then and are now. Sometimes it helps to discuss these with someone who can allow you to explore all that is going on. I wonder if you might like to talk about how things are going now."

Allowing at least a year for the postdivorce adjustment permits an individual to go through the cycle of important annual markers, such as the birthday of the ex-spouse, the wedding date, the birthdays of children, holidays, and other times which typically carry a considerable emotional load. The first time each of these dates occurs, an ex-partner is likely to engage in a process of remembering what it was like on this day a few years ago. Through this recalling and talking about each event, a person can emotionally disengage from the former marriage.

We have examined in detail the sequence of processes from the first consideration of divorce through the postdivorce period. In most individuals, this process will cover approximately two to four years. One or several crisis points will occur during this lengthy span of change, and at each of these points the pastor-counselor has specific tasks.

Divorce Crises

The six stages outlined here could be condensed into fewer or expanded into more, since they are merely guideposts along the road of becoming disengaged from another with whom one has been extensively involved in many complex and pervasive ways. In this process there are at least three major crises.

1. The crisis relating to the process of making a decision about divorce (stages one, two, and sometimes three above). This is a crisis because it usually involves a radical shift in one's self-concept, major changes in living arrangements, and affects one's acceptability with most of the significant persons in one's life. For example, one young man was very upset because he was the only person in his family whose marriage had ended in divorce. As a result he was deeply disturbed, the root cause being the shattering of his own self-concept and the feeling of having disgraced the family.

2. The crisis of the divorce process itself (stages four and five). If the feelings between the divorcing spouses are mutually cordial and if no legal contest occurs, this crisis may be the least difficult of the three. On the other hand, if the spouses engage in the legal charges and countercharges of a contested divorce, this crisis may assume major proportions, possibly generating secondary crises involving loss of self-esteem, anxiety, anger, and possibly threats of physical harm. In this situation, the pastor will at times be supportive, at other times try to enable both partners to consider the effects of the battle on all concerned, and sometimes seek to place the current conflict in the longer-time perspective of adjustment to the changes that are occurring.

3. The crisis of postdivorce adjustment (stage six, although it may begin in stage four). This includes the readjustment to physical separation, moving personal items and clothes (and perhaps furniture) out of what one thought of as "home," changes in daily

routines, sometimes much idle time, and other aspects of readjustment to living either alone or with relatives or friends. This also may precipitate secondary crises, such as failure of one of the ex-spouses to keep promises made as part of the divorce agreement, reentry into dating or other singles activities, relationships with friends who are still married, family pressures, financial needs, care of children, and other potential problems.

The Minister's Role

Now that we have traced the process of divorce, it is important to emphasize the pastor's role in these crises. Although objective events may appear to be similar when the pastor compares two or more couples, the focus in divorce counseling is upon the meaning of these events for the individuals concerned. Crises in the divorce process occur when the spouses interpret the events as overwhelming and beyond their control in some way. The pastor's task is to assist them to distinguish clearly among the confused meanings and organize their personal resources to respond constructively to the divorce situation.

The pastor's role as counselor in this situation is to assist the individuals to discover and articulate personal meanings of divorce. Is divorce forbidden among a person's relatives, or is it perhaps almost expected? Does the divorce trigger earlier feelings of rejection by or alienation from parents? Is the divorce an ineffective effort to return to adolescence or possibly childhood? Does the individual feel that God and/or the church will reject him or her because of divorce? These and related feelings of failure and rejection may be a central theme in the divorce crisis.

The pastor must be prepared to let the individuals examine any personal feelings of being in a double-bind situation. Since at deep levels the individual has sought acceptance in marriage, perhaps even fleeing from other friendships, the person may feel unable to please the mate but cannot live without the mate, either. How realistic is this interpretation? Are there sources for friendship and support other than the marriage? Is the pattern of "damned if I do, damned if I don't" related only to the marital partner, or is it generalized, in other situations as well? Does it have its roots in the individual's childhood? With sufficient training in pastoral counseling, the pastor may provide limited counseling in these areas. When it becomes obvious that the divorce is only one symptom of some type of personality inadequacy or conflict, the minister may consider securing consultation or referring the individual to another professional who is more qualified and has the time to work with a longer-standing personality problem.

If the individual feels rejected by the mate, there probably will be a grief process similar to that which occurs in the loss of a loved one by death. In this situation, typical grief reactions may occur. These include (1) initial shock and disbelief that divorce could "happen to me." This may result in futile attempts to ignore, repress, or reject the reality of divorce. (2) A crisis situation follows, in which the individual frantically seeks help from any source in correcting the situation or in adjusting to the "news" of the divorce. (3) A period of generalized passive acceptance may follow, in which the reality and inevitability of divorce comes home to the individual. This may occur two to six months after the initial announcement by the mate of an intention to divorce. This phase may also be accompanied by depression, hostility, and/or counteraggressive moves toward the "offending, rejecting" spouse. (4) A period of readjustment during which the individual is able to reorganize the ego resources to cope more constructively with the divorce and the resulting changes in life-style. This readjustment may include neurotic defenses as well as coping mechanisms, and its success will depend heavily on the development of healthy coping processes.

The minister's role in this process depends on the point at which she or he first comes in contact with the individual. If at reaction "1," the minister will need to provide stable support to let the person know there are others who will stand with him or her in receiving the shock of the mate's desire for a divorce. Allowing the counselee to repeat the unbelievability of the divorce request will help the person accept the reality of the situation.

The minister who enters the scene at "2" may represent one of the resources to which the person facing divorce can turn in the crisis. The minister may also need to remind the individual of genuine personal resources and strengths which the counselee actually does possess in order to confront the divorce crisis. In addition, the minister may assist the individual to secure legal or other resources that may be necessary in the divorce proceedings.

In "3" and "4," the situation is often such that no genuine reconciliation efforts are possible. If the other spouse refuses to participate in counseling or other adjustment efforts, or if other conditions make divorce the only constructive solution to an intolerable situation, the minister may need to help the individual understand the attitudes of the church and other significant groups concerning divorce. From the church's perspective, divorce is not a reason for excluding a person, but rather an admission that the marriage is no longer viable, and its termination seems to be the least harmful solution. At every point the minister must convey to the persons that they, by God's grace, continue to be just as acceptable now as formerly and that possibilities for new life can come out of the ashes of a destroyed marriage.

In contrast, the individual who feels relief and satisfaction as a result of a divorce will face psychological adjustments of a different type (see stage six above). Typically, they occur in sequence: (1) Initial relief at being away from what was perceived as an intolerable situation. This may express itself in a refusal to date others, an attitude that the mate never really understood "my" feelings, or perhaps a flight into much dating and many other activities. (2) This may be followed by a growing attitude that it was primarily the mate's fault that the marriage did not succeed. The most serious consequence of this attitude may be that the individual becomes convinced that he or she was "right" and that there is no need to make any changes in his or her own style of living and/or personality. (3) The person who lacks insight into the dynamics of the divorce process may seek either a mate who is totally opposite from the first mate, or one who interacts in the same manner as the first.

The minister's task in counseling with this second type of reaction to divorce is, again, to enable the individual to separate fact from fantasy. Was the marriage situation actually a very painful experience? In what way? To what extent was the divorce precipitated by the individual who now considers everything to have been the ex-spouse's fault? How accurate is the counselee's insight into the real reasons for divorce? Is the individual able to benefit from these insights and make changes in behavior to improve chances for relating more constructively with another person? Does the individual have any plans for remarriage? If within a year of the divorce, is it probable that remarriage is, in part, a reaction to feeling unhappy in being divorced, rather than a genuinely healthy acceptance of the new mate? These are issues the individual needs to consider. The pastor, of course, will not present the questions in the form outlined here, but must be aware of these issues and allow, even at times encourage the counselee to face them.

Some divorced persons may experience a variety of guilt reactions, expressed as "If only I had done differently . . . " or "It was all my fault." There is also the problem of aligning the divorce situation with one's original marriage vow, "Till death us do part." This vow is a statement of the intention of the individuals at the time they enter marriage. In the face of divorce, one must now decide whether the original intention was well-founded and whether in some way one has gone back on that promise. At deeper levels, it may be a way of asking whether one is still acceptable to family, friends, and others. Both psychologically and religiously, guilt must be resolved through forgiveness and a renewed acceptance of the individual by significant persons in his or her life.

When guilt reactions occur, the minister can be a channel of this forgiveness and renewal through the counseling process. The pastor can also assist the individual to become involved in appropriate group relationships that will confirm his or her acceptability as a divorced person. At deeper levels, the minister may assist the person to explore theological issues of marriage and divorce, perceived failure and guilt, and God's forgiveness. This is appropriate as part of the broader counseling process, although the pastor must be careful that this intellectual discussion is not used as a way of avoiding painful emotional feelings.

Divorce often results partly from changes in status in the life of one or both spouses. Many divorces begin in the first year of marriage—this is a period of rapid adjustment to the major change from single to married life. Other critical periods are the arrival of the first child (thus forming additional triangles and two-against-one situations); a spouse's graduation from university or other educational programs; establishing of a spouse in a job, business or profession; a change to different duties in a job; major financial adjustments or reversals; loss of a job or career status; moving to a new community; anticipation of middle age; death of close relatives or friends; opportunities for becoming involved in an extramarital affair; and major changes in relationships with family members and friends. None of these is actually the basic reason for divorce, but in each situation, underlying inadequate adjustments may be exposed by the added stress of a crisis in the life of one or both mates, thus leading to the additional crises of divorce.

In counseling with an individual for whom a major life change has precipitated consideration of divorce, the central task is to enable the person to clarify the sources of stress and identify the threats involved. Once this occurs, the person can be assisted to find more constructive ways to handle the original crisis. In addition, both spouses may be helped to discover how essential support, comfort, and care can be given to the one who is under stress. If this does not occur, then the counselee needs the aid of the pastor in making realistic plans to resolve each crisis—first the precipitating event and then the divorce.

Divorce is usually a more or less permanent separation. Although it is possible that former spouses can sometimes shift into a stable acquaintance or friendship pattern, it is very unlikely that this will occur. The circumstances of divorce usually can be handled much more simply and adequately if the parties involved consider the divorce to be a permanent and absolute severance of any relation whatsoever. It is not too extreme to suggest that divorce should be as complete and permanent as the death of a spouse. However, practical problems of child support or property may force ex-mates to continue contact with each other, hopefully on a cooperative basis, for the care of their children or in order to maintain child support or alimony payments. If a couple decides to terminate their marriage, then it should be a clean and complete break.

In the planning and anticipation of the postdivorce adjustment, the pastor has the opportunity to assist the individuals in clarifying any lingering hope or dependency needs in relation to the ex-spouse. If an individual hopes to continue on a friendly basis with the former mate, the pastor should gently confront the individual with the meaning of these relationships. Is continuing to see the ex-mate a result of guilt about the divorce, a way of "fixing" or undoing an undesirable divorce? Is it a diffused hostility toward the other partner, being expressed in subtle comments, depreciating comparisons, or a flaunting of the individual's "better" life now that the divorce is over? Is it related to dependency and anxiety about being left alone or being unable to succeed in any new relationships with the other sex? Is it a way of continuing to use the ex-mate after divorce?

In some postdivorce situations, the person may feel especially vulnerable emotionally and harbor a hidden fear of being left alone. This may cause the individual to avoid any further contacts with the other sex, to reject her or his own sexuality, or to be very defensive in relation to potential future mates. More severe psychological reactions may trigger a variety of acting-out behaviors calculated to secure attention, while at the same time punishing the attender.

The pastor has an opportunity to assist the divorced person to feel accepted through the pastor's own contacts, as well as by enabling each individual to become involved in appropriate support groups. A variety of divorce adjustment groups are available in many larger communities.[13]

The minister can also guide mature lay people in the church or community to initiate friendships with divorced persons to let them know they are still wanted and desirable as persons for whom God and the church cares. There is the possibility also that other persons who have successfully readjusted to their own divorces may be enlisted, under the minister's guidance, to maintain friendships with newly divorced persons. In this relation of empathetic sharing, the person adjusting to divorce may be able to receive support from others who have gone through similar experiences, and may also be able to talk more freely about personal feelings surrounding the divorce. In some churches, church school classes and other groups, which typically include many divorced persons, may be organized especially for single adults. Traditional couples' classes might be sensitized to the need to reach out to divorced persons in helping them feel accepted. Sometimes the minister may enlist the divorced person in volunteer activities in the church or community as part of the readjustment process.

Regardless of the circumstances of the divorce, each partner will need some postdivorce counseling. Some writers even suggest a formal ceremony of "uncoupling," somewhat parallel to the wedding ceremony in its psychological function of having the community acknowledge and accept the new status of the divorced person. Since divorced persons are in considerably different psychological circumstances from those who have never married, the minister can be available through counseling to help them find their way in this new life situation, which is different in several respects from either single, married, or widowed life-styles.[14]

As has been described in earlier chapters, the general format of crisis counseling by the minister consists of short-term contact with an individual experiencing major acute life changes that tend to overwhelm the person's typical coping patterns. Since the process of divorce extends over a period of time—from at least one year to perhaps several years—it should not be inferred that this constitutes one long, almost chronic crisis (a contradiction in terms). Instead, there are at least three rather specific and separate crises that typically occur during this period. These were described above as the crisis of deciding about divorce, the potential crisis of the actual legal actions necessitated by the divorce decision, and the crisis of postdivorce adjustment. The concepts, procedures, and suggestions of this chapter must be understood as based upon the fundamental principles of crisis intervention and counseling, as well as placed in the context of both an individual's life history and the family dynamics he or she has experienced in both the childhood family and the adult marriage.

With this interrelationship in mind, we will briefly consider five situations which are closely related to the crises of divorce: desertion, children of divorce, remarriage, multiple divorce, and annulment.

Desertion

Desertion has often been termed the poor person's divorce. Except for the legal aspects, desertion is very similar to divorce in its psychological dynamics. There is a period when the deserting mate first begins to consider this action as a possible solution to an unhappy marriage. He or she may not announce this impending absence, which creates for the deserted mate an ambiguous situation, in that the spouse does not know whether to expect the partner's return. As a result, the remaining spouse may be left with unpaid bills, children to support, little or no income, and other serious problems in addition to the basic crisis of shock, loss of self-esteem, and related psychological damage from the desertion itself.

The pain and problems of desertion are often compounded because it is likely to happen to persons who have less than average personal and psychological coping ability to meet a situation that is more difficult and ambiguous than a clearcut divorce. The pastor of a deserted person will need, first, to be sure that basic necessities such as food, housing, and daily needs—of that person and usually of children—are met.

Once the daily needs are stabilized, the pastor can begin the counseling intervention described above under stages two, three, and four. In addition, there is the important task of helping the remaining spouse clarify and work through the feelings of sudden rejection, loneliness, and anger. In this process the minister may also enable the spouse to identify any of his or her own behavior that may have helped to cause the desertion. Efforts at reconciliation may also be appropriate. If the deserting party can be located, the pastor may initiate contacts to help that person work through personal feelings about the remaining spouse, as well as discover constructive ways of either rebuilding the marriage or making a clear divorce decision. If financial expense is a problem, the pastor can assist in locating inexpensive legal clinics for the parties as needed.

Children of Divorce

When children are involved in a divorce, the divorcing partners are usually very concerned with the impact upon them. There are several decisions to be made: which mate will have custody and daily responsibility for the children, the extent and schedule of visits (if any) with the other parent, provision of child support, and many practical matters. In addition, the divorcing mates usually wonder what to tell the children about the divorce and how having only one parent present will affect the children's development.

The effect of divorce on children is a very broad topic, which can be mentioned only briefly here. Each year in the United States, about one percent of all children under eighteen years of age experience the divorce of their parents; approximately 10 percent of white and 35 percent of nonwhite groups are not living with both parents. Estimates are that between one-third and one-half of all children will spend some of their childhood years in a one-parent family situation, usually the result of divorce. It now appears that most children experience acute feelings of anger, anxiety, and conflict during the first year or two after their parents' divorce, and negative impacts continue for at least two to five years afterward.[15]

Perhaps the central task of the pastor is to enable the parents to examine their own feelings about the children in relation to the divorce. Does the divorced person blame the children for the marriage breakdown? Is there an attempt to overcompensate in subtle ways for the child's having only one parent? Does the parent feel, perhaps without acknowledging it, that she or he really did want to eliminate the influence, and hence the threat, of the mate on the children's lives? Does the remaining mate feel adequate to the task of parenting?

The pastor may assist the parent to discuss, and possibly role-play difficult situations relating to the divorce. The parent must be aided to be both supportive and honest in answering their children's questions. For example, if the child asks, "Why don't you and (Daddy/Mommy) live together so we can all be happy?" the parent might answer, "I love you and will continue to be with you, and (Daddy/Mommy) loves you also. We just could not seem to work together, like you and (name of a child) sometimes have difficulty playing. We felt we could all be happier as we are now than if we had stayed together and fussed with each other all the time." It is important that the answer convey to the child that the parents are still definitely dependable and available (according to the circumstances of the divorce), that the child is sincerely loved, and that as much as possible, the child will have a normal childhood.

At a deeper level, the child really has, in a sense, four "parents." These are, of course, the father and the mother, and in addition, the mother as presented and described by the father and the father as presented and described by the mother. Even if one parent is now gone, the child continues to have both the remaining parent and the "other parent as interpreted by this parent to the child." What, then, are the feelings of the remaining parent toward the divorced spouse? What can he or she reply to the child and still be honest?

The pastor can provide opportunities for the divorced parent to consider these deeper feelings, their impact on the children, and specific ways in which to convey the most constructive interpretations of the situation. In this way the pastor can assist the individual to avoid or resolve the crisis of relating to the children as being in some way responsible for the partial loss of their other parent.

The pastor needs to be alert to the stresses and possible crises which the children in a divorce situation may experience directly. There are a variety of ways in which children may express their feelings of crisis, depending upon their ages. Preschool children may experience restlessness; bad dreams; intensified fears of being left alone in church school, day nursery, or other situations; and related changes of mood. Older children may demonstrate crisis feelings by failing to do as well in school as formerly, moodiness, enuresis, acting-out, increased health problems, nailbiting, bursts of inappropriate anger, and noncooperativeness. Adolescents may be overtly rebellious or aggressive, withdraw from former friends or activities, use alcohol or other drugs, or become overly involved in romantic affairs. These and other behaviors are ways the children of divorced parents usually communicate anxiety, anger, and shock.

Noting such unusual behavior in children and adolescents in a divorce situation, the pastor may take the initiative in discussing these changes with the parent in counseling or pastoral care contacts. The pastor may also initiate counseling directly with older children and adolescents. Sometimes a family counseling situation may develop. In other situations, the pastor may need to suggest referral to an appropriate professional, a psychologist or psychiatrist. Usually the pastor can discuss with one or both parents the possibility of a crisis impact on the children so that they too can be alert for these signs of excessive stress.

Helpful suggestions concerning children of divorce are available.[16] Much depends upon the quality of both spouses' parenting skills and their commitment to continuing parenting relationships with each child. It now appears that parental divorce permanently affects children in many ways. Some children may reach the same levels of emotional and personal maturity that they would have reached anyway, but even then the scars of loss seem never to heal completely. With increasing awareness of the influences of one's family of origin, it is easy to see that divorce and the events that follow will have great influence on the children in their own adult lives.

Often overlooked are the adult children of divorcing and recently divorced parents. It has often been unthinkingly assumed that their parents' behavior has little or no impact upon them. Quite the opposite seems to be true. There are a number of ways in which these grown children's psychological equilibrium is adversely affected. Anxiety, anger, guilt, the loss of "home," feeling caught in the middle and not knowing how to handle this difficult and uncomfortable situation—these and other reactions may be a part of their response. The sensitive minister will not overlook opportunities to call on these persons to offer pastoral services.

Remarriage

Most divorced persons eventually remarry. If the remarriage of a divorced person occurs after that period of time which allows for adequate readjustment and recovery (usually a year or more), the pastor will utilize the basic premarital counseling approaches. The major changes involve the careful consideration by the two potential mates of their feelings about the previous marriage. How will the anticipated marriage be different from previous unsuccessful ones? What was learned that will enable this marriage to be happier and more successful?

Other areas that will probably be modified in premarital counseling with divorced persons include a discussion of relationships of the new parent to the former parent, who may still be visiting the children, and the combining of two families, if both partners have children from a previous marriage. If one partner has children but the other does not, the childless partner must adjust to a ready-made family in which the children may have ties with the absent original parent. Matters of living arrangements are also involved, since the new mate may be "invading" the home of the children and be seen by them as an interloper. The pastor, through premarital counseling sessions, can allow consideration of and help to defuse these problems that are unique to the remarriage situation.[17]

Multiple Divorce

In some instances the pastor may be confronted with individuals who are terminating a second unsatisfactory marriage, or even a third or fourth. The basic divorce process and crises are still likely to be present. In addition, however, there is the possibility that a second divorce may indicate more severe personality maladjustments, which prevent the individual from living intimately with another person for an extended period of time. If the pastor suspects this, a referral to a psychologist or psychiatrist for a personality assessment may be important at some point to clarify whether crisis counseling by the pastor is the most appropriate primary therapeutic intervention. This does not diminish the need for pastoral care of such persons, since they continue to face the crises of divorce, sometimes in greater severity. The person's greater sense of failure and inadequacy may be expressed in statements such as "Anybody can make a mistake once, but if twice or more, there must be something seriously wrong with me."

With a second divorce, the chance of a successful third marriage drops to less than 40 percent. With multiple-divorce persons, the additional task of the pastor is to determine how much of the person's troubled behavior results from crisis and how much is due to long-standing inadequate personality and coping processes.

Annulment

The process of annulment is similar to that of divorce, since in many cases annulment is only a technical legal term for divorce. The three basic stages of decision, legal proceedings, and postannulment adjustment crises are very likely to be present in the person who is terminating marriage in this manner. In addition, since annulment is likely to involve younger (often teenage) mates, the pastor may need to deal with additional crises involving one or both mates and one or both sets of their parents or other relatives.

Annulment may also indicate a marriage that was hasty, ill-considered, or in reaction to parental pressures; thus it is likely that the pastor will have the further task of assisting reconciliation or adjustments between the child whose marriage is annulled and his or her parents. Here principles of family dynamics and counseling are central, in addition to crisis intervention skills.

Summary

In applying the principles of crisis intervention to the divorce process, the pastor's basic step is to clarify his or her own understanding of divorce in our society—as a legal procedure, from a theological and philosophical perspective, and in the pastor's own personal experience.

The three basic crisis situations of divorce—decision about divorce, legal procedures and other changes relative to the actual divorce decree, and postdivorce adjustment—are high-visibility points of the total divorce process, which may extend over a period of at least one or two years, usually three or four years, and in some cases a much longer span of time. As an aid to the details of this process and the pastor's opportunities for ministry, six stages of this total sequence have been described. The minister, of course, needs to keep in mind that these stages actually may overlap, merge, or be skipped in a specific divorce situation.

CHAPTER 9

INTERVENING IN THE SUICIDAL CRISIS

M ost ministers do not often become involved in helping a highly suicidal person. Nevertheless, in every community and congregation are numerous persons who periodically have suicidal thoughts and/or impulses with varying degrees of intensity. Most often these recurring thoughts and feelings arise as the result of depression or in a severe situational crisis. Ministers are not more often engaged in working with people in regard to this potent aspect of their lives because of some collusion between the persons and the ministers. Many people are ashamed of or feel guilty about their suicidal thoughts or feelings and therefore hide them from their ministers (and from many other persons as well, for that matter). On the other hand, many ministers are afraid to ask people directly whether such thoughts and impulses are a part of their depression or crisis experience.

The appearance of Paul W. Pretzel's *Understanding and Counseling the Suicidal Person* (Abingdon Press, 1972) was the first comprehensive and competent book by a minister, designed for clergy and providing material to assist them in doing exactly what the title suggests. Other useful books for clergy appeared at about the same time.[1] It looked as if clergy involvement with suicidal persons might increase and ministers would continue to have available material that could lead to greater effectiveness. Unfortunately, the publication of such books abruptly stopped. This is not to say that there are no written resources. In fact, there is a great deal of material—books, specialized journals, articles in other journals—but these do not usually come to the attention of ministers. Excellent chapters in pastoral-care books have occasionally appeared, but these have been far too infrequent.[2]

Suicide and the Clergy: Opportunity and Problem

The word *suicide* as used here refers to death as a result of one's intention to kill oneself, for some presumed benefit to one's self. It does not include martyrdom or accidental death in high-risk situations or poor health care or heroism in war.

The subject of this book requires a focus on working with persons' suicidal feelings in the context of situational crisis. Slaikeu comments on the fact that "most people are suicidal for only a short period of time, usually a matter of days, and often change their minds about killing themselves; crisis intervention aims at getting people to postpone irreversible decisions until other help may be brought to bear on the situation."[3]

Just as in any situational crisis, the clergy are in a unique position to be of significant help to large numbers of severely distressed people, for the reasons given earlier in this book: visibility, availability, mobility, flexibility of procedure, prior relationships with many, the custom of pastoral initiative, and the resources of faith and the community of faith. How tragic, then, that so many people who are dealing with some of the most powerful feelings of despair in human life, who are facing the ultimate issue of life and death itself, do not call upon us with the frequency with which they seek our assistance in many other crises. Lives could be saved; severe crises might be resolved more quickly and with less suffering.

It might be important to look in more detail at the collusion between clergy and other persons in the failure to talk about suicide. What are the feelings and attitudes that we as persons and ministers have about people killing themselves? What do we communicate about our attitudes by our behavior, words, silence? What view do others have of us and the church, regardless of our own actual personal feelings and attitudes?

First, to the extent that we have anxiety about any death, our own death in particular, and such anxiety is repressed or denied or otherwise distorts our relationship with persons in many situations, the same would be true in regard to suicide.

Second, such a response tends to be even more intense when the death is by suicide. In fact, relatively few people have been to the funeral of a person whose death was by suicide, but my personal experience and reports from others indicate that there are too many of these funerals during which either no reference at all is made to the mode of death (silence about suicide) or the minister exhibits anxiety or anger about the mode of death in other ways. These occasions are reflections of the feelings of the ministers, feelings of fear or even dread. Such ministerial behavior communicates very clearly that suicide is still a taboo topic. A person is "wrong" to have these thoughts and feelings; such a person will be condemned by the minister; the minister cannot handle it emotionally.

Third, during several centuries of the church's history, it very clearly forbade suicide and its response to suicide was quite vindictive. Certain forms of worship would not be held as a funeral; burial in the church cemetery was denied. Major church leaders wrote and spoke very vehemently in support of these and even more radical practices such as public desecration of the body.[4] Far too much of this image of the church, if not its actual practice, remains in the thinking of many.

Fourth, some ministers and other Christians do believe sincerely that suicide is morally wrong, that under all circumstances it is sin, and that the person is eternally condemned. To the extent that this is believed by a pastor, or that someone thinks that it is, would a suicidal person talk with that minister? Very likely not.

The complexities of the ethics in regard to suicide are far too many to be discussed here, as are the issues with regard to whether it is a sin, or whether it may be at some times and may not be at others. It is very important, though, for any minister to recognize that the issue is not resolved by clear biblical commandment, since the seven suicides recorded in the Bible contain no additional word of moral judgment one way or another (Judg. 9:54, 16:30; I Sam. 31:4, 5; II Sam. 17:23; I Kings 16:18; I Chron. 10:4, 5; Matt. 27:5.) The commandment "Thou shalt not kill" is so obviously limited in its application (in its particular context not applying to war, capital punishment, the protection of one's self and others) that it could not have been intended to apply to suicide. The biblical contribution to ethical judgments concerned with our killing ourselves are those that relate to the process of suicide prevention, as well as a whole host of other behaviors (such as driving while intoxicated, driving too fast or recklessly, abortion, and many others): God is the creator and giver of human life; life is to be lived not only for ourselves but for God and the neighbor; we are not entirely our own, but as Christians are "bought with a price"; the body (including the physical body) is a temple of the

Holy Spirit. Life is sacred, to be valued, and we are responsible to God for the way we use our lives. Detailed discussions of ethical and Christian perspectives on suicide can be found in other writings.[5]

There are two major points here. First, the attitude of condemnation in all cases of suicide is one that fits neither the biblical message nor what we understand about the complex dynamics of suicide. Such an attitude is a handicap to ministers who might otherwise genuinely want to be as helpful as they can to persons in distress. Second, there are strong warrants for us to engage and intervene as fully and effectively as we can with those whose distress involves suicidal thoughts and feelings, in order to prevent them from killing themselves, insofar as it is reasonably possible for us to do so.

Although there have been barriers which have stood in the way of the open discussion of suicidal impulses with ministers, they remain in a unique position to be of assistance. These barriers can be reasonably well broken down by ministers' communication of understanding, shown in public and private words and other behavior; by their alertness to the verbal and other behavioral clues to suicide; and by their willingness to take the initiative to respond with clear words and acts to these clues.

What Ministers Need to Know

Given the willingness to work with suicidal people and an attitude that will allow such work, ministers still need to have accurate information and be reasonably skilled in the most facilitative communications of pastoral care. Much has been written about the dynamics of suicide (how it is that persons can come to the point where they will actually make an attempt to kill themselves), the characteristics of suicidal persons, the interpersonal situations, the sociological conditions.

The Ten Commonalities of Suicide

The simplest scheme to remember, though profound in its total content and implications, is a proposal by Shneidman which he calls the "Ten Commonalities of Suicide."[6]

I. *The Common Stimulus.* Unendurable psychological pain may take a number of forms. The common fear is that there will be even more pain and/or that the pain will never cease. The person has the experience of not being able to continue at all.

I. The common stimulus in suicide is intolerable psychological pain.

II. The common stressor in suicide is frustrated psychological needs.

III. The common purpose of suicide is to seek a solution.

IV. The common goal of suicide is cessation of consciousness.

V. The common emotion in suicide is hopelessness-helplessness.

VI. The common internal attitude in suicide is ambivalence.

VII. The common cognitive state in suicide is constriction.

VIII. The common interpersonal act in suicide is communication of intention.

IX. The common action in suicide is egression [escape].

X. The common consistency in suicide is with lifelong coping patterns.

II. *The Common Stressor.* The pain is caused by frustrated psychological needs. Shneidman states elsewhere, "Every suicide act is addressed to certain unfulfilled needs."[7] If the needs are met, the suicide will not take place.

III. *The Common Purpose.* Shneidman emphasizes that suicide is not a random act. It is understood by the person as the way out of a problem. The task of the helping person is to discover the problem and, if necessary, help clarify it for the other.

IV. *The Common Goal.* The solution is the cessation of consciousness. In death, the problem no longer exists. When a person's mind begins to see the solution in terms of the cessation of consciousness, that person has taken a major step in the direction of the act.

V. *The Common Emotion.* Shneidman believes that hopelessness-helplessness is a central characteristic of suicide, regardless of the other elements present for any given person (although these characteristics may also appear as factors in persons other than those who are suicidal). Hopelessness has been isolated as the single most accurate predictor of suicide. Shneidman refers to "the penchant for precipitous capitulation."[8] Hopelessness is closely associated with loneliness.

VI. *The Common Internal Attitude.* All persons who think about committing suicide are ambivalent. They want to kill themselves, but at the same time they want to cry for the help they need in order to be saved from their perceived hopeless situation. Persons who have committed an act that is usually lethal, but who have not died, report that they had fantasies of being rescued. One young woman said to me, following a serious suicide attempt, "I wanted to kill myself, but I didn't want to be dead." There is, according to Shneidman, a conflict between survival and unbearable stress.

VII. *The Common Cognitive State.* At one point Shneidman uses the term "constricted desperation." Constriction refers to "dichotomous thinking," the suicidal person's mental trap. It is *either* this extreme or that extreme. The person sees only two choices:

Joan: I just can't continue to live like this. I can't stand this much pain all the time. The *only* possible thing left to do is to kill myself.

Minister: You *have* suffered a lot. It *is* painful. No one would want to go on just like that. But the way you've said it doesn't allow the possibility of some different way of seeing yourself and relating to others which doesn't keep you in so much pain all the time.

The following exchange between a minister and another woman illustrates both the ambivalence and a possible response to it. On two or three occasions during the session, Carol had said she could not go on. At other times she had stated she was afraid to kill herself, that each time she was close to committing the act, she became very fearful of what would happen to her after death. She had never put these two contradictory statements together, but the minister begins to do so here:

Minister: Your alternatives, as you put them a while ago, were suicide, and yet you *do have* some conflict about that . . .

Carol: Yes.

Minister: Your alternatives were suicide, which you really were afraid to do, don't want to do, or staying alive. And yet you don't see how you can do that either, and . . .

Carol: I can't . . . I don't see how I can stay alive . . .

Minister: But in those terms, you either *will* be alive or you will *kill* yourself, and right now you don't see how you can do either one.

Carol: Uh-huh.

Minister: Therefore it seems to me that one thing we're going to have to do is see if there is yet *another* alternative within the context of your being alive.

In this interchange, the minister sharpens the ambivalence (the common internal attitude) for her by putting her conflicting feelings together (she wants to; she can't because she's afraid). He then points out the discrepancy between her radical statements reflecting her constrictive thinking (it's *impossible* for her *both* to kill herself and stay alive, yet she doesn't see any alternatives). Finally, he begins to try to open her thinking to *other* possibilities. It does not have to be either live like *this* or kill yourself. It could possibly be that she could live *another* way. In his statement the minister also reveals his bias toward Carol's staying alive and their working together toward the middle ground. Shneidman believes the presence of constriction is "one of the most dangerous aspects of a suicidal state."[9]

VIII. *The Common Interpersonal Act.* Most persons who begin to think seriously about suicide or who have strong suicidal impulses are sufficiently troubled by these either to talk explicitly with someone about them or to make implicit (perhaps unconscious) verbal communications or other behavioral communications to a person or persons who are in some way significant in their lives. Such communications will be discussed in more detail later. Shneidman reports that in retrospective investigations ("psychological autopsies") of unquestioned suicide cases, 90 percent of the persons had given some clear communication of their intent.

IX. *The Common Action.* Shneidman refers to egression, meaning escape. He states that "suicide is not so much a movement toward death as it is a movement away from something,"[10] that "something" being the "frustrated psychological needs" and the concomitant "unendurable psychological pain."

X. *The Common Consistency.* Suicide is consistent with each suicidal person's lifelong patterns, though at times these inconsistencies may be very subtle. To find them, one looks at the way the person has *characteristically* responded to threat, stress, failure, or pain when these have been experienced previously. Has the person, to any degree, tended to withdraw, escape, act impulsively, engage in some self-defeating or self-damaging behavior in any of the many ways in which these can be expressed? Suicide is the radical form of these types of behaviors.

The Dynamics of Despair: An Invitation to Theology

An additional dimension which can provide an overlay through which ministers may view the psychodynamics of the suicidal person, as they have been presented in the Ten Commonalties, is elaborated by Gerkin. He speaks of suicide as "both a self-imposed condemnation and punishment for failure at living, on the one hand, and a defiant act of taking one's future into one's own hands, on the other." It is the radical expression of hopelessness and despair, "the experience of loss of a sense of future in which the person can have any confidence or a sense of expectation."[11]

Gerkin describes the experience of despair, if I understand correctly, as not being the same existential phenomenon as the psychiatric category of depression, although the two experiences can be overlapping. All persons have discrepancies between whom we see ourselves to be and the person we would like to be or become. Most people have some capacity for tolerating a reasonable amount of discrepancy between our awareness of the reality concerning ourselves and the ideal self as we have defined it. Many of us are also able to view our individual behaviors as being expressions of *part* of the self but not as *being* or *reflective of* the *whole* self. (I failed in this task or that assignment, but I am not *a failure*. I behaved very badly in that situation, but I am not a *bad person*. I am in the process of learning from these experiences of failure or obnoxious or hurtful behavior and am coming closer to what I would like to be more of the time.) The threat of despair comes when the discrepancies are too great to be tolerated and/or the learning from the individual experiences becomes blocked by persons' increasingly pessimistic interpretations of themselves. The gap between the actual (as interpreted by the person) and the ideal (whether relatively realistic or quite unrealistic) cannot be bridged. The result is the loss of selfhood.[12] As one suicidal woman put it several times in conversations, "I am a zero." She genuinely felt there was truly nothing worthwhile in the makeup of her own self.

Gerkin discusses the several losses which characterize the experience of the despairing person: loss of trust; of integrity; of mutuality; of fulfillment, or opportunity for self-realization; and finally, loss of future. These absences in a person's life, whether they were never a part of his or her selfhood as a result of lack of adequate self-defining experiences provided within the family of origin, or whether they arose gradually or erupted suddenly out of a particular set of life experiences, become the cognitive set which produces "a despairing interpretation" of all subsequent events in the person's life, reinforcing the negative picture of the self. Both the underlying impetus and the new interpretations are those of "judgment and condemnation of the self."[13]

Explicit and implicit in Gerkin's analysis of the dynamics of despair are a number of the "commonalities of suicide": psychological pain, frustrated psychological needs, hopelessness-helplessness, constricted thinking, the desire for a solution, the value to the person of the cessation of consciousness. Beyond this type of overlapping, human despair, in Gerkin's development of it, offers the minister a particular perspective that is invitational to a theological view of the suicidal person in her or his sickness of soul (selfhood). Therefore, in addition to the psychological and interpersonal terms used in discussing a particular person's condition, appropriate theological expressions and biblical images can be utilized to facilitate self-understanding and point to relevant directions in the helping process.

Evaluation of Lethality Potential

A suicidal person's lethality potential is the degree of probability that the person will make an attempt on his or her life within a very short time and with some means that is very deadly. The lethality potential scale developed by the Los Angeles Suicide Prevention Center lists nine criteria and assesses each on a 9-point scale, with 9 being the most lethal.[14] The type of intervention is guided by the ability to determine whether a person who talks about committing suicide is low, moderate, or high risk.

Age and Sex. At all ages, males kill themselves at a higher reported rate than do females. This seems to be the case in all countries and for all races. For whites in the United States, although the ratio in the various age categories varies somewhat depending on the particular year the data is gathered, males are never at a lower ratio than 2 to 1, and may go as high as 8 to 1 or more at age 75 and older. Females make more attempts, with 3 to 1 being the usual stated figure, but men are definitely more successful in their attempts. Although the rate for women also rises with age, their rate peaks during the 45–54 age range, then decreases slightly with each succeeding decade. For all ages, the white male to white female mean ratio was 3.3 to 1 in 1980. White males killed themselves at a higher reported rate than black males, white females at a higher rate than black females, and black males at a higher rate than black females. *Even though children and youths have low rates in comparison with adults, and females in comparison with males, all suicidal clues and verbal communication should be treated with the utmost seriousness and brought out into the open.*

Plan. More weight is to be given to aspects of a person's possible suicidal plan than to any of the other criteria: whether there is a plan; the specificity versus the generality of its detail, if there is a plan; the lethality of the means; and the availability of the means. This criterion gives more clues to the person's intent than any other. If details relating to this criterion do not arise as the person is talking, it is imperative to ask direct questions in order to elicit the necessary information.

Stress. Stress refers to contemporary external events: some form of loss—a loved person, place, thing, activity, position, role, limb, and so on; disfigurement, failure, accident, arrest, or any other environmental change. Are there none of these, one, or several? How does the person interpret the meaning of these events to him or her? The severity of the person's reactions is important to explore in detail.

Symptoms. Psychotic persons, especially those who hear voices telling them to destroy themselves or to engage in high-risk acts, or those who have other severe distortions of reality, have a high probability of being dangerous to themselves. The same is true of severely depressed persons. These persons should be hospitalized as quickly as possible for their own protection. Chemically dependent persons, including those who are alcoholic, have a higher rate of reported suicide than the general population.

Resources. The fact that a person has some family members and friends, is an active member of one or more formal or informal groups, has at least some minimal amount of money available, knows a minister or has a family physician, puts that person in a much better position to cope with and get help for problems and to deal with stress. Persons who live alone are more likely to kill themselves, and widowers more than married men.

Life-style. Life-style is to be read in terms of stability versus instability: number of marriages, jobs, moves; whether there is a specific home or the person is on the street and on the move; previous psychotic episodes or prior suicide attempts. Those with the greatest number of life disruptions are of higher lethality.

Suicidal Communication. Those who are willing to talk directly and in detail and length about their suicidal feelings with one or more other persons are less likely to kill themselves than those who do not

take such initiative or who are not responsive to another person's
invitation to talk about their thoughts and feelings.

Reactions of Significant Others. Are family members and friends
genuinely concerned, take the person seriously, willing to talk, to take
action? Or are they ambivalent, indecisive about taking action or what
action to take, make light of the person's communications, evade the
issues in conversation? Or are they, on the other end of the
continuum, hostile to the person, rejecting, punitive in their
behavior, and in some ways contribute to the worsening of the
situation and thus to the intensity of the suicidal impulses?

Medical Status. Is the person in good health or with perhaps only
minor transient illness, or is there a chronic, debilitating, painful,
terminal illness, very often cancer? These latter sometimes do kill
themselves in order to avoid pain and suffering, the facing of life
without former activities, and the other negative aspects of lingering
illness and long hospitalization. They sometimes want to spare family
members more suffering and expense. In addition, there are persons
who have delusions of such illness, which persist even in the face of
medical diagnosis to the contrary. Sometimes they too commit
suicide.

These nine areas of observation and investigation can provide the
minister with an assessment of a person's potential for suicide. Precise
numerical values have not been assigned to each item on the scale, so
there can be no single total score. Yet by giving primary attention to the
plan, much weight to symptoms and life-style, and realizing the
importance of the other items, at least there are some reasonably
accurate guidelines for both conversation and assessment.

The preceding discussions about the thinking, feelings, and
motivation of a suicidal person and the evaluation of lethality are not
without their theological dynamics and implications. In fact, issues of
faith can be identified throughout: the fact of human suffering to
such a radical degree, in the face of belief in a loving, redeeming God
revealed in Jesus the Christ; human hopelessness, even while the
person is being called to faith; the meaning of faith, when the person
is confronted by situations of human limitation and helplessness; the
worth of human life, when understood as being created by the God
who continues to value that life; the possibility of human growth in
both emotional strength and faith, in the situation of helplessness.

The pointing out of these theological issues in this context is not for the purpose of leading to a superficial "faith is the answer" conclusion, but to suggest the possibility, and frequently the appropriateness, of a theological or "pastoral diagnosis," as suggested by Pruyser.[15] The perceptive minister can be attentive to the suicidal person's affirmations of faith, doubts about God and the meaning of life, anger at God, belief in life after death, depth of hopelessness compared with stated beliefs that suggest hope, degree and meaningfulness of participation in a community of faith, and other faith issues. These may be woven into the lethality scale (stress, resources, life-style, reactions of significant others). They might, even better, comprise an additional category which may give relevant information concerning the relative strengths of a person's motivation toward suicide in comparison with that person's reasons and resources for living as indicated by the expressions of faith.

Intervention Procedures

The Ten Commonalities, some of the items of the Lethality Potential Scale, and an understanding of despair which invites a theological response suggest a number of the directions a minister would need to take in conversation with a suicidal person. In addition, with moderate and highly lethal persons, other actions are necessary.

The First Interview

There are several goals essential to keep in mind during the very first discussion with a person who is talking with the minister about his or her suicidal feelings, or one whom the minister thinks might be suicidal. As these are listed and discussed here, their number and critical nature may seem overwhelming. However, merely keeping in mind the facilitative conditions of all helping relationships as these are applied to situational crises, as discussed in Chapters 2, 3, and 4, will go a long way in addressing the suicidal situation. To these, of course, will be added the evaluation of lethality potential and only a few other considerations.

The Facilitative Conditions. First, as in all occasions of pastoral care and counseling, the provision of the facilitative conditions of the helping relationship is essential. (see pp. 58-62). Except in certain extreme circumstances, the accurate communication of empathy is the starting point. The following is the beginning of the conversation with Carol referred to earlier (p. 208). She had called for an appointment and indicated there was a serious problem which she wanted to discuss with the minister.

Minister:	Carol, I wonder if you would be willing to share with me something of what your feelings were that led you to call for an appointment and come by to see me.
Carol:	I . . . am very unhappy.
Minister:	What are the feelings of unhappiness? What goes into this?
Carol:	I just don't want to live.
Minister:	You're feeling very desperate, then.
Carol:	Yes (*pause*) very desperate, very depressed. I don't really want to live.
Minister:	When you say depression, what is depression for you? How do you feel when *you* are depressed?
Carol:	I feel like I'm down at the bottom of a deep hole and I can't get out.
Minister:	Just feeling very helpless, very hopeless.
Carol:	It's just that every time I try to get up, it's like the walls are made of mud and I just keep sliding back.
Minister:	You have the sense of really struggling to do something . . . catch hold of some sort of meaning for your life, but you just can't do it.
Carol:	Absolutely! Yes!
Minister:	And . . .
Carol:	I just . . . I can't make it.
Minister:	You really are at the point of giving up right at this moment, then.
Carol:	Yes, if I weren't such a coward (*pause*) I would kill myself.
Minister:	This is a strong impulse in you, and yet you have some conflict about whether to do it or not.
Carol:	Yes. I feel suicide is murder . . .
Minister:	Uh-huh.
Carol:	I guess I don't know . . . I just can't go on. (*pause*) Absolutely nobody cares.
Minister:	You're feeling *very* alone in all of this.

Even though the woman made a suicidal statement in her second response and again at responses eight and nine, the minister patiently sought to communicate his understanding of her experience, his second and fourth responses being concrete in the service of empathy. He did not panic at the mention of suicide, immediately plunging into the lethality potential evaluation process or problem solving or referral procedures, or change the subject. The way he responded to her explicit statement of thinking about killing herself indicates that he heard her words and the desperation behind them.

Such communication of understanding, and the willingness to move into this sense of desperation, meaninglessness, pain—whatever the combination of powerful feelings that comprise the person's experience—has the effect of breaking through the person's increasing sense of isolation. He or she no longer feels so entirely alone. The ground is now being cultivated for the first seeds of hope. With even a slight amount of hope, the person feels less suicidal, the "want to live" side of ambivalence is strengthened, beginning the experience that someone cares, someone understands, someone is willing to be with me, to be for me.

Later in the conversation the minister talked with Carol very explicitly about suicide. But the beginning point was the establishment of a working relationship of trust, assisting fuller self-exploration of her internal experience and eliciting a more detailed expression of her feelings.

Attentiveness to Suicidal Communications. The second requirement of pastors entering into a conversation with a distressed person is that they be attentive to suicidal language and other behavior. Only a few persons are as quickly open about suicide as Carol. Her part in the conversation rather quickly got across what was on her mind: "Just don't want to live. . . . If I weren't such a coward, I would kill myself." Later in the interview she was even more explicit. It is imperative that ministers take this language at face value and reply in similarly concrete words.

It is easy for us to allow our own fears to control us, replying with words similar to those used by friends of another woman. That woman told her friends what a difficult time she was having following the death of her husband. She added that she had been thinking about killing herself.

One friend replied, "You don't really mean that!"

"But I do," she answered.

"You *can't* mean it. You have so much to live for." But she *did* mean it, and a few weeks later had been very close to accomplishing it when she was brought to the hospital.

Ministers who respond as did those frightened and misguided friends frustrate the person even more, increase the sense of not being understood and the feeling of isolation, the overall impact pushing the person closer to the act. Even when a pastor does not answer with language that directly denies what the other person has aid, it is easy to move into general terms and language that considerably diminish the intensity of the other's feelings. Someone says, "I'm desperate! I've thought several times that I might be close to killing myself." A diminishing response might be, "Sounds as if you've been feeling a bit down." In contrast, it is much more effective to meet the person's statement head on: "You don't see any way out; thoughts about suicide keep pushing into your head."

The first response communicates that the pastor cannot tolerate feelings of desperation and is unwilling to talk openly with the person about suicide. The person hears this as being told to go back into the shell, put on the mask, pretend not to be feeling as bad as he or she really is. The second response, while not the only possible helpful one, meets both the desperation and the suicidal thoughts directly and openly.

Even easier not to hear, and thus to avoid, is the *implicit* language of suicide. If Carol had not been so explicit in two or three places in the conversation, some of her statements might havv been bypassed.

> "I just . . . can't make it."
> "I just can't go on."
> "Life is really nothing."
> "I don't want to live."
> "You can't count on anything. Sometimes you wonder why you even bother to live."

People may make other such statements:

> "Sometimes I think my family would be better off without me."
> "I'm so tired of fighting it (or life, or my problems)."
> "Some day I know I'm just going to give out of energy."

When people use language like this, they may be thinking about killing themselves, or they may not. It is clearly the helping person's job to find out. Many people occasionally make statements like these during a bad day or in the midst of a particular problem. But in conversation, each time a person uses an expression such as this, the alert pastor, seeking concreteness, asks what the person means. Even if the person does not reply in explicitly suicidal terms, after the second or third similar statement, it is imperative that the pastor respond with something like this:

"You've just said that life is nothing. Earlier I remember you said you don't see how you can go on or how you can make it. My experience is that many people who talk like this are thinking about killing themselves. I can't help but wonder if that's in your mind."

The cumulative experience of experts in the field of suicidology is that only rarely will a person fail to answer truthfully. If people who have said these things are not thinking about killing themselves, the pastor's words will serve at least as a mild shock, to help them hear how they have been presenting themselves: "Oh, no! I'm not thinking about killing myself. Things are bad, but not that bad." The minister may then reply, "Well, since your words led me to wonder, perhaps you can clarify for me just exactly how intensely you *are* feeling."

If the person *has*, in fact, been having suicidal thoughts or feelings, when the minister makes quite explicit the implicit language that has been used, at times the person's sigh of relief is quite audible. Even if not, there is a great sense of relief that the minister has recognized the hopelessness to which the words were referring and has now made it clear that this representative of the church is willing to talk quite openly about the person's hopelessness, desperation, and thoughts or feelings about suicide. The gates of a particular dam in the pastoral conversation have just been opened, and a flood of new material flows through. It is the essential task, then, to respond to explicit suicidal language with equally concrete language and to seek to make the other person's implicit language explicit, so that the other may hear the actual words and now be required to respond to them. Concreteness and clarity are necessary.

It is not uncommon for ministers to have some anxiety about directly questioning another as to that person's thoughts about suicide, fearing that they might be putting dangerous ideas in the other person's head. Reflect on this. If it is already in the other person's thinking, it is clarifying, relieving, and productive of more constructive conversation when the helper has provided the explicit words. If a person has *not* been thinking about committing suicide, does not intend to do so, she or he will not do so merely because we have mentioned it. In fact, our questions concerning what we recognize as possible suicidal language will, once again, assist in the clarification of the person's thinking, feelings, and intensity of feelings.

There are, of course, other ways of communicating suicidal intention than the two types of verbal language just discussed. Certain acts are themselves a type of implicit language. Like other implicit language, these acts may have other meanings also, but since they are acts which people who are thinking about killing themselves often actually do, it is imperative that the minister ask directly about the meaning.

Someone may come by the pastor's home or office and, after a brief interchange, say something like, "I've just been thinking. I'm not going to live forever, you know. I was just wondering if you would help me work out some details of my funeral, so that when the time comes my family won't have to worry with it (or since I don't have any family, it will be taken care of)." This move may be a very thoughtful, courageous, commendable act on the part of a person who has never thought of suicide. On the other hand, it may be reflective of suicidal thoughts. The same could be said about drawing up a will after many years of refusing to do so, or other similar acts.

There are a number of ways a minister might respond:

"I'd be glad to talk with you about that. I wonder if you'd be willing to share with me the specific thinking that's gone into making this decision."

"That could be a useful thing to do. I wonder, though, what has led you to be thinking about it right now."

If the conversation that grows out of these types of responses does not produce any clues to possible suicidal thinking, then the minister might say:

"Thanks for taking the time to tell me what had been going on in your mind. I really asked for two reasons. One, it just helps me know you better, and that can help in the plans we make. But sometimes people will take this sort of action when they've been having some thoughts about killing themselves, and if you have been, it's crucial that I know about it and that we talk about it."

Even without having given other clues until this time, occasionally someone will answer, "Well, as a matter of fact . . . ," and then go on to talk about the thoughts or feelings he or she has been having about

committing suicide or, even more clearly, the intent to do so.
There are other acts which require some clarification if the
minister happens to notice or hear about them: withdrawal from
activities which heretofore had been enjoyable and/or meaningful to
the person; ceasing a favorite form of recreation; giving away things
the person frequently used in work or recreation and which have
some special meaning; or even a rather sudden and unusual sense of
calm, when up to that point the person has been noticeably troubled,
agitated, distressed, or quite tense. The minister seeks the person
out and says, "This is what I've noticed (or heard about), and I'm
concerned. I was wondering what it means (or what has happened)."
Then the minister patiently stays with the person until sufficiently
concrete language is used to clarify what the person is experiencing
and doing and planning. Most people do not continue to cover up
their suicidal impulses when a trusted and respected person makes
this approach, and they very rarely openly lie and deny such thoughts
and feelings if they actually have them. There are, of course,
occasional exceptions when the person's mind is clearly made up, no
element of ambivalence is apparent, the impulse seems irresistible,
and the person does not want anyone to interfere. In these few
instances, the minister still will have done all that reasonably could
have been done with the perceptiveness and knowledge and skill and
courage that she or he has.

A Situational Crisis, or Not a Situational Crisis? Third, it is crucial to
determine whether the person is in a situational crisis, or whether the
person's difficulties—including, in this case, the suicidal feelings—
are long-standing, or cyclical in nature with no apparent precipitating
event. If it cannot be determined that the person is in a situational
crisis, the person needs to see some professional in addition to the
minister. It may well be that the person will need some psychotropic
or antidepressant drug or other medication. It may be that the person
needs to be hospitalized. Or if the person is chemically dependent, he
or she may need to go to a detoxification center or into a drug-abuse
treatment program. Although the pastor may continue to play an
important role in this person's life, the primary administrator of the
person's treatment plan will be a psychiatrist or other physician, a
psychologist, or someone else related to a mental health center or
hospital.
When the person is in situational crisis, even though the presence
of suicidal ideas and impulses will require a variety of special

arrangements and the minister will want the person to be in touch with some other professional, both for the potential additional help for the person and for the minister's own protection, the pastor skilled in crisis counseling may be in an excellent position to help the person in the resolution of the crisis itself. When the suicidal feelings are a part of the situational crisis, they will usually diminish and disappear fairly rapidly, along with the other feelings and behaviors of crisis, during the usual process of identifying the precipitating event and the nature of the threat, catharsis, and problem solving.

The seriousness of the suicidal elements in situational crisis is not to be downplayed merely because they may be amenable to fairly rapid change. The drive for suicide may be very intense and the person may very well be in danger. The usual assessment of the lethality potential needs to be made and protective measures appropriate to the level of lethality taken. But usually the time period during which the person is truly suicidal is quite brief in *situational* crisis. (It can be longer in crisis reactive to loss by death or divorce.) It is quite useful for the minister to be in touch with the person frequently, with counseling sessions only a day or two apart, and with brief telephone contact between face-to-face conversations; the minister should invite the other to call if feelings become extremely intense, with arrangements made with someone else to be contacted if the minister cannot be reached; and the person should be monitored in his or her appointments with other professionals (agencies, etc.) selected according to the person's particular needs.

As has already been suggested, the combination of accurate communication of empathy, with its necessary concreteness, and the willingness of the pastor to engage the person in candid discussion of suicidal thoughts and feelings will begin to break down the suicidal person's isolation and loneliness, the sense of not being understood. This in turn usually leads to diminishing the person's fear of the suicidal impulses themselves and some reduction of the extremity of hopelessness. Contributing to the stimulation of hope, Schneidman emphasizes the value of the suicidal person's seeing the helper (and for many such people, clergy have a head start) as being powerful. Under most circumstances a counselor wishes to *reduce* any magical thinking the troubled person may have about the counselor's ability to take care of everything, and certainly wants to avoid playing into such thinking so as to cultivate it. However, at least *early* in the work with a highly lethal person, it is useful not to tamper with *anything* that may be keeping the person alive. It is possible to move from such trust in the minister's omnipotence to yet another transient and helpful stage in the relationship, as the minister shares his or her ego strength (competence as a person, as a helper, as one who is not fearful of the suicidal thoughts and impulses of another, who has a sense of meaning and purpose and hope) with the battered and weakened ego of the suicidal person. That person experiences safety and then, increasingly, strength of his or her own through the relationship. In a situational crisis, it is common and to be expected that movement will take place—from dependence upon the counselor (although not always magical thinking in regard to him or her), through a stage of the counselor's sharing his or her ego strength with the other, on to the resolution of the crisis, with the former strengths of that person now coming into full experience and use. When suicidal feelings are also involved, they will usually diminish and disappear with the resolution of the crisis itself. Along with the usual methods of crisis counseling, the minister adds any and all procedures necessary to keep the person from committing suicide during the relatively short time they are working together for crisis resolution.

Evaluation of Lethality Potential. By the time the minister has spent a substantial portion of the first interview with the accurate reflection of empathy, being attentive to implicit and explicit suicidal language and responding to either or both in concrete words which communicate understanding of the other person's thoughts and feelings about suicide, determining whether the person is in a situational crisis or not, the degree of lethality is frequently quite apparent. Recent stress, especially loss or failure or other significant changes in the person's life will have been identified, in determining whether the person is in crisis. Aspects of the communication of suicidal intent, other symptoms, the reactions of significant others, life-style, and resources will frequently have been referred to, sometimes in considerable detail. However, if any critical elements of the lethality potential scale have not been touched upon, it is essential that the minister say or ask whatever is necessary to elicit this information:

> "We've been talking together about your feelings in regard to killing yourself, but I haven't heard you say anything about how you might go about doing it."

> "You've told me quite a lot about yourself, but I haven't heard you mention much about your family. Are you living with them at this time?"

"How are different family members responding to you during this difficult time?"

A concrete example of a move into the pursuit of relevant detail is provided by the minister who was talking with Carol. He had been trying to sharpen for her the mutually exclusive outcomes she had posed for herself. Only about ten minutes remained in their scheduled time together.

Minister:	But put in those terms, you either *will* be alive or you will *kill* yourself, and right now you don't see how you can do either one.
Carol:	Uh . . .
Minister:	Therefore it seems to me that one thing we're going to have to do is see if, you know, there is yet another alternative within the context of your being alive. (pause) You, of course, have thought of suicide . . .
Carol:	Oh yes!
Minister:	I wonder . . .

(*Here the minister was in mid-sentence, apparently beginning to propose something for Carol to consider, when she interrupted.*)

Carol:	I even have a plan. All I need is the courage.
Minister:	Could you tell me how you have planned this?
Carol:	I have a lot of pills.
Minister:	What sort of pills do you have?
Carol:	Well, pain pills, sleeping pills; I have enough to do the job.
Minister:	Have you had times when you really were very close to taking them?
Carol:	Yes. I have had them in my hands.
Minister:	How was it at that time you chose not to take them?
Carol:	I don't know what's facing me after I die, and I was scared of it. For so many years you're brought up with this thought . . . and you get scared.
Minister:	And so right now you're staying alive only because you're afraid.
Carol:	That's right. I am more afraid, I guess, of dying, but some day it's going to be a day, I think, when it is going to be too much.
Minister:	You think that you *could* just go ahead and take them.
Carol:	All I have to do is look in that mirror or have my husband look at me in the way he does . . .

The minister responded without pausing when Carol completed her statement that had interrupted him. Whatever the point he was trying to make, he judged it to be of far lesser value than the immediate pursuit of her startling statement that she had a plan. Within the next few minutes their conversation closed, but not before arrangements were made for her to discuss her suicidal desire fully with her husband, to make an appointment with a psychiatrist for further evaluation and possible medication, to see the minister again three days later, and to call the minister during that time if she thought she needed to do so. The minister also knew, in his own mind, that he would be taking some initiative to be back in contact with her by phone or visit in the interim.

By the end of the first session, it is imperative that a reasonably accurate evaluation of lethality potential be made.

Hospitalization. This has already been referred to briefly under the discussion of whether the person is or is not in a situational crisis. If the person is psychotic and/or psychiatrically depressed and/or of extremely high lethality potential, although all aspects of the situation may not be clear, hospitalization will usually be necessary. This is not a final decision that ministers would ordinarily make by themselves, although with increasing experience, they can usually make a fairly accurate judgment as to the necessity. In most states, only a physician can hospitalize a person, although an increasing number of state laws allow a psychologist to do so. There is no question that in these severe cases, a minister must see to it that the highly suicidal person sees someone who can make a further evaluation, a decision concerning hospitalization, and the necessary arrangements. If no such person is fairly quickly available, the minister may need to take the person to a hospital emergency room where a physician will either be on duty or on call.

Ministers have no choice in this matter. It is morally imperative to protect persons from their own suicidal impulses, and it is professionally necessary in order that ministers may protect themselves. There have been and will be an increasing number of malpractice suits filed against clergy who have not taken such a decisive protective action. On occasion, in the absence of other resources, the minister will need to call appropriate law enforcement officials authorized to handle such severe cases.

Some people will respond to the minister's suggestion that they see a physician (or psychologist) with full cooperation; and the majority of others will go, also, though reluctantly and after some verbal resistance. Many of these people do not want anyone else to know about their situation and do not want the inconvenience and/or stigma of being hospitalized. Confidentiality will be discussed in the next section, but the point here is that through the minister's kind, concerned persistence, most people will see the point. Hospitalization, while somewhat drastic, is considerably less drastic than a person's suicide. In the face of any resistance, the minister continues to state in clear terms that the person has sought his or her help or has responded, until this point in the conversation, to the minister's initiative. It is obvious that the person needs help beyond that which the minister alone can provide, and the minister is responsible for seeing that the person gets it. In a variety of ways, it is clearly communicated that the minister is responsible for acting in behalf of the other person's well-being, and will do so. Only a very few people will continue to resist actively. In these few instances, the minister may need to call a family member, a close friend, or, as already suggested, the appropriate law enforcement or other official.

Unfortunately, many of us ministers are uncomfortable with direct resistance to our suggestions and do not want other people to be angry at us. In the case of highly suicidal persons, our own discomfort *cannot* be a consideration. We *must* act to protect them. Sometimes they will be angry at us—occasionally, very angry. Nevertheless, we are called upon to do whatever is necessary to try to prevent these people from killing themselves.

Confidentiality. Is it not a universal assumption, if not always the actual case, that what a minister is told in private will be kept absolutely secret? Most of the time this would be true. This assumed confidentiality allows, even encourages people to talk freely with ministers and other professionals about the most intimate details of their lives. Such secrecy, then, is obviously in the best interests of the person who is talking to the pastor. But which is the higher value—secrecy, or the best interests of the person? Careful reflection tells us that we are committed to the *person*, not a *principle*. The principle of confidentiality usually assists us, but there are some situations in which this secrecy is detrimental to the person.

If someone reveals his or her suicidal impulses to a pastor and the person is judged to be of moderate to high lethality, the minister is under obligation *not* to keep this entirely secret. A response might be: "Is your wife (husband) aware of how you feel about this? (or of the fact that you've been thinking about killing yourself? or of what you're planning to do?)" Whether the answer is Yes or No, then, "How about giving her (him) a call right now and asking her (him) to come over? (or telling her [him] that we'll be over in a few minutes to talk?)" If there is no spouse, this procedure might involve other persons (a parent, grown child, sibling, best friend). It is essential that a family member or members, if there be any at all, be drawn into the situation—the process of seeking to understand, and any treatment decisions that need to be made.

Ministers, like other helping professionals, are bound by the "duty of care" to do what they can to help a person in the most responsible way possible. The Everstines discuss those situations in which there is also the duty to hospitalize, the duty to warn, or the duty to report. It has already been stated clearly that when ministers discover someone is suicidal, it is critical, in order to produce the best care, that we bring that person in contact with a professional who can evaluate his or her lethality and psychological state, with a view to the administration of medication and, if necessary, hospitalization. That professional, then, has the obligation to hospitalize when the person is judged "to be dangerous to other people . . . to himself or herself . . . [or] to be 'greatly disabled.' "[16]

At any point prior to the suicidal person's contact with such a professional, ministers have the moral, professional, and probably legal obligation to inform some responsible member of the family. (The same is most certainly true when the person seems to be a danger to someone else.)

(Although "duty to report" refers to matters such as child abuse and neglect, sexual abuse, and other such situations, it is well to digress briefly here to say clearly that ministers are citizens as well as professionals. Many states and communities have laws requiring the reporting of such situations when they are known, or even suspected, and ministers are not exempt.[17])

Often essential, toward the latter part of the first interview, is the suicidal person's promise to the minister not to kill himself or herself. Such a promise may be proposed in various words and for varying periods of time, but it must be specific and clearly understood by both parties. Usually in the case of moderate- and high-lethality persons, shorter periods of time will seem more reasonable and thus are more likely to elicit a positive response. These short-term commitments may be renewed as necessary.

Here is an example of the way such a suggestion might be made :

"We've been talking for an hour or so now, and we've both just indicated that we believe we've made a good start in working together and that we're going to get together again day after tomorrow. You've been very candid with me that your desire to kill yourself is definitely there, even though not real strong right at this moment. I wonder, though, if you would be willing to make a promise to me that you won't kill yourself during this time between our appointments."

Most people, most of the time, will make such an agreement, based on the part of themselves that desires to live; on the developing, seemingly productive relationship with the minister; and on the hope, however small or great, that this process now seems to hold for them. Very few people will make such a commitment knowing they will not keep it. Most people, having promised, will not kill themselves. People who are most likely not to promise, or to promise and not keep that promise, are also those whom ministers will probably be transferring to a psychiatrist or psychologist and who will, in all likelihood, be hospitalized—the psychotic, the deeply depressed, and the highly impulsive persons (low frustration tolerance, low ego control, poor reality testing).

Even after the promise is made, it gives the person an additional sense of security to have two or more alternative plans of action in case the intensity of the suicidal impulse increases: The person might call the minister (if the minister will be fairly available during that period of time), talk with a spouse or other family member or friend, go to the hospital emergency room, call a crisis intervention or suicide prevention center, or take some other course of action which the two of them can think of and agree upon.

Very occasionally, a person will not make such a commitment. The minister may respond by asking, "What are you aware of that's standing in the way of your making this promise to me?" If the person answers in such a way that a profitable discussion can ensue and the barrier be eliminated, then it is imperative that the minister take the time to accomplish this goal. Inform any person who might be waiting for the next appointment that you will be late. Call your spouse with the same information about dinner. Postpone your sermon preparation. Miss the business meeting scheduled for this time. Life-and-death issues take priority. Usually with a few more minutes' discussion, or in another half hour, such a promise will be made.

If the person refuses to make the commitment and suggests that the time is up and that he or she really needs to leave, the minister, in some clear, direct form, says, "No way! Not until the promise is made." If the person still refuses, the minister then says, "If your feelings are so strong or so unpredictable, even to yourself, that you can't make this promise, then it seems to me it would make the most sense for us to go on out to my car and go to the hospital."

This cannot be said as a threat. It is the *minister's* promise. Also, the person has the option of calling a family member from the minister's home or office and explaining the situation, or, if the person refuses to do so, the minister will call. There can be no giving in on a gamble with a person's life. If the person now reflects that he or she has just been exaggerating the situation, so the minister ought not to be taking it so seriously, the minister comes back with the same alternatives: talking about suicide is *always* serious, so the only choices are either promise or hospital (or some effective substitute, such as going directly to a psychiatrist's or psychologist's office or informing family members who will be responsible for being with the person at all times until some other provision is made).

For the minister's own well-being, he or she needs to be aware that some persons will delay agreeing to a no-suicide contract merely in order to keep the minister in conversation longer, and longer, and longer. It is not good for either the minister or the other person to allow that person to manipulate the minister. It is imperative that the minister be able to set and keep some time limits. As already indicated, it may be productive to talk longer with a person about possible barriers to the no-suicide commitment, but if after fifteen or twenty minutes the conversation seems to be entirely nonproductive, the minister can speed up the process:

> "I'm really going to need to stop in another fifteen or twenty minutes. I hope we can discover the source of your hesitation so we can resolve it and you can agree that you won't kill yourself. If we haven't accomplished that in that amount of time, we're going to need to (call the doctor, go to a hospital, call a family member, whatever), because I simply can't let you leave here without that promise."

If some persons continue to resist—become angry, say that the minister does not trust them or does not care for them, or take some other approach—the minister is called upon to respond in kind:

"I guess it is hard for me to trust you on this matter since you've been very clear with me that you don't trust yourself. I have to do what I think is necessary to help you."

"The fact that I'm not just going to let you go out without your commitment not to kill yourself *is* the way I'm caring for you right now. You've asked me to help, and that's what I'm doing, even though you seem not to like it."

Regardless of the way the other person is responding, this pastoral behavior communicates that the minister is taking the other person and what he or she is experiencing and saying with the utmost seriousness. When any person talks in any type of suicidal language, the minister can do no other than act as if this is what the person means.

Further Pastoral Counseling of the Suicidal Person

A first pastoral conversation with a person who reveals suicidal thoughts or feelings, then, may end in one of two major ways, although in many instances these will overlap. The person who is moderately or highly lethal, or about whose degree of lethality we are unsure, who is or may be psychotic and/or severely depressed, or whose problem(s) is not related to a situational crisis, is *transferred* to a medical or psychological professional for additional evaluation, perhaps hospitalization, and appropriate treatment. This is accomplished after conversations with other responsible members of the family, when they are available. In these instances, the other professional will be the primary therapist. The minister continues with pastoral care of the person and the family in ways consistent with their needs and the situation, in consultation with the other professional, if at all possible, and guided by the insights presented in this chapter. When the person's suicidal thoughts and feelings are a part of a situational crisis reaction, and when the minister is clear that the lethality potential is low, there are other procedures to be followed.

Solving the Problem. If suicide is a solution to a person's problem, then clarification of the problem that needs to be solved is obviously a part of the process. Problem definition and resolution were discussed in detail in the chapter "Methods of Crisis Counseling." Schneidman has noted the common stimulus, "unendurable psychological pain," and indicates that "a just noticeable difference" toward tolerability may make the difference in a person's decision to live longer and work toward further pain reduction.[18]

Even though the first phase of helping as described in the previous section will not be sufficient for most suicidally distressed people, it plays its dynamic role in the reduction of pain for many and provides the groundwork necessary for much problem solving.

Identification and Resolution of Powerful Feelings. During the first phase of the helping process, but necessarily extending beyond it, catharsis is taking place. This refers to the identifying, feeling, targeting, and expression of emotions. What constitutes the "psychological pain" for this particular person? Is it sadness over a loss; guilt; shame; a feeling of failure, fear, rejection; repressed anger or anger the person is aware of but has been frustrated in expressing; some other emotion or some combination of these? As feelings are identified, along with the event, situation, and/or persons involved in the eliciting of them, and as the interactions between the feelings themselves begin to be understood, many persons begin to experience some relief from the inner pressure, inner pain. "Reduce the individual's anguish, tension, and pain, and his (her) level of lethality will concomitantly come down, for it is the elevated perturbation that drives or fuels the elevated lethality."[19] In a situational crisis, this reduction may take place quite quickly, within one or two conversations. At other times, of course, it may take longer.

A particularly important emotion often dynamically connected with suicidal feelings is that of anger. Although Freud's own views of the dynamics of suicide recognized several different possible motives and the interactions between them, certainly anger, even rage experienced by a child toward a parent and then directed toward one's self as the parent is introjected, is one that has received considerable emphasis over the years.[20] However, Litman offers a very appropriate word of warning that we ministers need to take seriously.

> Less experienced therapists should be cautioned against the simplistic psychodynamic cliché that suicide essentially represents hostility turned against the self ("Murder in the 180th Degree"),

particularly if this theoretical formula leads the therapist to interpret the patient's unconscious hostility prematurely, especially against someone he loves and needs; this lowers his self-esteem, increases the regression, and activates suicidal trends. Frequently the patient breaks off contact with the therapist, and the therapeutic opportunity is lost.[21]

Actually, the attempt to deal with a person's unconscious self-destructive anger is an area ministers would do well to stay out of. It is not a matter of a situational crisis, but a deeply entrenched disorder.

A very compelling case is made by the Everstines—that the anger of suicidal persons, rather than being directed *inward*, is usually very specifically directed toward someone *outside* the self. They, as have others, view suicide (with some exceptions, which they note) in an *inter-* rather than an *intra*actional context. They state three premises:

1. Suicide is an event which is intended to send a message from one person to another;

2. There is one specific person who is expected to receive the message of suicide; for that person, above all, the suicidal act is performed; and,

3. The primary content of the message being conveyed is anger.

In summary, a suicidal person progresses through these stages: (1) wishing the death of another; (2) being prevented from actualizing that wish; and (3) "killing" the survivor by means of the effective technique of killing him/herself. The survivor is forced to live on, and the life that he or she lives will be marked by an indelible brush.[22]

They obviously understand much suicide to be "a direct, deliberate, and hostile act." Based upon this view, work with suicidal persons who are not clearly psychotic or dying of an incurable disease, whose motivations produce an emphasis more on selfmutilation than on self-killing, and a few other types, entails a concentration on a person's most significant relationships. This investigation would be expected to lead to a recognizable target, a specific person who is the intended victim of the suicidal person's act. These relationships may be present or past; persons may be substituted for the original object of the anger; there may be fantasies involved in the person's perspective on the relationship. It is essential to discover, by detailed exploration if necessary, who is supposed to receive the message from the suicidal person. The Everstines then indicate that the focus of counseling at this point is the "pathological relationship" and the attempt to reduce the rage. The prior frustration of any channels of expression of the anger has contributed to its buildup to the point where suicide is seen as the *only* course of action ("constriction"), the *only* way to send the message and hurt the other irreparably. The reduction of the anger, of course, means the reduction of the lethality.[23]

Ministers are in a position, with a number of people with whom they may be involved, to be particularly attentive to the possibility that *God* is the "person" at whom the anger is directed. This was the case with Carol. The minister had asked what it had been like for her when she had seen herself for the first time after a disfiguring facial operation six months before.

Carol:	I couldn't believe it.
Minister:	You felt somehow it wasn't really you.
Carol:	Right. I cried, but . . .
Minister:	Very bitter tears, I imagine.
Carol:	And I screamed! I screamed in frustration and horror.
Minister:	Just outraged that this had happened to you.
Carol:	Yes! Outraged, absolutely! I felt like I was going to explode.
Minister:	I wonder if you could direct that anger in any way. Were you aware of who it was you were so mad at at that time?
Carol:	At God!
Minister:	At God, that God had allowed this for you.
Carol:	Well, I hadn't done anything to him.
Minister:	You felt as if God had been punishing you, or was punishing you.
Carol:	Yes. If I could understand why. Then when my husband turned against me, that was all.
Minister:	That was the end; that was the end.
Carol:	That was the end.
Minister:	I wonder if this outrage at God that you're talking about is . . . might be one of the reasons that you came to see me as a minister.
Carol:	I came to see you . . . I need God. I just don't have anybody to turn to. I have got to have someone pulling. I need help.

Those who have believed that God's work in the world is to protect them from suffering and failure and rejection might have direct and primary anger at God, although any fuller exploration will also find significant anger at some other person or persons, or even at themselves. Sometimes, however, God is the most available, yet intangible substitute for intense anger at another person, a needed person. Yet it is an anger which in any number of ways literally cannot be, or is perceived as being impossible or too threatening to express directly. The minister as a representative of God provides a unique opportunity to elicit such anger from the other person, sometimes as the person transfers it to the minister, to "give permission" to the person to be mad at God, assist the person to express such feelings directly to God in what is truly prayer, or help the person, when such is the case, to understand that the anger is really at another human being and has been displaced onto God. It is necessary, of course, that the minister have enough faith in God to be confident that God can handle a human being's anger without ministerial defense. The pastor who was talking with Carol obviously did not feel called upon to try to protect God, but rather sought to help Carol express herself more openly and fully about this previously unexplored area of her life.

Although considerable reference has been made to frustrated anger as a prominent dynamic in suicide, it is interesting to note that Shneidman does not mention it among his Ten Commonalities. I am not aware of his reason, but I believe it is most useful to discuss anger under the category of "the common stimulus," "unendurable psychological pain." Even though there may be instances when persistent self-destructiveness is an expression of anger toward the introjected object, and even though the discussion of the Everstines' provocative presentation clearly suggests that their observations and procedures are useful for ministers to keep in mind while working with suicidal persons, we must always beware of becoming so enamored of any single theory that we ourselves work with mental blinders on, missing the complexities and variances of human motivation and behavior.

Anger in one form or another, conscious or unconscious, directed inward or outward, seems prominent in many suicidal persons. However, it always seems to be as a result of some great pain and/or is productive of pain. Often the anger itself has arisen out of some hurt or series of hurts which the person has experienced as a result of another person's attitude and behavior. These may be specifically remembered or the occasions may have faded from memory, with only the wounds remaining. The other person may or may not have intended hurt. The suicidal person's perception of the other may be relatively accurate or considerably distorted. But whatever the circumstances, the hurt is real for the person involved, and so is the anger in response to it. In this case, any reduction of the hurt in the helping process also reduces the anger. That reduction may come about in any of several ways: through clarification of any distortions of the relationship, through change in the behavior of the other person, through change in the suicidal person's perception of the meaning of the relationship, through direct conversation between those in the relationship, or through other ways that may be suggested by a particular situation.

Shneidman gives a variation on this theme. He states that "when suicide is a hostile act, it is often not the hostility of the perpetrator but rather the hostility of the significant others who have provoked or permitted the act."[24]

This is an important point, not to be overlooked. Sometimes people are hostile toward another and behave in ways that have the uncanny knack of thrusting sharply into another's areas of peculiar vulnerability. This is not to deny the suicidal person's anger, but it is the end of a line to which another's hostility has significantly contributed, producing the hurt, with anger in response, the development of the suicidal feelings, and increased anger by the other, in a vicious circle.

A final point is that to live with chronic hostility, whether conscious or unconscious or a combination of both, is also to live with chronic pain. Persistent anger equals unhappiness. It takes its toll on the sufferer. The word *chronic* is the key here. It is not necessarily painful to become angry, or even to become angry frequently, as circumstances may elicit it in certain people. Anger is basically purposeful: It energizes to constructive action. But when that energy finds no constructive expression, and when the stimuli to anger, understood in terms of "frustrated psychological needs," have been frequent, or even chronic, then the backlog builds up and chronicity of anger ensues. The result is frequently depression or, if not clinical depression, an awareness of "intolerable psychological pain." While a well-trained and sensitive minister might be very helpful to these persons in a number of ways, when such chronic anger-pain expresses itself in suicidal thoughts and feelings, it is critical that the person also see another professional.

Broadening Constricted Thinking. Although it has already been referred to, it should be noted again that it is very important for the helper to be aware of the other person's constricted thinking. The helping processes just discussed will tend to contribute to its breakdown, but the minister's constant attention to any reference by the other person to the constriction will alert the helper to respond by pointing out the unnecessary nature of such limited alternatives, reframing and suggesting additional perspectives on the person and the situation.

Identification and Meeting of Needs. Since the pain, whatever its component parts, is a result of frustrated psychological needs, an obvious part of the detailed exploration must be designed to identify and make explicit those needs, and to work to find ways the person might begin to have them met. This calls for the problem-solving phase of looking at the person's internal and the actual or potential external resources, the latter most frequently present in terms of people: professional people, family members, present friends and group memberships, potential new friends and group activities, relationship repairing, personal faith, and the community of faith. Out of such exploration of possibilities, it is most important that the suicidal person make the first decision to do something for himself or herself, then act in some nondestructive way. What takes place in so doing is legitimate self-assertion. The act of self-assertion, no matter how insignificant it might otherwise seem, communicates to the person that he or she is no longer helpless. This act is the first contribution to the person's growth in renewed self-esteem. When a minister helps in such a way in the resolution of a situational crisis, the momentum toward acting for one's self and the growth in self-esteem usually pick up quite rapidly, and soon the minister can step out of the picture, except for the usual pastoral (and/or friendship) contacts. On the other extreme, when a person has had long-term problems with passivity, a sense of helplessness, and low self-esteem (these are all tied together), many "baby steps" will need to be taken, with the minister holding the other person's psychological hand for awhile, balancing, supporting, leading, affirming.

Faith Response to Despair. If Gerkin's analysis of the dynamics of despair is valid, then "the importance for maintaining a hopeful, lively lifeline of implicit and explicit faith in that relationship with God by which the person is finally identified is of ultimate importance."[25]

An acceptance of one's self by oneself has the potential for taking place as one experiences acceptance by God. God's acceptance is communicated and demonstrated by a person's acceptance by a pastor, who, in their relationship, is a living symbol of God, functioning in an incarnational ministry. Gerkin properly suggests the starting point for the process is the pastor's willingness to step down into the pit of despair with the other person, sharing the depth of this particular type and intensity of suffering as much as any other human being can. In such a relationship an opening is made to the world outside the despairing person's closed circle of rigid negative interpretation, of isolation of the self from others, of blindness to a future. Without a sense of the future, the person is shut off from the God who stimulates hope by coming into our present out of the future and confirming for us both the present and the future, regardless of the wounds we have received in life.[26]

Gerkin characterizes the pastoral process with the despairing person in outline form:

1. The pastoral relationship is symbolically interpreted by the despairing person as representative of or incarnating the relationship of God to the self.

2. A process is set in motion which involves an enlargement of and enlightening change in the context within which the person experiences the suffering of his or her despair.[It] loses some of the isolated, hopeless quality.

3. A process is set in motion involving the bridging or gathering together in some greater whole of those splintered, separated aspects of self and life experience. . . .

4. The interpretation of new experience as God's activity seems to take place at points in the process. . . .

5. The process of finding new solutions to old sufferings, a new and hopeful style of interpretation, is sometimes experienced by the person as a symbolic process of dying and being reborn.[27]

Eliciting Commitments. Throughout the entire process, it is very helpful for the minister to seek from the other person a series of commitments for a number of actions: talk with a family member about the problem before the day is over, call the next morning to let the minister know how the conversation went, make an appointment with a doctor, see the minister again after two days, start back to Sunday school, share the struggle with a trusted friend, make a long distance call to someone the person misses, begin exercising, and so on. With a large percentage of people, the relevant possibilities are almost endless.

With every act, some need of the person is touched in some positive way, even if only slightly. There are multiple contributions to the sense that one can do things for oneself; there is less helplessness and therefore less hopelessness, a bit more self-esteem. Thus the person begins to feel that he or she is *worth* doing something for, worth caring for. In addition, with each commitment to action, the minister is helping the person buy more time, which the process itself needs in order to move to the point where the person no longer wants to attempt suicide, though all problems may not be resolved. Such a time is very brief during most situational crises, with longer and varying time frames for persons not in this type of crisis. The series of commitments to action also forces the person to begin thinking in terms of some future, a process which had been blocked before.

In terms of the inner resources, the type of exploration in feelings and needs and relationships that has been referred to will probably have revealed some ego strengths dynamically connected with the person's "want to live" side of the ambivalence. Every aspect of that part of the person's life needs to be pointed out clearly, discussed in detail, and reinforced in order that the person recognizes his or her own strengths, establishes them more firmly, and is enabled to draw upon them.

For a number of people there may be aspects of faith to emphasize and build upon: the givenness of life by God; God's love for this particular person, whatever he or she has done, experienced, thought, felt; God's forgiveness; God's mission in the world to which that person might make a contribution; the impact of that person's life or death on the community of faith; and others. It is obvious that these are not possible subjects for a series of mini-sermons to the person, but relevant responses to the person's indications of faith that may appear in interaction with the minister. As these are raised and responded to, further discussion might have the impact of suggesting alternative interpretations of events, other perspectives on situations and oneself and one's future, other possible solutions to problems, additional resources. Such discussion may then contribute to the reviving of hope; an increased sense of worth; a new view of the purposefulness and meaningfulness of life; the value of the person to God, to others, and to the church; and other life-affirming dynamics.

Naturally, as in all pastoral involvement, follow-up contacts appropriate to the situation are to be made. What this means specifically in terms of pastoral visits to home or place of work, and phone calls which express caring and interest, will vary from person to person. Such conversations at the pastor's initiative will be fairly frequent at first, diminishing in frequency over a period of time—the time obviously being shorter following a situational crisis and longer in other situations. These continuing conversations very often offer the greatest opportunities for focused discussions of the role of faith in the person's life, giving greater emphasis to growth in faith and to the consolidating of such growth in terms of firm commitment and increased resources to draw upon in future crises.

After the Suicide Attempt or Suicide

Though the suicide attempter may or may not have been in a situational crisis, it is rare that the attempted or completed suicide is not the precipitating event for such a crisis. This situation is an opportunity for the minister, if not already contacted, to go to people to represent God and the community of faith in an intervention. Attempters will frequently be more highly lethal in any future attempts, and they are more prone to make other attempts.

Family members of the person who killed himself or herself are, as a group, more prone to suicide themselves. Rapid response, sensitive and skilled pastoral care and counseling, and follow-up over a period of time are all called for.

Pastoral Care of Attempters and Their Families

Pastoral care and counseling with an attempter follows very closely the process of helping any suicidal person, although some people in the aftermath of an attempt will be more open to help than they were earlier. Certainly this time provides an entrée to some persons with whom such a possibility had not been previously available. Many persons at this moment will be relieved that they are alive, although not necessarily less suicidal. It does need to be noted that some will be angry that they did not do the job well or that they were rescued. There may be relief and anger at the same time, with one of these being visible, the other hidden.

Such reactions, whatever they are, provide opportunity for the minister to demonstrate caring by close involvement with the person, by personal presence, by being a living symbol of the caring of God and the church, and by the accurate communication of empathy, with the potential power all these indications of caring might have for establishing a meaningful and helpful pastoral relationship.

Some aspects of facilitating a person's self-exploration more fully immediately following a suicidal act from which the person did not die will be somewhat different from a conversation with a person who has become suicidal but has never attempted, or has not attempted for a long time. It is potentially quite useful to focus on the act itself and the period of time before and following the act. What were the significant events and relationships leading up to the intensity of the suicidal impulse and/or the desire to cry for help in this particular way? What were the feelings the person had for significant others and in reaction to certain events? Did the attempt appear to take place in the context of a situational crisis? If so, what was the precipitating event and the identified threat to the person? In what ways had the person already tried to resolve the problem and reduce the pain? How much did the person really want to be dead? Did the person commit the act and then tell someone else? If so, how does the person understand the connection between these two acts? Did his or her feelings change after committing the act? What sort of fantasies did the person have? Were they of being rescued? By whom? What took place in the rescue fantasy? Were there fantasies of being dead and then observing the reactions of others? What others, and how were they reacting? What clues do the responses to all these questions give to the person's past and present needs?

Further pastoral conversations with the attempter will follow something of the outline and procedures suggested in this chapter for any suicidal person, whether the pastor is the primary helper or the person is hospitalized and/or seeing a psychiatrist or psychologist.

Another difference, however, exists when the attempter is living with, is near, and/or has been closely involved with family (a spouse, parents, children, or some combination of these). Most of the time, regardless of the context of the attempt, the act itself will trigger a family crisis. At this point, the various issues discussed in the chapter "Intervening in Family Crises" will arise and family crisis intervention procedures will be applicable. Nothing will be different in terms of the minister's evaluation of or functioning with the family, except for the specific attention given to the family's reactions to the attempter, the attempter's feelings about himself or herself and his or her reaction to the family's reactions, and the continued monitoring of lethality potential and the taking of those actions necessary to protect the highly suicidal person.

Reactions in the family will be similar to those in response to many other events which trigger family crises: shock, disbelief, anger, fear, guilt, shame, although frequently more intense than in other situations. It is always wise to be aware that the intensity of one feeling may cover up others. The pastor's goals and the procedures for working with the family are the same as those given in the earlier chapter.

Some cities have organized groups of suicide attempters, led either by professionals or trained lay volunteers. Occasionally it may be a self-help group. It is important for the minister to know whether such a group exists and enough about it to make some judgment about its potential usefulness to a particular attempter. Many attempters are helped by talking with, being supported by, and getting feedback from other attempters.

Ministry to Survivors of Suicide

With the family and other significant persons in the life of someone who has just committed suicide (survivors of suicide), all the usual schedules and procedures of ministry to the bereaved, as these have been discussed in Chapter 6, would be followed. Of course, it is necessary to give special attention to the probable higher intensities of anger and guilt, the greater possibility of suicidal thoughts or feelings, the greater ambivalence toward the dead person, and thus the probable greater complexity of the grief reaction itself.

Stone, when he assessed generalized feelings of anger as expressed in heightened irritability, found no difference between the spouses of a suicide and those whose spouses had died in some other way. However, 54 percent of the survivors of suicide were aware of being angry at the dead person, in contrast with 22 percent of the other group. In the assessment of guilt, only a very small number of the nonsuicide respondents felt that they had in any way contributed to the death of the spouse; however, over 50 percent of the suicide survivors had that feeling. Survivors of suicide believed they should have done more for the spouse while still alive than did the others (65% to 35%). Of the survivors of suicide, 69 percent felt guilty about things they had said and done to the now-dead spouse, in contrast with 32 percent of the other group.[28]

In that same research, only 12 percent of the nonsuicide group indicated they had thought of killing themselves, but 32 percent of the survivors of suicide had such ideas and feelings.[29] Sources of this reaction may be "identification with the deceased, an attempt to rejoin a lost one, or a learned reaction to stress."[30]

The minister working with persons whose family member has committed suicide needs to pay special attention to the fact that frequently the survivors will become much more emotionally fixed on the *cause* of the death than on the *death itself*.[31] They are so preoccupied with the *suicide* and their feelings of anger and guilt and shame that they do not allow themselves to experience the *loss as such* and whatever genuine sorrow (or sometimes relief, or a combination of the two) is present, which must be felt and expressed if the grief is to be resolved constructively. As a matter of fact, such preoccupation may even be employed as a way to avoid the greater pain of loss.

The pastor can be guided in ministering to these persons by the information just summarized. Anger and guilt are to be listened for and responded to with understanding and acceptance—both are natural. Even though many of the expressions of guilt may sound unrealistic, it is most useful to allow and even to encourage its full expression, with the minister's first responses being statements of accurate empathy and questions of clarification. It is not wise to offer our perspectives prematurely, however valid we believe they might be. As some bit of time goes by after the funeral and we have already had several conversations with the person, both we and they will be in a position to distinguish more clearly between guilt that is relatively realistic and that which is not. One realistic factor is that two people are always in a relationship and that the behavior of one does have an impact on the other. Being human, persons are not perfect, and hurtful behavior and neglect can be pointed to in any relationship. Gradually, through detailed discussion, it can be seen which were genuine violations, truly hurtful to another, and forgiveness may be sought and experienced.

These situations are different from the many others in which people wish they had handled themselves differently with another person, and for which they may have *regret*, different from guilt, and therefore for which the experience of guilt is inappropriate. The pastor can be very helpful in this process of sorting out the differences between guilt and regret and discussing which reaction goes with which behavior.

However, even with behaviors and omissions in the relationship for which there may be guilt or regret, *the survivor did not cause* the other person's death. Whatever the degree of freedom of choice of the suicidal person (and suicidal persons differ from one another in that degree of freedom), he or she committed the act. Surely some survivors played their role in contributing to a poor relationship, and for this they may feel guilt and need forgiveness. But they did not *cause* the suicide. Sooner or later, the minister will need to work intensively with some persons on this issue.

The funeral need be no different from any other, except that special care needs to be taken that persons' realistic feelings and questions as a result of this kind of death are brought into the open and recognized as being inevitable and natural.

If the facts surrounding the death are unknown or ambiguous, any speculation one way or the other is out of place at the funeral. There was a sudden death, and it can be responded to only as any other sudden death.

When it is clear that the death was by suicide, but the family (or some members of the family) is still actively denying that fact, the minister is in the difficult position of needing to respect their defenses at this time, while recognizing the reality of the questions and feelings of most of the people present.

When the family acknowledges the fact of the suicide, it is particularly important that the anger and sorrow and guilt be openly recognized, along with the "why" questions. There may be no clear answers, but the fact that people have questions needs to be raised. It is critical that the minister not be led, by whatever reason, into assuming the prerogative that belongs only to God and declaring that he or she is privy to the dead person's eternal destiny. Faith does not declare that ministers have such information. What faith *does* clearly declare is that "God is love," that God's attitude and action towards God's creatures are like those displayed in the obedient behavior of Jesus, and that this God and this God alone handles issues dealing with eternity. It is in this God that we trust.

Close consultation with the family prior to the funeral is especially important in order that the minister be clear as to how different members view the mode of death and how they feel about that mode of death and the deceased person.

Finally, the minister is in the unique position of being the teacher and guide of the congregation. This provides the opportunity to draw the congregation's concern and active support around the survivors. The minister must not be trapped by the expectation that he or she will do all the supporting. Approaches to understanding and helping may be communicated in the worship service, the church letter or bulletin; in a special meeting with the official governing body of the congregation; by an appearance in the person's or family's Sunday school class or classes; and by specific phone calls to certain individuals who might be capable of helping in various ways. This building of support begins with encouraging the congregation to attend the funeral; it includes food, child care, visits to the spouse, parents, children, and other services appropriate to the needs of the particular person or family.

Many persons' fears of death (suicide in particular), of the intensity of another person's grief, of not knowing what to say or do stand in the way of the people of faith fulfilling their ministry to others who have lost someone close to them by suicide. The minister may need to suggest, encourage, teach, and even have follow-up conversations with members of the congregation, if they are to comfort and support the bereaved. More important than any other response in its impact on the survivors is the *withdrawal* of people at this particular time of need and their unwillingness to talk at all about the grief and the survivors' memories of the deceased. Once visitors have in mind only a few things *not* to say, their time with the survivors can be comforting, regardless of what else might be said or done. Therefore, they are to avoid:

"It's such a tragedy that he's in hell now."
"Somehow it must all be God's will."
"You don't really *mean* what you just said."
"It'll all turn out just fine."
"There's really no need for you to feel that way now."

In contrast, people are to be encouraged to go just to be there, to listen, if possible to help the other express herself or himself more openly and fully, to do some job or errand that needs to be done, to say in some way, "I care for you."

In terms of the pastoral care schedule, in most instances more frequent contact and a longer period of time for follow-up are called for than in most grief situations.

In some cities, there are ongoing groups for survivors of suicide. These may have been established by some agency or professional or concerned lay person (usually a family member of someone who killed himself or herself). Just as with attempers, it helps the minister in serving distressed people to know whether such a group exists. If it does, it has the potential of being quite useful to persons who are grieving because of the suicide of a family member.

Summary

Though most ministers will not often find themselves working with highly lethal suicidal persons or conducting funerals of persons who have killed themselves, when these occasions do arise, they are times of intense emotion and unusual opportunity, and call for even greater sensitivity and skill and courage and persistence than most other pastoral situations. In addition, ministers very frequently are in touch with people who have had or who are presently having suicidal thoughts and/or feelings. They are in the congregation on any given Sunday. We greet them casually in the church or around the community almost every day. We make pastoral calls on them, almost always for some other reason. They see us for counseling, dealing with other issues. All too often the subject of suicide does not arise. It is the responsibility of the ministers to present themselves to the congregation and community and to respond to people in pastoral conversations in ways that are invitational to bringing such suicidal thoughts and feelings into the open. Unique opportunities await such ministers.

This chapter has attempted to survey some of the most important understandings and procedures ministers will need in order to maximize their effectiveness in such situations: the psychodynamics of the suicidal person, the evaluation of lethality, counseling with suicidal persons in situational crisis, effective referral, the clarification of the meaning of confidentiality in such situations, working with attempters and the survivors of those who have killed themselves, and the funerals of those who have killed themselves. In addition to what the minister has to offer by way of technical knowledge and counseling skills, and in addition to the unique characteristics of the minister's context and methods of operation as a helping person in contrast with other helpers, the minister's own faith and the power of the gospel itself, as it is shared in the helping relationship, can be a potent force in leading to the healing of hurt and brokenness.

CHAPTER 10

THE MINISTER,
THE CONGREGATION, AND
COMMUNITY CRISIS SERVICES

This book has pointed to some of the aspects of the total context of operation, the tradition, and expected functions of the clergy which show them to be uniquely suited for the role of crisis counselor, a role in which they already spend a large amount of their time. In order to assist them in developing their effectiveness in this task and opportunity to a higher level of competence, details of crisis theory, the crisis counseling process, and some specific forms of intervention have been presented.

It now remains to consider the larger context of the minister's arena of functioning, with regard to the nature of the congregation and the minister's relationship to other crisis agencies and mental health professionals. This last chapter will seek to sketch that picture briefly.

The Minister and Community Crisis Services

Ministers are called and ordained not only to serve their own congregations directly, but the larger community within and for which the congregations exist. They ordinarily perform this service through direct helpful contact with persons and families, through a variety of educational activities, and through a number of functions within other established helping agencies.

Fulfilling the Traditional Role of the Clergy

The emphasis of this book has been on the ministers' own work, operating within their own congregations as crisis counselors—one of the functions both they and their congregations expect them to perform. This does not mean, of course, that the only persons pastors see are members of their congregations, but it is the institution within which they do their work and from which they go to serve the larger community. The point has been made that by fulfilling this role conscientiously they are not only being faithful to the ministry of the church but are also to be viewed as very important frontline mental health professionals. In several places the unique advantages of the clergy over other mental health professionals have been mentioned, presuming that they capitalize upon these advantages and do so with competence. An excellent presentation elaborating this point has been made, happily enough, by a nonministerial professional in the field of community psychiatry. In summary, she states that pastors have a population focus (the congregation and its constituency), are known by this population and know them, are less threatening for many people to approach than is a psychiatrist or anyone else in a psychiatric clinic, are likely to see people at an early stage of disturbance or in crisis, may respond within a short time to a distress call, and, because of their knowledge of a person, may assess the situation or condition more rapidly, do not expect a fee, have the initiative to intervene, are expected to call in homes, remain close to those they have counseled through other forms of relationship, offer a variety of modes for continuing care, have a position of authority that may be sensitively utilized in some instances, are in a context in which guilt may be effectively dealt with, and have rituals that are helpful to many people.[1]

When ministers do persistently and well what is given by their situation as pastor, they are making a significant contribution to persons and to the mental health of the community.

Working with Community Crisis Services

However, ministers also have additional opportunities by relating themselves to mental health agencies in general, and to crisis intervention and suicide prevention centers in particular. Many ministers should associate themselves with these agencies in forms specific to the minister's own interests and abilities and the needs of those organizations. This directive, while important, should not be misunderstood. Although ministers who have no concern whatsoever for the effectiveness of the operation of mental health services in their community should examine the quality of their own caring for persons, it is not being suggested that every minister could or should actually work in some way with these agencies, or that they are the only, or even the most important community services that should be supported with the ministers' money, time, and talent. The major point of this exhortation is merely to declare that each of us exists in the midst of many distressed and disturbed persons. There are a variety of ways in which these needs might be met. A number of different types of agencies or programs, including crisis intervention and suicide prevention centers already are or could be operating in every community of any size, either as separate agencies or as an important and available function of a broader agency or institution such as a general mental health clinic, public health clinic, hospital or Council of Churches counseling center. Many ministers have this type of service to persons as one of their high priorities and also have the training and experience to be useful to such a program. Such ministers can increase their usefulness by actively searching out these opportunities.

One study clarifies the great gap between the stated care and actual behavior of ministers in this regard. In a survey taken of a hundred ministers in order to get a picture of their mental health activities as defined by prevention, counseling, and referral, only two felt they were forced against their own desires into such a role. On the other hand, ninety-eight expressed great interest and concern for this aspect of the minister's work and felt they should be involved. Yet even though a majority carried on counseling and other preventive activities within the church, only seven belonged to any type of mental health organization, and it might be presumed that some of these were not even direct service agencies.[2] Recognizing the tremendous demands on a minister's time and the existence of other high priorities, this picture remains a bleak commentary on what we claim our concern to be.

One word of warning: The response by other mental health professionals and even by lay people will not always be an enthusiastic welcome to ministers who volunteer. However, this realism should not deter the clergy from proposing that they are legitimate and important professionals in this field, especially that of crisis, and that they are available. The pastor will often, if not always, find significant opportunity for helping.

Ministers are, in fact, working with satisfaction to themselves, with value to agencies, and with both direct and indirect advantages to persons in need, in a number of different capacities. Clergy may carry to board membership their knowledge of effective organizational behavior, personal relationships, program supervision, or finances. As members of a personnel committee they may use their own congregation, and organize other ministers to use theirs, as resources for the selection of volunteer workers of high quality. If they happen to have clinical skills, they may be on a clinical services committee, do face-to-face or telephone counseling, make emergency visits to persons who have called a telephone crisis center, or become trainers of lay volunteers.

Since there has been an explosive increase in the number of such telephone crisis services, the church itself being the initiator and sponsor of many, and with many of the others looking to ministers for different forms of support, it might be appropriate to comment upon the pastor's role in and responsibility to them, along with some dangers of which to be aware.

The point has already been made that such a form of helping is an appropriate place for ministers to invest themselves, and some of the ways in which they might do so have already been listed. In some communities, individual ministers or groups have initiated discussions that have led to the development of telephone services. In these instances, one would assume that they have consulted from the very beginning with mental health professionals in their area, for several reasons. The most important are, of course, to profit from their insights in the surveying of community needs, to plan for the selection, training, and supervision of the workers, and to implement day-to-day operational guidelines and procedures.

This is not to suggest that everything every mental health professional says should be accepted as final law. That becomes quite clear as we observe the differing among themselves as to whether the community needs such a service, whether it can accomplish the purposes proposed, whether lay people can do such work, how much training is necessary before work on the telephone begins, and other issues. Nevertheless, such input is important in making those decisions necessary for getting an agency underway.

Second, effective strategy suggests that the professionals in a community always be kept fully informed of what is taking place, even if some of them are in disagreement with the whole or parts of the project. A professional's suspicions concerning the operation may often be more damaging to its usefulness in the community than his or her knowledge of its actual weaknesses.

Third, it is important that some of these professionals be involved in some way in the ongoing program through board membership and policy-making, training, supervision, and consultation. Most of those telephone agencies that have sought, with whatever good intentions, to offer their services to a community without having these forms of relationship with mental health professionals have had significant barriers to overcome, have often done as much harm as good, and occasionally have failed to overcome the barriers and have passed out of existence.

It has not only been the case that some of the telephone services, through a lack of wisdom, have failed to have adequate professional consultation and supervision, but others have actually had an antiprofessional tone. The assumption of some, particularly those who are youth-oriented, is that any young person can automatically communicate well with any other young person, that any former drug user by virtue of that fact can help a drug user, and that mere openness, acceptance, and unstructured relationships are therapeutic. These assumptions are not substantiated by the actual data. As a matter of fact, they may cause harm.[3] Ministers should associate themselves with such unsupervised activities and unchallenged assumptions only with the greatest caution, and then only in personal consultation with a mental health professional and with the view of upgrading the service through the introduction of professional supervision. While volunteers in such services may very well be young people, former drug users, members of the counterculture, it is still essential for effective service that they be selected on the basis of their therapeutic potential for those in distress, be trained, and have professional supervision.

Community Crisis

One area in which most ministers have very little training, and only by coincidence any experience, is that of community-wide crisis, such as geographical areas might suffer as a result of earthquakes, tornadoes, hurricanes, or floods, or in community crisis reactive to the significant and sudden loss of a number of lives through an explosion, fire, or other accident.

The minister, along with other community helpers (doctors, nurses, social workers, schoolteachers), is in a unique position to work to alleviate overwhelming community needs.

John Reed has offered helpful material to ministers, growing out of his own personal experience and reflection. He refers to the intense, persistent needs of persons in the aftermath of disaster: the stress of uprootedness, the loss of possessions, the loss of boundaries. He does not specifically discuss massive loss by death of family members and friends, but one may presume the issues he would emphasize. Loss of possessions is more than a financial loss, since so many are symbolic, self-extensions, linked with persons' ego structure. By the same token, loss of physical or geographical boundaries are often experienced as the loss of ego boundaries. In the midst of all this there tends to be a preoccupation with the disaster that leads people to neglect certain of their own needs and many of their usual responsibilities. There is the need, Reed states, "for enlightened long-term pastoral care following disaster." The pastor can play a critical role in assisting people in mobilizing their own resources, gaining some balanced perspective on their needs and responsibilities, accepting their losses, and finally, readapting to a more "everyday" manner of living, in which the individual is no longer a victim or a "special" person. These pastoral tasks are accomplished by regular and frequent home visitation, getting people to talk, helping guard people's privacy, being patient with typical transient crisis behavior, and continuing to show concern over a period of months.[4]

A newspaper feature has reported the service of the Center for Preventive Psychiatry in White Plains, New York, in the aftermath of the flood suffered in the city of Corning following Hurricane Agnes.[5] The mental health team identified these as the basic psychological needs of the people: to express fully their feelings about their loss of homes, possessions, family, friends, their feelings of helplessness, anxiety, despair, anger. The people in the community who did not have such direct losses often were troubled by guilt over having escaped—an irrational, but nonetheless real and troublesome feeling.

The primary methodology of the mental health team was to get people to share their feelings with one another in groups, utilizing as far as possible the natural and already organized groups that exist in any community—professional societies, civic and service clubs, church groups, etc. A second methodology was to meet with the teachers and school administrators to help them work effectively with the types of problems they would have when the children returned to school, enabling these natural community leaders to assist those for whom they are responsible in expressing their feelings and in dealing with the realities of the situation without denial. A third means of meeting the psychological emergencies of the area was to set up a twenty-four-hour "help and rumor" line, alleviating people's anxieties both by crisis counseling and by simply giving accurate information.

Following the disaster and during the whole emergency period, only a very few suicides and psychotic breaks were recorded in Corning, in contrast with another city which had suffered equally from the flood but where no similar intensive mental health services were rendered. There the rate of suicide and psychotic reactions doubled. This has been interpreted as one bit of evidence of the value of the procedures. It requires no imagination to see where ministers would fit into such a situation, with their already established community leadership, their relatively open door to civic and service clubs, their meaningful symbols of the church and the faith, their congregations smaller units, their visiting of families and groups of families, and their participation on newly organized emergency mental health teams.

Considerable study has been made of the Buffalo Creek flood. Early Saturday morning, February 26, 1972, a dam made of slag from a mine gave way, and thousands of tons of mud and water roared down that narrow valley in southern West Virginia, leaving 125 dead, hundreds injured, and 4,000 or more homeless. Within hours, the National Guard sealed off the area and medical units from nearby hospitals evacuated the injured. Volunteer rescue teams began work, and the Red Cross and Salvation Army brought in food and supplies.

At first people stayed with friends, family members, or in a school gymnasium just outside the area. Later the Department of Housing and Urban Renewal provided trailers in thirteen different sites in and near the valley, but these were allotted on a first-come, first-serve basis, so the separation of persons from their families, friends, neighbors, and original homesites became institutionalized. The state quickly decided to build a highway through the valley, thereby tying up the land so that many people were prevented from moving back to their own homesites and rebuilding. Two years later, many were still waiting for decisions to be made concerning the use of their land.

A number of systematic and sophisticated psychological studies were made of the dislocated survivors. Titchener and Kapp found disabling psychiatric symptoms (anxiety, depression and despair, delusions, occasional hallucinations, repetitive nightmares and other sleep disturbances, impotent rage, a sense of dehumanization, and other symptoms) in over 90 percent of the people they interviewed more than two years after the flood. The various ways the people themselves tried to cope with these feelings and experiences became maladaptive, producing unhappiness and interfering with relationships, work, and play. These results were attributed to the impact of the disaster itself, with its multiple losses of family and friends by death, of home and possessions, and to the subsequent disruption and failure to reestablish the sense of community that had been so much a part of their lives.[6]

These findings were substantiated by Gleser and others in a later study, using a different design and some different procedures but identifying some of the same and some additional negative psychological effects.[7]

Unfortunately, these reports fail to make any mention of systematic visitation on the part of ministers, pastoral care, grief counseling and other crisis intervention, community-building activities, or advocacy with the mining company or governmental agencies. As a matter of fact, ministers were available and active. Jordan has indicated that local pastors contacted the chaplains at Appalachian Regional Hospital, who then came to the scene and assisted with emergency pastoral care and crisis intervention. An ecumenical program of pastoral care and counseling follow-up was established, including home visitation. Undoubtedly these ministers rendered significant help, but the tasks of social reorganization in this particular disaster, exacerbated by the break-up of families and close communities over a long period of time, were formidable.[8]

Among the many other needs people have in the face of any crisis, and certainly a community disaster, is the need for meaning. Human beings seem naturally compelled to try to make sense out of their experiences. There are a number of different ways of framing the questions and the attempts to answer them—scientific, philosophical, religious—which may be mutually exclusive for some persons, but are not necessarily so. These three often complement one another within the same individual.

The Perrys investigated family and community determinants of children's responses to the impact of a tornado which destroyed two rural Mississippi schools in 1955, killing a number of children. The Perrys state that part "of the social expression of disturbance . . . centered around the attempt to see the meaning of the disaster. There were expressions of confusion and perplexity, bewilderment and incoherency."[9] The authors affirm that the many questions which arise in such situations . . .

must somehow be answered in a way that makes personal and social sense to the survivors. Naturalistic or scientific explanations are sufficient to some people, but many survivors need another sort of explanation, generally one couched in terms of their religious traditions. They need an explanation that answers "why" and not merely "how."[10]

The Perrys' report speaks at one point of the role a minister played, but it was an ambiguous one. Everyone spoke of him as something of a hero in the rescue operations. Yet after those efforts had been completed, the minister seemed to withdraw, be uninvolved, and have either a reluctance or an inability to discuss his or other people's feelings, or to serve as a guide in the struggle for meaning in which the people were involved. The people reacted to this behavior with confusion and anxiety, followed by an increased rigidity in thought and behavior.[11]

While ministers are not the only professionals or designated or natural community leaders involved in working with people in the realm of meaning, collectively they are very significant in most communities and therefore have a unique opportunity to take a major role with congregations, other community groups, and individuals, as people very naturally respond to the shattering of their "assumptive worlds" with an intense search for some meaning that can help reconstruct their lives.[12]

The Minister's Relationship with Other Mental Health Professionals

The way this section heading is phrased assumes what has already been made clear to the reader—that by virtue of being an effective and faithful minister of the church, the pastor is in fact an important mental health professional with a unique contribution to make. However, it should not be misinterpreted as suggesting that all, or even most psychiatrists, psychologists, and psychiatric social workers and nurses accept this as self-evident. To the contrary, some have had early personal experiences or contacts with ministers, or with their own clients, which have caused them either to be dubious about the value of ministers' work with persons or to be downright negative about it. Others have not even considered the possible value of a close working relationship with the clergy.

Some of the psychotherapeutic professionals' suspicions concerning ministers are founded more on experience than on ignorance and prejudice, although these may also be present. There are ministers who are naive psychologically, ineffective as pastors and counselors, and who hold and communicate attitudes and utilize methods of handling emotions and drives that may be harmful to some persons. Certainly we all realize that the qualifications for ministers are much more varied than those for other professionals, and therefore the label *minister* says absolutely nothing about educational and other training prerequisites, in contrast with the medical, psychological, and, to a somewhat lesser degree, social work professionals.

Nevertheless, an increasing number of ministers are becoming better trained in dealing with people and their problems, and many others who are not formally trained are sensitive and competent and helpful human beings within the framework of their vocation. These persons form a great pool of helping resources for a large percentage of our population, and their lives and ministry do in fact touch more persons in some ways than does the service of other professionals. At the same time, since the training of ministers is so varied, when they get into the area of assisting persons in crisis, there is still much to learn from other professionals.

The following diagram shows some of the lines for interprofessional support and collaboration in a full therapeutic program for meeting the needs of individuals and families in crisis.

First, the teacher-learner relationship presumes what is usually true, that the professional psychotherapist has accumulated a certain body of knowledge concerning personality development, psychodynamics, psychopathology, and interpersonal relationships, and has developed certain insights and skills related to therapeutic communication which the majority of ministers have not had the opportunity to obtain, even though we may have considerable experience in dealing with people. Since ministers are so strategically located throughout most communities and, by virtue of their position, are related to such a large number of people and so readily available to additional numbers, it only makes good sense for the mental health professionals of every community to offer, and the ministers of every community to seek, specialized continuing education in the area of understanding individual and family dynamics and improving counseling skills.

Second, simply in performing their usual expected work, ministers frequently will be the primary crisis counselors to many persons and families (in grief, loss of job, change of residence, family conflict,

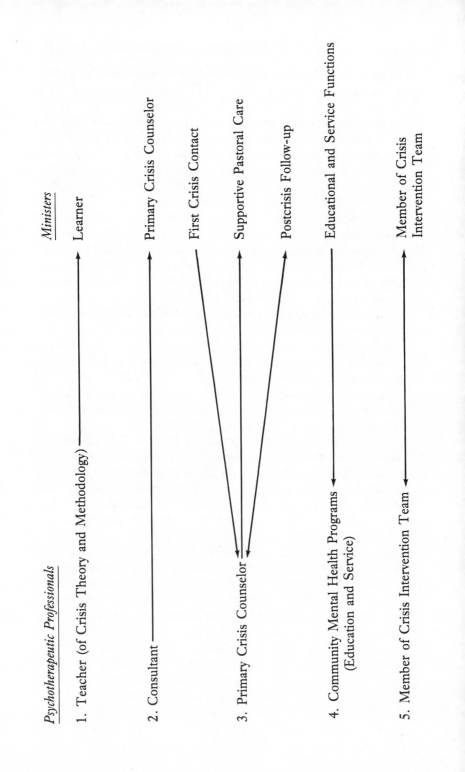

divorce). In many instances they will be able to assist persons through these crises successfully, anxiety will diminish, mood will lift, decisions will be made, constructive action initiated. They will do this through the meaning of their ordination (their symbol power), the strength of their genuine humanity, and whatever knowledge they have of crisis counseling. On occasion, the nature of the person or family undergoing crisis, or the intensity of the crisis itself, combined with a lack of clarity concerning the issues involved, the interventions to utilize, the possible directions to take, may lead the minister to seek one or more consultation sessions with another professional. In such a case, the minister would make an appointment with the other professional, describe the total situation, discuss all the issues, and receive guidance as to procedures in working with the person in crisis. The minister continues to be the primary counselor, with assistance from the psychotherapist.

There may be several sources and forms of this arrangement. Some ministers may be fortunate enough to have, in their own congregations, one or more such professionals who would be willing to provide this type of consultation to their own pastor, without charge, as a part of their own lay ministry. Or outside the congregation, some professional might be found who would be willing to donate some amount of time. Most ministers, however, will probably not be so fortunate.

Three other routes remain open. If the mental health professional is in private practice or working for a private institution or agency, it is proper for that person to expect a fee for consultation services. Either the minister would need to pay this, or the congregation could see the value of such a procedure and put this item in its budget. Only a few hundred dollars would purchase quite enough time for most ministers' needs over the period of a year.

A second route is described by Ruth Caplan: A particular denomination could purchase regular group consultation services for its ministers within a geographic area.[13] Most denominational or faith groups have such administrative budgets, as well as the contacts necessary to employ competent professionals, neither of which do most pastors of small churches have.

A third route is available in those cities and counties with an organized Mental Health-Mental Retardation program, where, in order to receive federal funds, the agency is required to provide consultation for the various helping persons of its area.

The third form of interprofessional relationship occurs when ministers are confronted with crisis situations in which a family is deeply disturbed, with strong and rigid dysfunctional communication and behavior patterns, or an individual has elements of psychopathology which render a particular minister's usual crisis counseling procedures ineffective. In such cases ministers would move toward referral or transferral to a psychiatrist or psychologist or other appropriate professional, with the latter becoming the primary therapist.

However, it should be clear that more often than not, the minister involved stays in the picture. He or she remains the pastor to the person or persons through appropriate phone calls and visits, maintaining personal interest, representing the congregation and the faith, and supporting commitment to counseling. The pastor may, in mutual understanding with the primary therapist, be in a situation to make emergency personal calls when the therapist or the person in crisis feels this is important. Finally, when formal counseling is completed, the other professional might be very happy to know that the minister will provide follow-up pastoral care.

In the area of community mental health programs, there are a number of functions the trained and sensitive minister might perform in support of the efforts of the psychotherapeutic professions. Some have already been mentioned in the discussion of the various roles of ministers in telephone-crisis agencies. In addition to these, the dialogue established between the various professions may give the minister the opportunity to clarify to others the particular view of human life that the community of faith understands, reemphasizing for all persons in the helping professions the ultimate value of persons, the role of faith in individuals' lives, the relationship of responsible (ethical) behavior to human well-being, and dimensions of being fully human that are not related only to materialistic pursuits. The frequent injection of this emphasis into interprofessional discussions and training programs, while not designed as a sneaky form of evangelism, should certainly have some effect of sensitizing mental health workers to how significant the religious perspective toward life might be to many of their own clients. This may then, occasionally, lead to other professionals' consulting with a minister whom they respect in regard to moral and religious dimensions of their clients' lives, or even making a referral to the pastor.

Finally, in some places, crisis intervention teams have been developed. The standard personnel are psychiatrists, psychologists, psychiatric social workers, and nurses. In the light of the third and fourth possible working relationships mentioned above, it would be logical for specially trained ministers to be members of such teams, for the mutual edification of all the professionals and for service to the persons in crisis.

The Congregation as a Context for Crisis Ministry

When we ministers consider the acting out of our vocation, a full understanding requires that we keep two things in mind simultaneously. First, we exist *not only* for our own congregations. Rather, as a part of and servant to and representative of the congregation, like the congregation, we exist for the world. Though "Christ loved the *church* and gave himself up for her," "God so loved the *world* that he gave his only Son" (Eph. 5:25; John 3:16, italics mine). The church as the Body of Christ exists for the same reason Jesus himself did, to be God's Servant to all persons, to all humankind. This is our mandate to be involved in the larger community in whatever forms of service are appropriate to our interests, abilities, training, and the needs that are apparent to us. This naturally brings many ministers into professional interaction with the mental health sector. Second, at the same time we participate in other agencies alongside other professionals, learning from them and working with them to meet human need, we must never lose sight of who we are and whose we are. We are a part of God's people, rendering our service out of commitment to God. Wherever we are, the congregation always forms the context for our activity. This is not only to speak of a particular mind-set with which we operate at all times, but much more concretely, it is a reminder to persons and families in crisis of the specific values of the community of faith in its organized life together.

Faith and Its Ritualistic Celebration

Every person lives by some internal impetus which might properly be called faith. It is that to which we commit ourselves as having some ultimacy, some overarching guiding significance for our lives. Individuals are not always fully aware of what this is for them or, if somewhat aware, do not clearly and fully articulate it and often do not celebrate it, either alone or with other persons who share a similar faith. But faith has a potency, provides motivation, suggests goals and behavioral guidelines, *is* in a sense why a person is living and why that person is living at a given time and in a given way.

The Judaeo-Christian faiths combine in a unique way for many people the dimensions of the long past, a tradition that includes their own individual briefer pasts, the high significance of the present moment, and a serious emphasis on the future, linked in some way with God's own future and thereby secured by God's love. Faith leads us into an experience of our own ultimate worth, since we are those whom God loves ultimately and without condition. It suggests that the present can always be viewed in the light of God's activity on our behalf both in the past and in the future, no matter how unaware we may be of God's caring at the moment. Thus there is always meaning in the present, though we may not *know* in the present precisely what that meaning is, and there is hope for the future. This hope is not knowledge of the form of our future life and its meaning, but an assurance that, without taking responsible decision and action out of our hands, the future belongs to the God who does love us and act for us, and all this without a denial of the reality of what is *now* taking place.

The implications of this faith for a person in crisis as it has been defined in this book are obvious. The person in crisis is one who has begun to lose perspective, feel anxious and helpless, often depressed and worthless, frequently without hope, one whose future seems to be blocked out, who even has lost sight of some of the past. Faith, as briefly outlined above, is a direct counterforce to the dynamics of crisis.

This should not be misinterpreted to mean that the needs of a person in crisis will be met by the mere mouthings of doctrines, religious catch phrases, or the quick and casual quoting of Scripture, although for some people appropriate verbalizations which reflect the realities of the experience of faith may be stabilizing. More effective is the ministry of the representative of the congregation, the pastor, with the symbol power that communicates the faith; being surrounded by the community of faith, joining with it in the group celebration of their common life, hearing and participating with this group in prayer, Scripture-reading, acts of praise in the midst of present suffering, hearing the Word proclaimed—all this reemphasizes for the person who she or he is, who her or his support is (both the Lord and the congregation), and what her or his future may be. In addition, there are the smaller groups within the congregation: the classes, the study groups, men's, women's, or youth organizations, and those individuals who express their care and concern in a variety of ways. Emotions may be expressed, perspective broadened, the future opened, direct present support given, all in the service of crisis resolution.

Ruth Caplan mentions "the role of regular religious observance in preserving mental health."[14] She speaks of the provision of a certain order in an individual's life that is of continuing therapeutic value.

> The fact that such observances are repeated at regular intervals steadily reinforces the message of discipline, structure, and identity. It regularly renews community contacts and devotion to that group's ideals by repeated exposure to signs of fellowship. As behavioral scientists have discovered, people need a *constant* flow of physical and social supplies and stimulation to maintain their well-being.[15]

Certainly for the person in crisis for whom such a faith and its celebration has had some meaning, even though that meaning may not in the past have been one of high emotional impact or constant conscious awareness, there is a way in which these symbols may reach deep into the person's life and stimulate hidden resources, reminding that person of the larger context of meaning within which he or she as a human being exists and bringing a strengthening, stabilizing power.

A Lay Crisis Ministry

In addition to the possibilities for the person in crisis growing out of the nature of religious faith itself and participation in the community of faith as it exists in its usual forms of life together, including that of simple personal friendship and support, there is a generally untapped source of power in specifically selected and trained lay persons who have much to give by way of help to other members of the congregation and to the larger community which the congregation also serves.

Lay people have always exercised a number of functions in the church, ranging from the trivial and dispensable to those of great significance and without which congregational life would disintegrate. However, other than their own spontaneous responses as individuals and families to others as they themselves have deemed appropriate, and some routine (routine does *not* mean unimportant) assigned pastoral care functions such as visiting shut-ins or occasionally the hospital, their potential helpfulness in many areas of severe human need has not ordinarily been utilized. One occasionally hears of congregations that have developed a program of lay pastoral care. These are increasing in number, but are still exceptional. Why should this be? While only a small percentage of lay people would have the training necessary to enter into long-term counseling with a person with chronic problems, congregations are full of persons who are relatively mature, have good judgment, can relate well to others, who themselves have experienced a variety of life's stresses and come through these successfully, and who genuinely care for others. An increasing accumulation of experience and a growing body of some precise data based on this experience have demonstrated that such persons, with only a small amount of training, can be extremely helpful in assisting persons in crisis, from mild to severe, and in other situations of need. At the present time, lay volunteers are being effectively used all over this country and in many other countries, in a number of different types of settings, in ways that are useful to persons in distress: crisis intervention and suicide prevention centers, mental health clinics, psychiatric hospitals, day-care centers, and others. The overall positive results are without question.

It should be made very clear that this is not an attempt to make low-level psychiatrists and psychologists. It does mean, however, that it is possible to capitalize on some persons' natural humanity, their own particular personality strengths, to help other persons accomplish significant changes in their lives.[16] It is high time the religious community drew on its own personnel to meet the vast needs of a hurting humanity.

We ministers, if we have not already done so, will need to shift our understanding of some of the ways we approach our tasks in the church and our relationships to the people of our congregations. The day when we viewed ourselves as the only persons capable of rendering pastoral care or engaging in important crisis counseling is past. If we find ourselves at all reluctant to share significant tasks in the congregation with lay people, we should examine our motivation very carefully. All too commonly, we have measured our own value by the amount of work we have done, and in order to do so have needed to guard some functions as belonging exclusively to ourselves. While this may have given us a certain satisfaction, it has often exhausted us, and besides, it is heretical. If we have competence in the pastoral care area (or any other, for that matter), our time and energies will be better spent in the selection, training, and supervision of lay people to share this ministry.

While this procedure will probably neither save time nor decrease the minister's load, the benefits both to ourselves and to the congregation will be many. Our own work will be multiplied, and the congregation will receive a greater amount of supportive care from a greater number of persons. Pastors will also receive satisfaction from teaching others to function in important areas of the life of the congregation, since their own knowledge and skills will be sharpened in the training and supervision process.

A clear understanding of the gospel would seem to lead naturally to increased motivation for the development of more thoroughgoing lay pastoral care in the congregation and in the surrounding community. Stone presents a very concise and convincing statement of the theological foundations, drawing from biblical and later historical sources examples of the creative and redeeming love of God in Christ, with our response to God's love being love of neighbor, expressed in concrete acts of caring.[17] Specific education of the congregation based on such a theological understanding is an essential part of the preparation for lay crisis ministry.

Finally, as a by-product, the very operation of such a program continues to educate the entire congregation as to the nature of the community of faith, the true nature of the laity, and the mutual ministry which persons committed to God owe one another by virtue of this commitment.

In most congregations, the minister's most effective strategy in beginning such a program would be to discuss the whole idea with a few key lay people. When there seems to be some interest, or at least a willingness to look at the matter in more detail, the program is offered for consideration, either to some established group in the church or to a committee especially appointed for this purpose by the appropriate body. Once a proposal makes its way through proper legislative channels in the congregation and is approved, a special committee can be quite important in identifying the functions the lay care givers will be carrying out, advising and guiding the preparation of the congregation, assisting in decisions concerning recruitment, helping to plan the training, and, in general, overseeing the program. Even though the pastor may be the major figure throughout, all such participation by lay people will emphasize the lay nature of the whole project.

Functions. The way ministers make use of the lay people may differ considerably from one setting to another. Most congregations, even relatively small ones, could probably use visitors for the sick in hospitals and at home. An individual or a couple might be assigned to a person or family in grief or to work with the pastor in a grief work group. Some might be on call for individual emergency crisis counseling sessions, either by phone or a visit to the suffering person. Someone might specialize in supporting and guiding persons undergoing divorce or during the period immediately following divorce. Since the move of a household from one community to another often initiates a crisis reaction, particularly in a spouse who does not work outside the home, and also in children, a group of church members might be developed to make regular visits to newcomers in the area. These plans, of course, will depend on the needs of the congregation and the community, the availability of persons to do the work, and the ability of the minister, either alone or assisted by other professionals, to do the selection, training, and supervision.

Selection. Careful and enlightened selection procedures are absolutely crucial.

Two major approaches to recruitment need to be considered carefully; both have advantages and disadvantages which can be openly discussed in the lay planning committee. One alternative is to invite all interested members of the congregation, through a number of public means, to attend an informational meeting, and those whose interest continues may then be invited to pursue the admission process. Details of a program using this method are described in detail by Detwiler-Zapp and Dixon.[18] As another alternative, the pastor and lay committee, having discussed the important characteristics for helping people, then identify and personally invite those persons whom they want to participate. In the first approach, it is sometimes necessary to discuss with some persons who have gone through a screening process that there are questions about their readiness. As difficult as this might be, these questions must be raised concretely and candidly and discussed individually with the person involved, both for the good of the persons themselves and for the quality of the caring program. Occasionally a person's entry into the program needs to be postponed until a later time. This takes place *prior* to the training.

Using the other approach, people are in some sense prescreened.

This avoids the difficulty of discussing with some people their lack of readiness, although at times such a lack may be revealed in the experiential elements of the training. There are other problems with this procedure, such as the possibility of overlooking some quite competent people in the congregation who might be interested in doing the training and work.

In either approach, the training itself should be of such a nature that it will serve as a further screening process, with some people discovering for themselves that they should withdraw from the program.

Several studies give important guidelines as to the characteristics a person should possess in order to utilize the training most completely and work with persons in crisis in the most helpful way. (As these characteristics are reviewed briefly, it might even be well for ministers to be evaluating themselves, and if they believe there are barriers to their own most competent functioning, they may want to seek the assistance of another professional in facilitating their own growth.)

Carkhuff reports a study which refers to "sincere regard for others, tolerance and ability to accept people with values different from one's own, a healthy regard for the self, a warmth and sensitivity in dealing with others, and a capacity for empathy."[19] The "healthy regard for the self" as a factor has been substantiated in a study in which forty-five crisis center directors responded to an adjective checklist as a means of evaluating their most and least effective volunteers, defined in terms of their actual performance in handling crisis calls on the telephone. The checklist did discriminate between the two groups, with the most significant factors statistically being the higher scoring of the effective volunteers on self-confidence and dominance, and their low scoring on abasement. They have, apparently, a more positive view of themselves and what they have to give in a relationship and feel. they have more control over what happens in their relationships with others than do the least effective workers.[20] The study of volunteer workers at the Los Angeles Suicide Prevention Center identified the following as the important criteria for helping persons: maturity, responsibility, willingness to accept training and supervision, ability to get along well in a group, motivation in terms of wanting to work directly with people and to learn and develop personally, and a willingness to give time and effort consistently over a long period.

Persons who are clearly unsuited for this work were identified as those who were looking for a way to gratify their own needs (as distinguished from a legitimate desire to *grow* as a person) and to push their own particular interpretations of human problems and specific solutions. Naturally, rigid persons who cannot adjust to new situations, who are hypercritical and defensive, are unacceptable.[21]

It is critical for the minister and/or lay committees to be very aware of these criteria for selection and apply them rigorously as they make decisions about whom to select, regardless of the process followed. They need to guard against other personal feelings that may influence their evaluations. This program is not something in which to place one's friends regardless of their personal characteristics, or in which to include individuals as a means of trying to help them. They must be persons whose impact on others is consistently therapeutic.

Training. The most effective setting for training is the small group. An appropriate beginning point would be to explore the individuals' motivations for responding to the minister's or committee's invitation, what they believe they have to offer, their fears and misgivings, how they feel about physical illness and hospitals, death and dying, how they have reacted at funerals, their feelings about suicide, how they typically react in the presence of strong emotion. This exploration, while important, must not consume an excessive amount of time, since the training program is much more than an encounter group. At this point, a very useful procedure, presented in detail by Carkhuff, should be followed if at all possible. This procedure is based upon highly sophisticated and well-developed exercises designed to improve one's empathetic sensitivities and communications.[22] These exercises are not effective, however, in the hands of a trainer who is not empathetic and who has not undergone this type of training. Such a minister will need to find someone else to lead this section, or go through these exercises under expert guidance before leading the group, or simply omit the exercises. Any pastor may, of course, read the relevant materials and discuss with the group the necessary ingredients of all helping relationships, with some benefit to the participants if they have been well selected initially.[23]

Additional input would self-evidently include crisis theory, crisis counseling procedures, and techniques of intervention. The methodology of training would be some combination of reading, lecture, listening to tapes of crisis counseling sessions, case study, role-play (or what Clinebell calls "reality practice"), and discussion. Specific problem areas such as physical and mental illness (the latter including an emphasis on depression), grief, family and divorce crises, suicide, and others that may be pertinent for the particular congregation. Obviously, the matter of confidentiality, its meaning and its necessity, will be discussed.

At this time the analysis of crisis counseling tapes, if such are available, and role-play become extremely important. Persons must begin to experience how it feels to be in the helping situation and forced to make specific verbal responses and develop a therapeutic plan for an individual in crisis. The situations should vary according to the specific assignments the lay counselors may later take and also should prepare them to respond flexibly to new situations they might encounter. The anxiety level of participants tends to rise during these sessions and some may decide to withdraw. Great sensitivity on the part of the pastor is needed here in talking with each of these persons individually, walking the fine line between assisting them to understand that the rise in anxiety is normal and that this alone is not sufficient cause to withdraw. But if their feelings are intense enough and continue to get in the way of their helpful responses, the pastor must be able to expedite their resigning from the program in such a way that they will not feel they have failed either themselves or the church. It is clear that not every person can do this sort of work. For those who withdraw, it might be quite helpful to have a few less threatening pastoral care functions for them to move into, helping them to realize that these other areas are also necessary and important and that their training, for the most part, will be quite relevant.

Finally, whenever possible, it can be very helpful for the lay trainees to observe real situations similar to those they will be called upon to enter. Some of these may be easily provided, such as a lay person accompanying the minister on several hospital or grief calls. In some cities it might be possible to work out an arrangement with a telephone crisis service for the church trainees to observe for a shift or two. Ministers will need to use their ingenuity at this point.

It should be noted that this type of training program includes aspects of self-exploration and growth in self-understanding, exercises that lead to greater empathy and empathic communication and some sense of familiarity with a feeling of doing the work itself, as well as instructional sessions of a more traditional didactic method. Summarized in this way, it becomes obvious that this could describe a year or more of full-time training. However, the time required for the *prework* lay crisis care program may range from ten to forty hours, depending upon the specific assignments the laity are to carry out. Hospital visitation alone may require fewer hours; some face-to-face emergency work, many more hours.

It is important to emphasize that this is the *prework* training. There will be supervision of the actual work later, and that will form the foundation of continuing training. Naturally, too little preparation would be unthinkable, but if the training period is too long (in length of time more than in total hours), people frequently begin to lose interest and motivation. An hour a week for forty weeks would probably kill the program, whereas two or three hours a week for twelve to fifteen weeks has been demonstrated to be quite workable. Some have used larger blocks of time: one or more Sunday afternoons and evenings of five or six hours each (the experiential beginnings), a few weekly sessions of didactic material, and a couple of several-hour sessions of tape analysis and role-play to conclude; or two or three whole weekends.

There are a number of models and schedules for training.[24] Stone has developed an especially detailed training program. Each of his chapters (4–11) is an outline of one of the training sessions. Each begins with a proposed schedule for each step of a particular session, homework for the session to follow, then both content and suggested procedures relating to each phase of the particular session. The entire program is chronologically systematic, with each activity within a session building on the one before, and each session building on the preceding sessions. Role-play is recommended as a way to practice the facilitative conditions of the helping relationship presented earlier, as well as to practice helping in certain specific types of situations. Critical to the training is Stone's suggestion that trainees make calls in a nursing home following Session 4, testing out what has been learned and practiced, then using the material growing out of that experience as a springboard to personal growth and greater skill.[25] In making pastoral care assignments such as this during the training process, it is wise to be sensitive to Clinebell's experience of having asked trainees to make a call before they were ready to do so. The result was such an increase of anxiety that Clinebell believes this was the reason "almost one-third of the group did not finish the training."[26]

Ministers and lay committees would be well served by familiarizing themselves with as many of the models as possible in order to tailor schedule, content, and procedures to the needs of the particular trainees in the particular congregation.

Supervision—Continuing Training. It is an absolute necessity for the minister, and some other professional if one may be found to volunteer his or her services, to be available on call to the lay persons after they have begun their work. From time to time their own anxieties and feelings of inadequacy, frustration, and even sense of failure will arise, and they will need the opportunity to talk these out as soon as they have been experienced. It will also be important for them to discuss with the pastor or another professional details of a particular person's life or an interpersonal situation, and their own functioning in that context. The minister needs to understand the significance of this type of availability as a most efficient use of her or his own time, since the crisis ministry to persons is being greatly expanded. The pastor will also begin to experience some of the satisfactions and benefits of the supervisory role.

In addition to supervision on a personal basis, it is important that there be regular group meetings of the lay persons for didactic input, for discussion and fellowship among themselves, and for case presentation and study.[27]

Such a lay crisis care and counseling program will expand and upgrade the pastoral ministry of the congregation to itself and to the larger community. Ministers will be using their time more efficiently and, while serving as leaders, will discover that they themselves are learning more and obtaining new satisfactions from their investment. The total congregational life will be lifted by the constant example of competent lay ministry and by the presence in its whole life together of a cadre of people who are increasingly sensitive to other human beings, in both the formal and informal meetings of the congregation. The lay crisis helpers will experience great satisfaction themselves as they become aware of developing sensitivities to others and insight into themselves, and as they experience their own significant role in the lives of individuals, families, and the congregation, through their expression of ministry to their Lord.

This book has sought to focus specifically on the dynamics of individual and family crisis, its purpose being to upgrade the level of effectiveness of ministers in this important aspect of pastoral work. The bulk of the material has also been relevant to the role of ministers as leaders in the selection, training, assignment, and supervision of lay persons to do some of this work as their faith commitment, thereby increasing the breadth of the pastors' own ministry and competence in their own skills, and deepening their satisfaction in their own calling.

The intent of the book is not to diminish the importance of any other function of the ministry or of any other phase of congregational life. Indeed, the whole center of the life of the community of faith is the context for, stimulus to, and support of crisis ministry: congregational worship with Word and sacrament; the education of children, youths, and adults; the prophetic Word to the larger community, including direct involvement in social change which involves the creation of a climate in which the well-being of persons is maximized.

Not only should crisis ministry itself be broader than the emergency services this book has dealt with, as Jernigan has so well pointed out,[1] but the total purpose for the existence of the community of faith is broader than that of present human crisis, although the relationship of major developmental and situational crises to the experience of personal faith and the forms of the community of faith are obvious: birth-creation-baptism; personal and social growth-education in the faith; puberty-personal faith decision-confirmation; love-marriage-celebration; death-grief-resurrection-funeral.

The congregation participates in the life of its Lord when we, ordained clergy and laity alike, commit ourselves to a "being for others," which we understand to be the characteristic attitude of God

269

in relation to us. This means that human distress and suffering cause agony for us, as we have been shown in faith that they do for God, and our only effective response is to be moved to action on their behalf. This means that in some way the love of God is literally expressed to persons through those meaningful relationships and communications and activities that are called pastoral care, of which crisis ministry is one important aspect. This book is a response to the call to the community of faith to be more self-consciously aware of certain forms of intense human need, of the inherent link between who we are called to be as God's people and our ministry to those in crisis, and to commit ourselves to the highest level of helping possible, realizing that this is one form of our seeking to express the love of God.

Preface

1. Howard Stone, *Crisis Counseling* (Philadelphia: Fortress Press, 1976); Charles Gerkin, *Crisis Experience in Modern Life* (Nashville: Abingdon Press, 1979).
2. Karl A. Slaikeu, *Crisis Intervention: A Handbook for Practice and Research* (Boston: Allyn & Bacon, 1984), pp. 171-81.

Chapter 1

The Minister as Crisis Counselor

1. Samuel Blizzard, "The Minister's Dilemma," *The Christian Century* (April 25, 1956). Although this is now an old study and new items would need to be added to the list of ministers' functions, there is no reason to believe that the emphasis on pastoral work (with counseling perhaps now being specified as one aspect of this) would be reduced. If anything, I would expect an increased value to be placed on it.
2. Paul Tillich, "The Spiritual and Theological Foundation of Pastoral Care," in *Clinical Education for the Pastoral Ministry*, ed. E. E. Bruder and M. L. Barb (Advisory Committee on Clinical Pastoral Education, 1958), p. 1.
3. Karl Menninger, *Theory of Psychoanalytic Technique* (New York: Basic Books, 1958), p. 10.
4. Robert Carkhuff, *Helping and Human Relations*, 2 vols. (New York: Holt, Rinehart & Winston, 1969), Vol. I, pp. 184-7.
5. Sidney Jourard, *The Transparent Self* (Princeton, N.J.: Van Nostrand, 1964), pp. 59-65.
6. Harry Stack Sullivan, *The Psychiatric Interview* (New York: W. W. Norton & Co., 1954), pp. 19-25.
7. For another discussion of the minister as a symbol, see Wayne Oates, *The Christian Pastor* (Philadelphia: Westminster Press, 1964), pp. 43-71.
8. Paul Tillich, *Dynamics of Faith* (New York: Harper & Brothers, 1957), pp. 41-43.
9. This understanding of the power of certain symbols as conveying unusual impact upon human life, when they have been learned early in life and in relationship with one's parents, is based upon the concept of "good" and "bad" objects proposed by Melanie Klein, "Mourning and Its Relation to Manic-Depressive States," *International Journal of Psychoanalysis* 21(1940): 127-28.
10. W. Robert Beavers, *Psychotherapy and Growth, A Family Systems Perspective* (New York: Brunner/Mazel, 1977), pp. 311, 312, 336-41.
11. Howard Clinebell, *The People Dynamic: Changing Self and Society Through*

Growth Groups (New York: Harper & Row, 1972); Joe Knowles, *Group Counseling* (Englewood Cliffs, N.J.: Prentice-Hall, 1964); Robert Leslie, *Sharing Groups in the Church* (Nashville: Abingdon Press, 1971).

12. Paul Pruyser, *The Minister as Diagnostician* (Philadelphia: Westminster Press, 1976), p. 45.

13. *Ibid.*, p. 10.

14. William B. Oglesby, Jr., *Biblical Themes for Pastoral Care* (Nashville: Abingdon Press, 1980); Donald Capps, *Biblical Approaches to Pastoral Counseling* (Philadelphia: Westminster Press, 1981).

15. Richard C. Cabot and Russell L. Dicks, *The Art of Ministering to the Sick* (New York: Macmillan Co., 1936), pp. 189-203; Seward Hiltner, *Religion and Health* (New York: Macmillan Co., 1943), pp. 167-205; Carl Rogers, *Counseling and Psychotherapy* (Boston: Houghton Mifflin, 1942).

16. Russell Dicks, *Pastoral Work and Personal Counseling* (New York: Macmillan Co., 1944); Seward Hiltner, *Pastoral Counseling* (Nashville: Abingdon Press, 1949); Paul E. Johnson, *Psychology of Pastoral Care* (Nashville: Abingdon Press, 1953); Oates, *Christian Pastor;* Carroll A. Wise, *Pastoral Counseling: Theory and Practice* (New York: Harper & Row, 1951).

17. Carl Rogers, *Client Centered Therapy* (Boston: Houghton Mifflin, 1951); *On Becoming a Person* (Boston: Houghton Mifflin, 1951).

18. Leopold Bellak and Leonard Small, *Emergency Psychotherapy and Brief Psychotherapy* (New York: Grune & Stratton, 1965); Peter Sifneos, *Short-Term Psychotherapy and Emotional Crisis* (Cambridge: Harvard University Press, 1972).

19. Henry A. Virkler, "Counseling Demands, Procedures, and Preparation of Parish Ministers: A Descriptive Study," *Journal of Psychology and Theology* 7(1979):273.

20. Irving L. Janis, *Short-Term Counseling* (New Haven: Yale University Press, 1983).

21. Howard Clinebell, *Basic Types of Pastoral Care and Counseling* (Nashville: Abingdon Press, 1984).

22. *Ibid.*, pp. 183-208.

23. Homer L. Jernigan, "Pastoral Care and the Crises of Life," in *Community Mental Health: The Role of Church and Temple*, ed. Howard Clinebell (Nashville: Abingdon Press, 1970), pp. 57, 59.

Chapter 2

Crisis Theory

1. Erich Lindemann, "Symptomatology and Management of Acute Grief," *American Journal of Psychiatry* 101(1944):141-48.

2. Anton Boisen, "Concerning the Relationship between Religious Experience and Mental Disorders," *Mental Hygiene* 7(April 1923):308-9.

3. Anton Boisen, *The Exploration of the Inner World* (New York: Harper & Brothers, 1936), pp. 54, 46, 56.

4. Anton Boisen, *Religion in Crisis and Custom* (New York: Harper & Brothers, 1955), pp. 42-43.

5. *Ibid.*, pp. 43-44.

6. *Ibid.*, pp. 44-45.

7. *Ibid.*, pp. 67-69, 3-4.

8. William James, *The Varieties of Religious Experience* (New York: Longmans, Green & Co., 1902); Edwin Starbuck, *Psychology of Religion* (New York: Charles Scribner's Sons, 1900).

9. Gerald Caplan, *Principles of Preventive Psychiatry* (New York: Basic Books, 1964).

10. Erik Erikson, "Growth and Crisis of the 'Healthy Personality'," in *Personality in Nature, Society, and Culture,* ed. Clyde Kluckhohn and Henry A. Murray (New York: Alfred A. Knopf, 1956), pp. 185-225.

11. Bruce A. Baldwin, "A Paradigm for the Classification of Emotional Crises: Implications for Crisis Intervention," *American Journal of Orthopsychiatry* 48(1978):538-51.

12. Lydia Rapoport, "The State of Crisis: Some Theoretical Considerations," in *Crisis Intervention: Selected Readings,* ed. Howard J. Parad (New York: Family Service Assn. of America, 1965), pp. 25-26.

13. Caplan, *Principles of Preventive Psychiatry,* pp. 31-33.

14. Peter E. Sifneos, "A Concept of 'Emotional Crisis'," *Mental Hygiene* 44 (April 1960):169-71.

15. Betty L. Kalis et al., "Precipitating Stress as a Focus in Psychotherapy," *Archives of General Psychiatry* 5(September 1961):221-24.

16. Caplan, *Principles of Preventive Psychiatry,* p. 39.

17. Wilbur E. Morley, "Treatment of the Patient in Crisis," *Western Medicine* 3(March 1965).

18. Caplan, *Principles of Preventive Psychiatry,* pp. 40-41.

19. H. H. Perlman, "In Quest of Coping," *Social Casework* 57(1975):13-25.

20. C. E. Hooker, "Learned Helplessness," *Social Work* 21(1976):194-98.

21. Karl A. Slaikeu, *Crisis Intervention: A Handbook for Practice and Research* (Boston: Allyn & Bacon, 1984), pp. 25-31.

22. Julian R. Taplin, "Crisis Theory: Critique and Reformulation," *Community Mental Health Journal* 7(March 1971):13-23.

23. Bertram R. Forer, "The Therapeutic Value of Crisis," *Psychological Reports* 13(1963):276.

24. *Ibid.,* p. 277.

25. Caplan, *Principles of Preventive Psychiatry,* p. 48.

26. Charles V. Gerkin, *Crisis Experience in Modern Life* (Nashville:Abingdon Press, 1979), pp. 32-33.

27. *Ibid.,* pp. 27, 31.

28. *Ibid.,* pp. 37, 35.

Chapter 3

Methods

1. David K. Switzer, *Pastor, Preacher, Person* (Nashville: Abingdon Press, 1979), pp. 55-69.

2. David K. Switzer, *The Dynamics of Grief* (Nashville: Abingdon Press, 1970), pp. 79-91.

3. Robert Carkhuff, *Helping and Human Relations,* 2 vols. (New York: Holt, Rinehart & Winston, 1969), Vol. I, pp. 33-74.

4. Gerald Caplan, *Principles of Preventive Psychiatry* (New York: Basic Books, 1964), p. 48.

5. *Ibid.,* p. 52.

6. Thomas F. McGee, "Some Basic Considerations in Crisis Intervention," *Community Mental Health Journal* 4(1968):323.

7. *Ibid.*

8. Nikolaus Nebl, "Essential Elements in Short-term Treatment," *Social Casework* 52(June 1971): 380; Betty L. Kalis et al., "Precipitating Stress as a Focus in Psychotherapy," *Archives of General Psychiatry* 5(September 1961):225; David M. Kaplan, "Observations on Crisis Theory and Practice," *Social Casework* 49 (March 1968):155.

9. McGee, "Some Basic Considerations," p. 323.

10. Donna G. Aguilera, "Crisis: Moment of Truth," *Journal of Psychiatric Nursing and Mental Health Services* 9(May 1971):23-25; Irene M. Burnside, "Crisis Intervention with Geriatric Hospitalized Patients," *Journal of Psychiatric Nursing and Mental Health Services* 8(March 1970):17-20.

11. McGee, "Some Basic Considerations," p. 324.

12. Carkhuff, *Helping and Human Relations,* Vol. II, pp. 5, 7-8; Vol. I, p. 45.

13. *Ibid.,* Vol. I, p. xi-xiv.

14. *Ibid.,* Vol. I, pp. xii.

15. *Ibid.,* Vol. I, p. xiv.

16. *Ibid.,* Vol. I, p. 45.

17. Sheldon H. Kardiner, "A Methodologic Approach to Crisis Therapy," *American Journal of Psychotherapy* 29(1975):8; Thomas N. Rusk and Robert H. Gerner, "A Study of the Process of Brief Psychotherapy," *American Journal of Psychiatry* 128(1972):882; Lewis Wolberg, "Psychiatric Technics in Crisis Therapy," *New York State Journal of Medicine* (June 1972):1269.

18. Nancy Mann Mulish, "The Effect of Sex of the Analyst on Transference," *Bulletin of the Menninger Clinic* 48(1984):95-110; Ruth M. Armstrong, "Women as Pastoral Counselors," *Pastoral Psychology* 31(Winter 1982); Ellen Berman, "The Woman Psychiatrist as Therapst and Academician," *Journal of Medical Education* 47(November 1972); Charlene A. Carter, "Advantages of Being a Woman Therapist," *Psychotherapy: Theory, Research, and Practice* 8(Winter 1971); Thomas V. Merluzzi and Bernadette Merluzzi, "Androgyny, Stereotypy, and the Perception of Female Therapists," *Journal of Clinical Psychology* 37(April 1981); Ruth Ann Turkel, "The Impact of Feminism on the Practice of a Woman Analyst," *American Journal of Psychoanalysis* 36(1976). I am grateful to the Reverend Abigail Carlisle for most of these references.

19. Emma Justes, "Women," in Robert J. Wicks; Richard D. Parsons; and Donald Capps, *Clinical Handbook of Pastoral Counseling* (Ramsey, N.J.: Paulist Press, 1985).

20. *Ibid.*

21. Emma Justes, *Pastoral Care of Women,* in publication.

22. Abigail Carlisle, "The Therapeutic Relationship Between Female Therapist and Male Clients," unpublished paper (1983).

23. Carl Rogers, *On Becoming a Person* (Boston: Houghton Mifflin, 1961), pp. 60-64; Charles Truax and Robert R. Carkhuff, *Toward Effective Counseling and Psychotherapy* (Chicago: Aldine Publishing Co., 1967), pp. 31-43; Carkhuff, *Helping and Human Relations,* Vol. I, pp. 33-45.

24. Carkhuff, *Helping and Human Relations,* Vol. I, pp. 35-39, 173-95; Vol. II, 82-95. See also Gerard Egan, *The Skilled Helper,* 2nd ed. (Monterey, Calif.: Brooks/Cole Publishing Co., 1982).

25. Gerald Jacobson, "Crisis Theory and Treatment Strategy: Some Sociocultural and Psychodynamic Considerations," *The Journal of Nervous and Mental Diseases* 141(August 1965):215.

26. Lydia Rapoport, "The State of Crisis: Some Theoretical Considerations," in *Crisis Intervention: Selected Readings,* ed. Howard J. Parad (New York: Family Service Assn. of America, 1965), pp. 29-30.

27. Karl A. Slaikeu, *Crisis Intervention: A Handbook for Practice and Research* (Boston:Allyn & Bacon, 1984), pp. 85-115. I am grateful to Slaikeu for the time he spent going over the first draft of the pages dealing with his work and for giving the detailed suggestions incorporated here.

28. *Ibid.,* p. 19.

29. *Ibid.,* pp. 122, 123.

30. *Ibid.*

31. *Ibid.,* p. 139; see pp. 177-80 for a discussion of the clergy's functioning with persons in crisis resolution.

32. *Ibid.*, p. 23.
33. *Ibid.*, pp. 177-80.
34. Bruce A. Baldwin, "Crisis Intervention: An Overview of Theory and Practice," *The Counseling Psychologist* 8(1979):49; Douglas Puryear, *Helping People in Crisis* (San Francisco: Jossey-Bass, 1979), p. 50-157.
35. Warren A. Jones, "The A-B-C Method of Crisis Management," *Mental Hygiene* 52(January 1968):87.
36. Thomas N. Rusk, "Opportunity and Technique in Crisis Psychiatry," *Comprehensive Psychiatry* 12(May 1971):252.
37. Paul Pruyser, *The Minister as Diagnostician* (Philadelphia:Westminster Press, 1976), pp. 34, 38-39.
38. Wilbur E. Morley, "Treatment of the Patient in Crisis," *Western Medicine* 3(March 1965).
39. C. Knight Aldrich, "Brief Psychotherapy: A Reappraisal of Some Theoretical Assumptions," *American Journal of Psychiatry* 125(1968):585.
40. Morley, "Treatment of the Patient in Crisis."
41. Wolberg, "Psychiatric Technics," pp. 1267-68.
42. Aldrich, "Brief Psychotherapy," p. 590.
43. Rusk, "Opportunity and Technique," p. 253.
44. Zane T. Nelson and Dwight D. Mowery, "Contracting in Crisis Intervention," *Community Mental Health* 12(1976):37, 38, 40-43.
45. Kardiner, "A Methodologic Approach," p. 7.
46. Kalis et al., "Precipitating Stress as a Focus," p. 225.
47. David L. Hoffman and Mary L. Remmel, "Discovering the Precipitant in Crisis Intervention," *Social Case Work* 56(1975):260.
48. Rusk, "Opportunity and Technique," p. 258.
49. *Ibid.*, p. 257.
50. *Ibid.*, p. 251.
51. Norris Hansell; Mary Wodarczyk; and Britomar Handlon-Lathrop, "Decision Counseling Method: Expanding Coping at Crisis-in-Transit," *Archives of General Psychiatry* 22(May 1970):464-65.
52. Louis Paul, "Treatment Techniques in a Walk-in Clinic," *Hospital and Community Psychiatry* 17(February 1966):51.
53. Rusk, "Opportunity and Technique," p. 262.
54. Michael E. Murray, "The Therapist as Transitional Object," *American Journal of Psychoanalysis* 34(1974):123, 125.
55. Bruce A. Baldwin, "Crisis Intervention in Professional Practice: Implications for Clinical Training," *American Journal of Orthopsychiatry* 47(1977):667-68.

Chapter 4

Intervention Procedures

1. Thomas C. Oden, *Pastoral Theology: Essentials of Ministry* (San Francisco: Harper & Row, 1983), p. 171.
2. *Ibid.*, pp. 172-73, 175.
3. David Rubenstein, "Rehospitalization Versus Family Crisis Intervention," *American Journal of Psychiatry* 129(December 1972):719.
4. Beverly Berliner, "Nursing a Patient in Crisis," *American Journal of Nursing* 70(October 1970):2156.
5. Frank S. Pittman et al., "Crisis Family Therapy," in *Current Psychiatric Therapies*, Vol. VI, ed. Jules H. Masserman (New York: Grune & Stratton, 1966), p. 190.

6. Rosemary Creed Lukton, "Myths and Realities of Crisis Intervention," *Social Casework* 63(1982):284.

7. Norris Hansell; Mary Wodarczyk; and Britomar Handlon-Lathrop, "Decision Counseling Method: Expanding Coping at Crisis-in-Transit," *Archives of General Psychiatry* 22(May 1970):464-5.

8. Rubenstein, "Rehospitalization Versus Family Crisis Intervention," p. 719.

9. Thomas N. Rusk, "Opportunity and Technique," *Comprehensive Psychiatry* 12(May 1971):259.

10. Rubenstein, "Rehospitalization Versus Family Crisis Intervention," p. 718.

11. Lukton, "Myths and Realities," p. 284.

12. Ruth B. Caplan, *Helping the Helpers to Help* (New York: Seabury Press, 1972), p. 20.

13. Ronald J. Catanzaro, "WATS Telephone Therapy: New Follow-up Technique for Alcoholics," *American Journal of Psychiatry* 116(January 1970):1024-47; A.J.R. Koumans; J. J. Muller; and C. F. Miller, "Use of Telephone Calls to Increase Motivation," *Psychological Reports* 21(1967):327-28.

14. Lewis Rosenblum, "Telephone Therapy," *Psychotherapy: Theory, Research, and Practice* 6(Fall 1969):241, 242.

15. Gene W. Brockopp, "The Telephone Call—Conversation or Therapy," *Crisis Intervention* 2(1970):73.

16. Catanzaro, "WATS Telephone Therapy," p. 1026.

17. Howard Clinebell, *Basic Types of Pastoral Care and Counseling* (Nashville: Abingdon Press, 1984), p. 311.

18. George H. Wolkon, "Changing Roles: Crises in the Continuum of Care in the Community," *Psychotherapy: Theory, Research, and Practice* 11(1974):368.

19. *Ibid.*, 369.

20. Clinebell, *Basic Types*, pp. 311-20; William B. Oglesby, Jr., *Referral in Pastoral Counseling* (Nashville: Abingdon Press, 1978).

21. Jean M. Allgeyer, "The Crisis Group: Its Unique Usefulness to the Disadvantaged," *International Journal of Group Psychotherapy* 20(April 1970):235-40.

22. Demetrius A. Trakas and Gertrude Lloyd, "Emergency Management in a Short-term Open Group," *Comprehensive Psychiatry* 12(March 1971):170-74.

23. Martin Strickler and Jean Allgeyer, "The Crisis Group: A New Application of Crisis Theory," *Social Work* 12(July 1967):32.

24. James M. Donovan; Michael J. Bennett; and Christine M. McElroy, "The Crisis Group: An Outcome Study," *American Journal of Psychiatry* 136(1979):906-7.

25. *Ibid.*, p. 909.

26. Wilbur Morley and Vivian B. Brown, "The Crisis-Intervention Group: A Natural Mating or a Marriage of Convenience?" *Psychotherapy: Theory, Research, and Practice* 6(Winter 1969):30-36. The outline that follows is theirs.

27. Strickler, "The Crisis Group," p. 31.

Chapter 5

Family Crises

1. Diana Sullivan Everstine and Louis Everstine, *People in Crisis: Strategic Therapeutic Interventions* (New York: Brunner/Mazel, 1983).

2. W. Robert Beavers, *Psychotherapy and Growth: A Family Systems Perspective* (New York: Brunner/Mazel, 1977), pp. 23-24.

3. Jerry M. Lewis et al., *No Single Thread: Psychological Health in Family Systems* (New York: Brunner/Mazel, 1976).

4. Beavers, *Psychotherapy and Growth*, pp. 132-55.

5. *Ibid.*, p. 153.

6. *Ibid.*, p. 155.

7. *Ibid.*, pp. 42-156; Lewis et al, *No Single Thread*, pp. 46-82, 99-138, 199-217.

8. Beavers, *Psychotherapy and Growth*, pp. 43-74; also see p. 79, refs. 6, 7, 8.

9. Jerry M. Lewis and John G. Looney, *The Long Struggle: Well-functioning, Working-Class Black Families* (New York: Brunner/Mazel, 1983).

10. Beavers, *Psychotherapy and Growth*, pp. 91-110.

11. Roseann F. Umana; Steven J. Gross; and Marcia McConville Turner, *Crisis in the Family* (New York: Gardner Press, 1980), p. 1.

12. *Ibid.*, p. 2.

13. Virginia Satir, *Conjoint Family Therapy* (Palo Alto: Science and Behavior Books, 1964); Brian Grant, *Reclaiming the Dream: Marriage Counseling in the Parish* (Nashville: Abingdon Press, 1986); J. C. Wynn, *Family Therapy in Pastoral Ministry* (San Francisco: Harper & Row, 1982).

The naming of specific books is problematic. There are many competent and useful works by numerous family theorists and therapists, most presenting somewhat different approaches. Those named here are only suggestions, with Grant and Wynn both being ministers writing for ministers. Those who are not already well acquainted with the different ideas and procedures of family therapy probably would be assisted in their next steps (in addition to reading Wynn's brief introduction to several theories) by reading a book such as James C. Hansen and Luciano L'Abate, *Approaches to Family Therapy* (New York: Macmillan, 1982), which summarizes in some detail thirteen major practitioners and their work.

14. W. Robert Beavers, "The Application of Family Systems Theory to Crisis Intervention," in Switzer, *The Minister as Crisis Counselor*, 1st ed. (Nashville: Abingdon Press, 1974), pp. 205-10.

15. For statements and illustrations concerning the need for such control by the intervenor in family crisis, see Douglas A. Puryear, *Helping People in Crisis* (San Francisco: Jossey Bass, 1979).

16. *Facts on Alcoholism* (New York: National Council on Alcoholism, 1983).

17. Sharon Wegscheider, *Another Chance: Hope and Health for the Alcoholic Family* (Palo Alto: Science and Behavior Books, 1981), p. 76; also pp. 76-88.

18. *Ibid.*, 150-62.

Chapter 6

The Crisis of Grief

1. Erich Lindemann, "Symptomatology and Management of Acute Grief," *American Journal of Psychiatry* 101(1944):141-48.

2. C. Murray Parkes, "Effects of Bereavement on Physical and Mental Health—A Study of the Medical Records of Widows," *British Medical Journal* 2(August 1964):274-79 (reprint, 4-5, 6, 13).

3. C. Murray Parkes; B. Benjamin; and R. B. Fitzgerald, "Broken Heart: A Statistical Study of Increased Mortality Among Widowers," *British Medical Journal* 1(March 1969):740-43 (reprint, 1, 35).

4. David M. Moriarty, *The Loss of Loved Ones* (Springfield, Ill.: Charles C. Thomas, 1965), p. 13.

5. C. Murray Parkes, "Recent Bereavement as a Cause of Mental Illness," *British Journal of Psychiatry* 110 (March 1964):202.

6. Norman L. Paul and George H. Grosser, "Operational Mourning and Its Role in Conjoint Family Therapy," *Community Mental Health Journal* 1(1965):340.

7. Norman L. Paul, "The Use of Empathy in the Resolution of Grief," *Perspectives in Biology and Medicine* 11(1967):161.

8. Leonard Moss and Donald Hamilton, "The Psychotherapy of the Suicidal Patient," *American Journal of Psychiatry* 112(1956):814-15.

9. T. L. Dorpat; J. K. Jackson; and H. S. Ripley, "Broken Homes and Attempted

and Contemplated Suicide," *Archives of General Psychiatry* 12(February 1965):213-16.

10. Irwin Gerber, "Bereavement and the Acceptance of Professional Service," *Community Mental Health Journal* 5(1969):487-95.

11. David K. Switzer, *The Dynamics of Grief* (Nashville: Abingdon Press, 1970), pp. 93-177.

12. Edgar Jackson, *Understanding Grief* (Nashville: Abingdon Press, 1957); C. Murray Parkes, *Bereavement: Studies of Grief in Adult Life* (New York: International Universities Press, 1972); Yorick Spiegel, *The Grief Process: Analysis and Counseling* (Nashville: Abingdon Press, 1973). For a provocative discussion of the dynamics of grief with a theological dimension, see Charles Gerkin, *Crisis Experience in Modern Life* (Nashville: Abingdon Press, 1979), pp. 142-61.

13. Switzer, *Dynamics of Grief*, pp. 195-207.

14. Parkes, *Bereavement, pp. 6-7.*

15. Wayne E. Oates, *Anxiety in Christian Experience* (Waco, Tex.: Word Books, 1971), pp. 52-55; Spiegel, *Grief Process*, pp. 62-83; Gerkin, *Crisis Experience*, pp. 155-61.

16. Granger Westberg, *Good Grief* (Philadelphia: Fortress Press, 1962).

17. Kenneth R. Mitchell and Herbert Anderson, *All Our Losses, All Our Griefs* (Philadelphia: Westminster Press, 1983), pp. 61-82; Edgar Jackson, *The Many Faces of Grief* (Nashville: Abingdon Press, 1972).

18. Elisabeth Kübler-Ross, *On Death and Dying* (New York: Macmillan, 1969).

19. C. Murray Parkes, " 'Seeking' and 'Finding' a Lost Object," *Social Science and Medicine* 4(1970):187-201; "The First Year of Bereavement," *Psychiatry* 33(November 1970):444-67.

20. Parkes, "The First Year of Bereavement," pp. 449-50.

21. Rita R. Vollman et al., "The Reactions of Family Systems to Sudden and Unexpected Death," Omega 2(May 1971):101.

22. *Ibid.*, pp. 104-5; also see W. Vail Williams; Paul Polak; and Rita R. Vollman, "Crisis Intervention in Acute Grief," *Omega* 3(February 1972):69-70.

23. Vollman, et al., "Reactions of Family Systems," p. 104.

24. Paul E. Irion, *The Funeral: Vestige or Value* (Nashville: Abingdon Press, 1966), pp. 117-19; Mitchell and Anderson, *All Our Losses*, pp. 139-48.

25. George Krupp, "Maladaptive Reactions to the Death of a Family Member," *Social Casework* 53(July 1972):433.

26. Hans W. Loewald, "Internalization, Separation, Mourning, and the Superego," *Psychoanalytic Quarterly* 31(1962):485.

27. Ibid., pp. 485-86.

28. Ibid., p. 485.

29. Ibid., p. 490.

Chapter 7

A Pathological Grief Reaction

1. This chapter is based on the author's article, "Repressed Affect and Memory Reactive to Grief: A Case Fragment," originally published in *Omega: An International Journal for Study of Death and Lethal Behavior* 3(Spring 1972):121-26.

2. Robert Carkhuff, *Helping and Human Relations*, 2 vols. (New York: Holt, Rinehart & Winston, 1969), Vol. I, pp. 173-75; Vol. II, pp. 94-95.

3. Switzer, "Awareness of Unresolved Grief: An Opportunity for Ministry," *The Christian Ministry* (July 1980):19-23.

Chapter 8

Divorce Crises

1. Sources of statistics on divorce: U. S. Bureau of the Census, "Marital Status and Living Arrangements: March, 1980," in *Current Population Reports*, Series P-20,

No. 365, 1981; Ira L. Reiss, *Family Systems in America*, 3rd ed. (New York: Holt, Rinehart, & Winston, 1980), pp. 365-71; Hugh Carter and Paul C. Glick, *Marriage and Divorce: A Social and Economic Study* (Cambridge, Mass.: Harvard University Press, 1976); Byron Strong et al., *The Marriage and Family Experience* (St. Paul: West Publishing Co., 1983); Jessie Bernard, "Present Demographic Trends and Structural Outcome in Family Life Today," in *Marriage and Family Counseling*, ed. James A. Peterson (New York: Association Press, 1968).

2. See R. J. Coogler, *Structured Mediation in Divorce Settlements: A Handbook for Divorce Mediators* (Lexington, Mass: Lexington Books, 1978); John M. Haynes, *Divorce Mediation: A Practical Guide for Therapists and Counselors* (New York: Springer Publishing Co., 1981). Robert Coulson, *Fighting Fair: Family Mediation Will Work for You* (Glencoe: Free Press, 1983) explains divorce mediation for couples considering divorce.

3. E. C. Hobbs, "An Alternate Model from a Theological Perspective," in *The Family in Search of a Future*, ed. H. A. Otto (New York: Appleton-Century-Crofts, 1970), pp. 25-41.

4. See B. Harvie Branscomb, *The Teachings of Jesus* (Nashville: Abingdon Press, 1931); Derrick S. Bailey, *The Mystery of Love and Marriage* (London: SCM Press, 1952).

5. For additional theological perspectives on marriage and divorce, see J. B. Nelson, *Embodiment: An Approach to Sexuality and Christian Theology* (Minneapolis: Augsburg Publishing House, 1978) for a Protestant view. For a Roman Catholic view, see Walter Kasper, *Theology of Christian Marriage* (New York: Crossroad Press, 1981).

6. For additional views on divorce, see Morton Hunt and Bernice Hunt, *The Divorce Experience* (New York: McGraw-Hill, 1977); Paul Bohannan, ed., *Divorce and After* (Garden City, N.Y.: Anchor Books, 1971); Harry F. Keshet, *Fathers Without Partners* (Totowa, N. J.: Rowman & Littlefield, 1981); Judith S. Wallerstein and Joan B. Kelley, *Surviving the Breakup* (New York: Basic Books, 1980); William V. Arnold, et al., *Divorce: Prevention or Survival* (Philadelphia: Westminster Press, 1977).

7. William J. Goode, *After Divorce* (New York: Free Press of Glencoe, 1956), p. 137. More recently, this finding has been confirmed in a study by P. Deckert and R. Langelier, "The Late Divorce Phenomenon: The Causes and Impact of Ending 20-Year-Old or Longer Marriages," *Journal of Divorce* 1(1977):183-87.

8. Since this chapter was first published in 1974, several authors have developed a variety of stage descriptions of divorce. An excellent overview of these can be obtained in Florence W. Kaslow, "Divorce and Divorce Therapy", in *Handbook of Family Therapy*, ed. Alan S. Gurman and David P. Kniskern (New York: Brunner/Mazel, 1981), pp. 662-96. Many journals now carry reports of studies of divorce, and the *Journal of Divorce*, begun in 1977, is devoted to the field of divorce studies.

9. For family systems approaches, see R. D. Laing, *The Politics of the Family;* J. M. Lewis et al., *No Single Thread: Psychological Health in Family Systems* (New York: Brunner/Mazel, 1976), See also the perspectives on family of origin as presented by James L. Framo, "The Integration of Marital Therapy with Sessions with Family of Origin," in *Handbook of Family Therapy*, ed. Gurman and Kniskern, pp. 133-58.

10. Elizabeth Ogg, *Divorce* (New York: Public Affairs Pamphlets #528, 1975) is an excellent brief resource. Some denominations now publish similar pamphlets on divorce, single parents, and related family issues. A wide variety of divorce help books is now available. In addition to those already mentioned, other helpful books for adults are Mel Krantzler, *Creative Divorce* (New York: M. Evans, 1974); Tom McGinnis, *More Than Just a Friend* (Englewood Cliffs: Prentice-Hall, 1981); William J. Goode, *Women in Divorce* (New York: Free Press, 1978); Stan L. Albrecht; Howard M. Bahr; and Kristen L. Goodman, *Divorce and Remarriage* (Westport, Conn.: Greenwood Press, 1983); Norman Shresky and Marya Manner, *Uncoupling: The Art of Coming Apart* (New York: Viking Press, 1972). A helpful research study has been done by

Graham B. Spanier and Linda Thompson, *Parting: The Aftermath of Separation and Divorce* (Beverly Hills: Sage Publications, 1984). Remarriage and related issues are discussed in Frank F. Furstenberg and Graham B. Spanier, *Recycling the Family: Remarriage After Divorce* (Beverly Hills: Sage Publications, 1984); Elizabeth Canhape, *Fresh Starts: Men and Women After Divorce* (New York: Basic Books, 1983).

11. Cheryl L. Strom; Robert Sheehan; and Douglas H. Sprenkle, "The Structure of Separated Women's Communication with Their Nonprofessional and Professional Social Networks," *Journal of Marital and Family Therapy* 9(October 1983):423-29.

12. See Charles Stewart, *The Minister as Marriage Counselor*, rev. ed., (Nashville: Abingdon Press, 1970); H. L. Silverman, ed., *Marital Counseling* (Springfield, Ill.: Charles C. Thomas, 1967); B.N. Ard and C. Ard, eds., *Handbook of Marriage Counseling* (Palo Alto: Science and Behavior Books, 1969); Gurman and Kniskern, eds., *Handbook of Family Therapy;* W. Robert Beavers, *Successful Marriage: A Family Systems Approach* (New York: W. W. Norton, 1985).

13. Many marriage and family therapists lead divorce adjustment and recovery groups. Some churches sponsor groups for divorced persons. One national network of groups for divorced persons is administered by Mel Krantzler, author of *Creative Divorce* (New York: M. Evans, 1974).

14. For an example and critique of divorce ceremonies, see Florence W. Kaslow, "Divorce and Divorce Therapy," in *Handbook of Family Therapy*, ed. Gurman and Kniskern, pp. 688-90.

15. Excellent research of the way stresses of divorce affect children is reported in E. Mavis Hetherington; Martha J. Cox; and Roger D. Cox, "Effects of Divorce on Parents and Children," in *Nontraditional Families*, ed. M. Lamb (Hillsdale, N. J.: Lawrence Erlbaum Associates, 1983); Judith S. Wallerstein and Joan B. Kelly, *Surviving the Breakup: How Children and Parents Cope with Divorce* (New York: Basic Books, 1980). Studies of the effects of divorce on other family members and relatives are presented in Esther O. Fisher, ed., *Impact of Divorce on the Extended Family* (New York: Haworth Press, 1982). *The Single Parent*, a magazine published by Parents Without Partners, a national organization of one-parent families, contains helpful articles on coping with divorce crises.

16. See Chapter 17 in Wallerstein and Kelly, *Surviving the Breakup* for an insightful description of some of these long-range issues. Among books on divorce addressed to younger children are Florence Bienenfeld, *My Mom and Dad Are Getting a Divorce* (St. Paul: EMC Publishing, 1980); Eric Rofes, ed., *The Kids' Book of Divorce: By, For, and About Kids* (New York: Random House, 1982); Eda LeShan, *What's Going to Happen to Me? When Parents Separate or Divorce* (New York: Four Winds, Scholastic Press, 1983). For older children and adolescents, these are available: Warner Troyer, *Divorced Kids: Children of Divorce Speak Out* (New York: Harcourt, Brace, Jovanovich, 1980); Bonnie Robson, *My Parents Are Divorced, Too: Teenagers Talk About Their Experiences and How They Cope* (New York: Dodd Mead, 1980).

17. Among helpful references are June Noble and William Noble, *How to Live with Other People's Children* (New York: E. P. Dutton, Hawthorn Books, 1979); Irving R. Stuart and Lawrence E. Abt, eds., *Children of Separation and Divorce: Management and Treatment* (New York: Van Nostrand Reinhold, 1981); Dorothy Cantor and Ellen A. Drake, *Divorced Parents and Their Children: A Guide for Mental Health Professionals* (New York: Springer Publishing Co. 1983); Sonja Goldstein and Albert J. Solnit, *Divorce and Your Child: Practical Suggestions for Parents* (New Haven: Yale University Press, 1984).

Chapter 9

The Suicidal Crisis

1. Doman Lum, *Responding to Suicidal Crisis* (Grand Rapids: Eerdmans Publishing Co., 1974); Howard Stone, *Suicide and Grief* (Philadelphia: Fortress Press, 1972).

NOTES TO PAGES 203-246   281

2. Charles Gerkin, *Crisis Experience in Modern Life* (Nashville: Abingdon Press, 1979), pp. 162-206; Robert Neale, *The Art of Dying* (New York: Harper & Row, 1973), pp. 49-70.

3. Karl A. Slaikeu, *Crisis Intervention: A Hankbook for Practice and Research* (Boston: Allyn & Bacon, 1984), p. 94.

4. Lum, *Responding to Suicidal Crisis*, pp. 29-34.

5. Stanley Hauerwas and Richard Bondi, "Memory, Community, and the Reasons for Living: Reflections on Suicide and Euthanasia," in Stanley Hauerwas; Richard Bondi; and David Burrell, *Truthfulness and Tragedy: Further Investigations into Christian Ethics* (Notre Dame: University of Notre Dame Press, 1977), pp. 101-15; Paul W. Pretzel, *Understanding and Counseling the Suicidal Person* (Nashville: Abingdon Press, 1972), pp. 200-25; Lum, *Responding to Suicidal Crisis*, pp. 61-82.

6. Edwin Shneidman, *The Definition of Suicide* (New York: John Wiley, 1985). I am very grateful to Dr. Shneidman for his permission to use the outline and some other materials based on this outline. I refer the reader to his book for the full explication of his ideas.

7. Edwin Shneidman, "Aphorisms of Suicide and Some Implications for Psychotherapy," *American Journal of Psychotherapy* 38(July 1984):321.

8. Aaron Beck, *The Diagnosis and Management of Depression* (Philadelphia: University of Pennsylvania, 1973), pp. 21-22.

9. Shneidman, "Aphorisms of Suicide," p. 323.

10. *Ibid.*, p. 322.

11. Gerkin, *Crisis Experience in Modern Life*, p. 163.

12. *Ibid.*, pp. 171-73.

13. *Ibid.*, pp. 177-79, 183.

14. Norman L. Farberow; Samuel M. Heilig; and Robert E. Litman, *Training Manual for Telephone Evaluation and Emergency Management of Suicidal Persons* (Los Angeles Suicide Prevention Center).

15. Paul Pruyser, *The Minister as Diagnostician* (Philadelphia: Westminster Press, 1976), pp. 60-79.

16. Diana Sullivan Everstine and Louis Everstine, *People in Crisis: Strategic Therapeutic Interventions* (New York: Brunner/Mazel, 1983), pp. 230-48; quote, p. 232.

17. *Ibid.*, pp. 239-48.

18. Shneidman, "Aphorisms of Suicide," p. 326.

19. *Ibid.*, p. 323.

20. Pretzel, *Understanding and Counseling*, pp. 72-79.

21. Robert E. Litman, "The Prevention of Suicide," in *Current Psychiatric Therapies*, Vol. 6 (New York: Grune & Stratton, 1966) pp. 271-72.

22. Everstine, *People in Crisis*, pp. 207, 208.

23. *Ibid.*, pp. 209, 213-19.

24. Schneidman, "Aphorisms of Suicide," p. 321.

25. Gerkin, *Crisis Experience in Modern Life*, p. 184.

26. *Ibid.*, pp. 37, 185, 30-32.

27. *Ibid.*, p. 187.

28. Stone, *Suicide and Grief*, pp. 41-43, 36.

29. *Ibid.*, p. 34.

30. Dean Schuyler, "Counseling Suicide Survivors: Issues and Answers," *Omega* 4(1973):316.

31. *Ibid.*, pp. 316, 320.

Chapter 10

Community Crisis Services

1. Ruth B. Caplan, *Helping the Helpers to Help* (New York: Seabury Press, 1972), pp. 16-36.

2. W. Kenneth Bentz, "Consensus Between Role Expectations and Role Behavior Among Ministers," *Community Mental Health Journal* 4(August 1968): 301-6.

3. Paul Torop and Karen Torop, "Hot Lines and Youth Culture Values," *American Journal of Psychiatry* 129 (December 1972): 730-33.

4. John R. Reed, Jr., "The Pastoral Care of Victims of Major Disaster," *Journal of Pastoral Care* 31(June 1977):97-108.

5. " 'Crisis' Therapy Tried in Corning," *New York Times* (October 29, 1972).

6. James L. Titchener and Frederic T. Kapp, "Family and Character Change at Buffalo Creek," *American Journal of Psychiatry* 133 (1976):295-99.

7. Goldine C. Gleser; Bonnie L. Green; and Carolyn Winget, *Prolonged Psychosocial Effects of Disaster: A Study of Buffalo Creek* (New York: Academic Press, 1981).

8. Craig Jordan, "Pastoral Care and Chronic Diaster Victims: The Buffalo Creek Experience," *Journal of Pastoral Care* 30(September 1976):159-70.

9. Helen Swick Perry and Stewart E. Perry, *The Schoolhouse Disasters: Family and Community as Determinants of the Child's Response to Disaster* (Washington, D. C.: National Academy of Sciences-National Research Council, 1959), p. 47.

10. *Ibid.*, p. 63.

11. *Ibid.*, pp. 50-51.

12. C. Murray Parkes, "Psycho-Social Transitions: A Field for Study," *Social Science and Medicine* 5(1971):103ff. According to Parkes, our "assumptive world" is the "total set of assumptions which we build up, on the basis of past experience. . . . [It] includes everything we know or think we know. It includes our interpretation of the past and our expectations of the future. . . . Any or all of these may need to change as a result of the changes in the life space."

13. Caplan, *Helping the Helpers.*

14. *Ibid.*, p. 35.

15. *Ibid.*

16. Robert Carkhuff, *Helping and Human Relations*, 2 vols. (New York: Holt, Rinehart & Winston, 1969), Vol. I, p. 6.

17. Howard Stone, *The Caring Church* (San Francisco: Harper & Row, 1983), pp. 11-22.

18. Diane Detwiler-Zapp and William Caveness Dixon, *Lay Care Giving* (Philadelphia: Fortress Press, 1982), pp. 42-45.

19. Carkhuff, *Helping and Human Relations*, Vol. 1, p. 8.

20. Steve Gerard, "Personality Associated with 'Good Volunteers,' " *Crisis Intervention* 4(1972):90-92.

21. Sam M. Heilig et al., "The Role of Non-Professional Volunteers in a Suicide Prevention Center," *Community Mental Health Journal* 4(February 1968):289.

22. Carkhuff, *Helping and Human Relations*, Vol. I, pp. 92-133; also 149-213.

23. *Ibid.*, Vol. I, pp. 35-39, 173-95; Vol. II, 82-95.

24. Howard Clinebell, *Basic Types of Pastoral Care and Counseling* (Nashville: Abingdon Press, 1984), pp. 400-411; Detwiler-Zapp, *Lay Care Giving*, pp. 38-62; Stone, *Caring Church*, pp. 32-100.

25. Stone, *Caring Church*, pp. 27-28, 56-59, 74-76.

26. Clinebell, *Basic Types*, p. 454.

27. For a detailed discussion of the supervision of the care givers, see Detwiler-Zapp, *Lay Care Giving*, pp. 63-79.

Conclusion

1. Homer L. Jernigan, "Pastoral Care and the Crises of Life," in *Community Mental Health: The Role of Church and Temple*, ed. Howard Clinebell (Nashville: Abingdon Press, 1970), p. 57-64.